THE MOTORWAY ACHIEVEMENT

*Building the Network:
The North East of England*

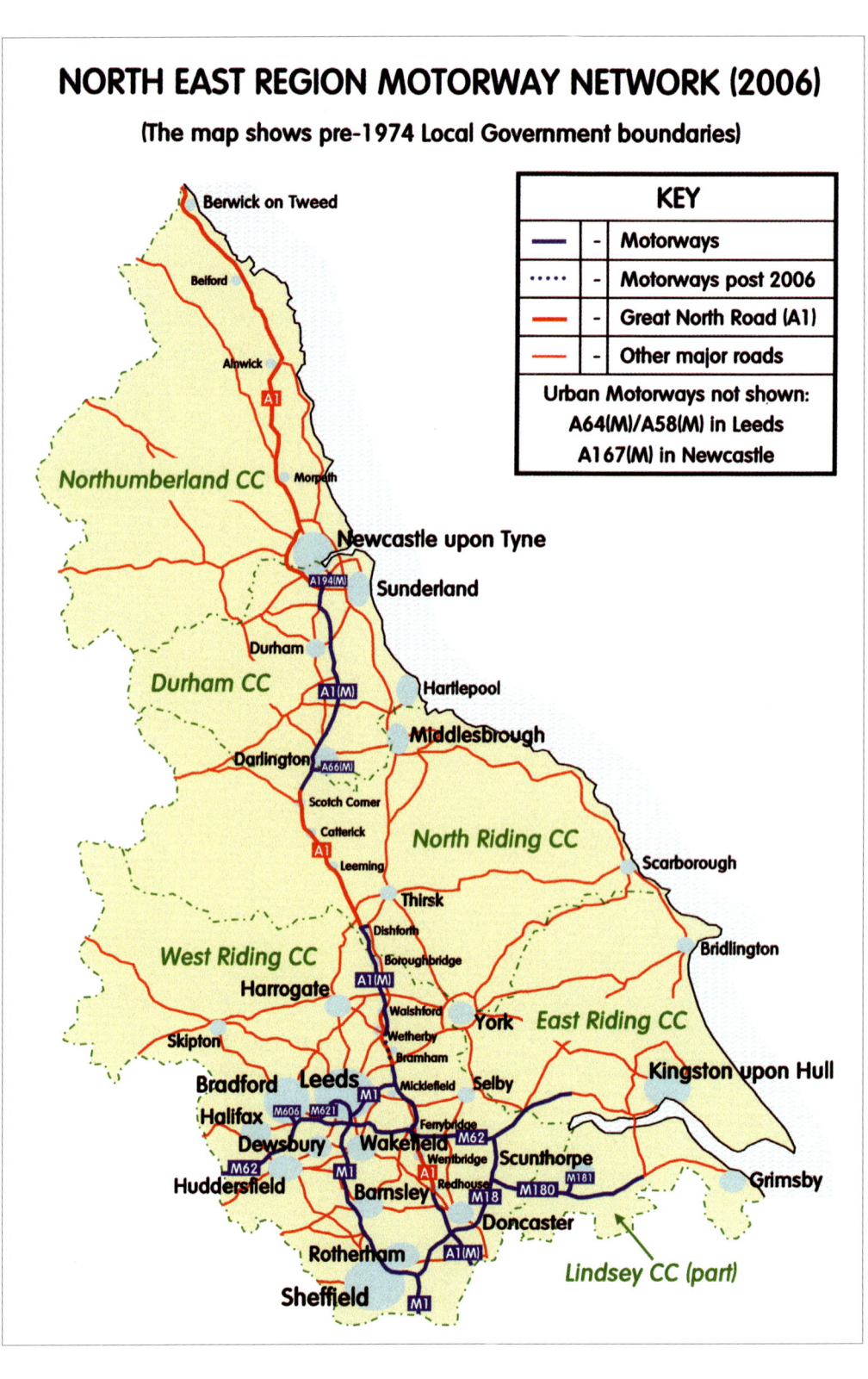

THE MOTORWAY ACHIEVEMENT

Building the Network: The North East of England

F.A. SIMS
OBE, BSc, FREng, FRSA, FICE, FIHT, FCIWM

Published for Motorway Archive Trust

PHILLIMORE

2009

Published for Motorway Archive Trust by
PHILLIMORE & CO. LTD
Madam Green Farm, Oving, Chichester, West Sussex, England
www.phillimore.co.uk
www.thehistorypress.co.uk

© Motorway Archive Trust, 2009

ISBN 978 1 86077 520 8

Copyright of the Motorway Archive Trust to whom all the authors identified herein have assigned their rights under the Copyright, Designs and Patents Act 1988. All rights, including translation are reserved by the Trust. Consequently, except as permitted by the Copyright, Design and Patents Act 1988, no part of this publication may be reproduced, stored in a retrieval system or transmitted in any form or by any means, electronic, mechanical, photocopying or otherwise, without the prior written permission of the publisher.

The Motorway Archive Trust (Registered Charity No. 1078890) is officially located at the Institution of Highways and Transportation, and operates in association with the institution of Highways and Transportation, the Institution of Civil Engineers, the Transport Research Laboratory from each of which the Trust gratefully acknowledges substantial material support and assistance. The Trust also acknowledges significant help from the Freight Transport Association and the RAC Foundation, the Rees Jeffreys Road Fund, and contributions, many in kind such as Russell Sunderland's reading of a draft text, and the donation of photographs and rights by the Highways Agency, the National Archives, *Transportation Professional*, Ordnance Survey, the Port of London Authority, Lord Montagu, Len Parker, Brian Hawker, Justine Taylor, InterRoute, Fitzpatrick, Union Railways and David Kidson of Winter and Kidson. Also particular photographic help from John Bird, Laura Wise and Trevor Hurst.

This book is published on the understanding that the authors and editors are solely responsible for the statements made and opinions expressed in it and that its publication does not necessarily imply that such statements and/or opinions are or reflect the views or opinions of the publishers. While every effort has been made to ensure that the statements made and the opinions expressed in this publication provide a safe and accurate guide, no liability or responsibility can be accepted in this respect by the authors or publishers. The publishers make no representations, expressed or implied, with regard to the accuracy of the information contained in the book and cannot accept any responsibility for any errors or omissions that may take place.

A full list of the photographic sources and acknowledgements of permissions is included at the end of this study. Further information is available in the captions.

British Library Catalogue-in-publication data and a catalogue record for this book will be available from the British Library.

Printed and bound in Malta

Contents

	Illustration Acknowledgements	ix
	Foreword	xi
1	**The Past and the Beginning**	**1**
	History	1
	Early Planning	5
	The Highway and Bridges Sections	9
2	**The First Motorway in the North East**	**12**
	Doncaster By-pass Motorway A1(M)	12
3	**The Improvement of the Great North Road, Trunk Road A1 in the West Riding**	**19**
	Redhouse–Wentbridge	20
	Wentbridge Viaduct and By-pass	22
	Wentbridge to Ferrybridge	26
	The Ferrybridge By-pass and Aire Bridge	26
	Brotherton By-pass	31
	Brotherton to Micklefield	32
	Micklefield By-pass	35
	Aberford By-pass	35
	Aberford to Wetherby	36
	The Wetherby By-pass and Wharfe Bridge	37
	Wetherby to Allerton Station	40
	Allerton Park Flyover Scheme	40
	Allerton to Boroughbridge	41
	A1 improvements by South Yorkshire Metropolitan County Council	42
	Redhouse Junction Improvement	42
	Barnsdale Bar Grade Separated Junction	42
	A1 improvements by West Yorkshire Metropolitan County Council	43
	Fly-over at Darrington Cross Roads	43
4	**Trunk Road A1 in the North Riding of Yorkshire**	**45**
	Introduction	45
	The schemes	46
	1960 onwards	49
5	**Trunk Road A1 in County Durham**	**51**
	The Darlington By-pass Motorway A1(M) and A66(M)	52
	Durham Motorway. A1(M)	54
	Birtley By-Pass A1(M)	62
	White Mare Pool to Black Fell A194(M)	63
	Newcastle Central Motorway East	64
	Newcastle Western By-pass	64
6	**Trunk Road A1 in Northumberland County**	**73**
	The County Surveyor's Department	73
	The improvement schemes	74
	Wide Open to Seaton Burn Diversion	74
	Seaton Burn to Stannington Bridge	74
	Stannington Bridge to Clifton Diversion	75
	Morpeth By-pass	75
	Morpeth to Felton	77

	Felton By-pass	77
	Newton on the Moor Diversion	79
	Hitchcroft to Cawledge	79
	Alnwick By-pass Stage I	79
	Alnwick By-pass Stage II	80
	Brownieside Diversion	81
	Warenford Diversion	81
	Pillars to New Mouson	81
	Belford By-pass	81
	Belford to West Mains	82
	Haggerston Diversion	82
	Berwick By-pass	82
	Conundrum to Marshall Meadows	84
7	**Motorways in the West Riding of Yorkshire**	**85**
	Aston–Sheffield–Leeds Motorway M1	85
	Surveys	87
	Statutory Orders	89
	Planning and Design	91
	The Construction Contracts	92
	Aston to Tinsley	93
	Meadowhall to Blackburn	93
	Blackburn to Tankersley	94
	Tankersley to Darton	95
	Darton to Wakefield	95
	Wakefield to East Ardsley	96
	East Ardsley to Stourton	98
	Bridgeworks	100
	Tinsley Viaduct – M1	107
	Tinsley Viaduct Construction	111
	The Strengthening of Tinsley Viaduct	112
	The Calder Bridge – M1	114
	M1 – Completed to Leeds	116
	Barlborough to Thurcroft Motorway M1 and Thurcroft to Wadworth M18	116
	The Barlborough to Wadworth Contracts	118
	The Wadworth Interchange Bridges	121
8	**The North Eastern Road Construction Unit and the West Riding and Durham Sub-Units**	**123**
9	**The Lancashire–Yorkshire Motorway M62**	**126**
	Prologue	126
	A View of the M62 in the 1990s	126
	Background	127
	The M62 Contracts Undertaken by the West Riding County Council and its Sub-Unit	134
	The Bulk Beam Contract	134
	The Construction Contracts	136
	The Pennine Contract, Lancashire County Boundary to Pole Moor Incorporating Scammonden Dam	138
	Pole Moor to Outlane	150
	Outlane to Hartshead	151
	Hartshead to Gildersome	155
	Gildersome to Lofthouse	157
	Lofthouse to Hopetown	159
	Hopetown to Ferrybridge	162
	Ferrybridge to Pollington	162

	The Reinforced Soil/Vidal Saga	163
	WYCET	166
	Pollington to Rawcliffe	167
	Rawcliffe to Balkholme including the Ouse Bridge	169
	The West Roads Contract	169
	The Ouse Bridge	170
	The East Roads Contract	172
	Balkholme to Caves	173
10	**Urban Motorways in the North East Conurbations**	**177**
	Land-use transportation studies	177
	Urban motorways	177
	A58(M). The Leeds Inner Ring Motorway, the First Urban Motorway.	178
	Stourton Link and M1 Interchange	181
	M1. Leeds South Eastern Urban Motorway	181
	M621. Leeds South West Urban Motorway	184
	M621. Gildersome Street to Leeds Motorway	185
	M606. Chain Bar–Bradford Motorway	187
	Newcastle Urban Motorways	188
11	**Rotherham to Goole Motorway M18 – East of A1(M)**	**189**
	Thorne to East Cowick	189
	Hatfield to Thorne (Thorne By-pass)	189
	Armthorpe to Hatfield	190
	Wadworth to Armthorpe	192
	Wadworth Viaduct	194
12	**Motorways in Humberside (formerly Lindsey County)**	**195**
	History	195
	South Humberside Motorway M180	195
	Tudworth to Sandtoft Advanced Earthworks	196
	Thorne to Sandtoft	196
	Sandtoft to Trent	197
	Continuously Reinforced Concrete Pavement (CRCP)	198
	Trent Approaches Advanced Earthworks	200
	Glued Segmental Bridge Construction in Yorkshire	201
	Trent Bridge	202
	Trent to Scunthorpe including M181	207
	The Scunthorpe Southern By-pass	208
	Brigg By-pass	209
	The Humber Bridge	211
13	**The Demise of the Road Construction Units**	**213**
14	**A1 Improvement Schemes Carried Out in the Mid-1980s to Early 1990s**	**215**
	Bramham to Wetherby	215
	Wetherby By-pass and Wetherby to Walshford Junction Improvements	217
	Wetherby to Walshford Junction Improvements	220
	Dishforth Interchange	220
	Baldersby Junction Improvements	222
	Gatenby Lane Junction Improvement	223
15	**The Up-Grading of Trunk Road A1 to Motorway Status in the North East Region After 1990**	**225**
	Redhouse to Ferrybridge	226
	Ferrybridge to Hook Moor	227

vii

	Hook Moor to Bramham	228
	Bramham to Wetherby Conversion	228
	Wetherby By-pass Upgrading	229
	Wetherby to Walshford	229
	Walshford to Dishforth	230
	Dishforth to Leeming	232
	Leeming to Scotch Corner	233
	The future – a brief note	233

16 The Role of the Department of State with Responsibility for Transport   **235**

17 The M1–A1 Link   **237**
History   237
The Private Finance Initiative   239
The Construction

18 Conclusion   **244**

Notes   247
Index   253

Illustration Acknowledgements

The following sources of photographs and diagrams are gratefully acknowledged:

Sir Alfred McAlpine & Son Ltd.
British Bridge Builders Ltd.
Bullen Consultants Ltd.
Cement and Concrete Association
Cerialis Press
Construction News
Dowsett Civil Engineering Ltd.
Mary Evans Picture Library
W.J. Harper
Harper Collins Publishers
The Hulton Deutch Collection
Huwood Ltd.
W.E. Middleton & Sons Ltd.
Ministry of Transport (H.A.)
Sir Owen Williams and Partners
Pell Frischmann Consultants Ltd.
Scott Wilson, Kirkpatrick and Partners
Stewart Bale Ltd.
Swan Photography
The Highways Agency
M. T. Walters & Associates Ltd.
Yorkshire Link Ltd.
North Yorkshire, Durham, Northumberland and the former West and South Yorkshire Metropolitan County Councils
Former colleagues Messrs. D. Bradley, R. G. Corby, T. England, D. Hunt, G. S. R. Hunter, J. Moglia, A. E. Naylor, G. Race and K. D. Williams.

Many of the photographs are taken from the writer's personal archive.

Footnote:
Most papers referred to in this Historical Record are to be found in the North Eastern Region Archive.

Foreword

The Archive for the North Eastern Region motorways comprises drawings, documents and papers from the following sources

- The West Yorkshire Archivist.
- Engineers employed by the West Yorkshire Metropolitan County Council successor Authorities.
- Engineers with North Yorkshire, Durham and Northumberland County Councils and Newcastle City Council.
- Personal contributions from engineers who wished to participate; many are now retired.
- The memoirs of A.T. (Hutch) Hutchinson entitled 'A Yorkshire Walkabout' and contributions from W.R. Varley and J. Shelbourn are of special note.
- The writer's personal archive.
- Published papers.

Successive re-organisations of local government have resulted in many documents being destroyed or yet to be unearthed. Many stories of those involved go untold.

I am indebted to the late Richard Coates former Assistant Director with Leeds City Council who arranged for the collection of archive material from the District Council Engineers, and to Ian Collinson for arranging for its temporary storage at the Ossett Laboratory, which he headed, and transfer to the County Archivist.

The West Yorkshire Archivist has agreed to take the archive collection and hold a copy of this record until a more permanent 'home' can be found.

I am grateful to all those who have contributed to the North Eastern Archive. I also wish to thank Mrs Eileen Hepworth of Active Solutions Ltd, formerly of Sawley, for her assistance with the word processing of the final text and Janet Booth for her perseverance with the typing, Christopher and Andrew Brennan for proof corrections and Len Parker for image processing. The hard work of Peter Hewitt in undertaking the final editing and indexing prior to publication is particularly acknowledged.

This historical record is a 'broad brush' attempt to cover the work done over almost half a century on the one hundred or so schemes comprising the present motorway system in the North Eastern Region, including

Trunk Road A1, which is being upgraded to motorway standards. In parts the early history of times and places are touched upon.*

In this account only a few people are recorded for their contribution to the motorway programme, a great many are not. Their contribution although unsung is warmly acknowledged. To those who read this and would like to contribute the Archive remains open.

This book is an edited version of my original text, which is half as long again and a much fuller account. The result of this essential editing process to meet commercial constraints is that much of the very technical detail has been edited out, individual contributions have been summarised rather than reproduced in full and many names have been omitted. A full set of References used for the original text is included in this edition. The full version has been deposited in the Archive, enquiries about which may be made to the Motorway Archive Trust by email to 'ner@ukmotorwayarchive.org'.

I hope this work will aid future researchers of the history of motorways and provide an enjoyable read for those who were involved or wish to know how the motorway network in the North East came about.

F.A. SIMS

Note: Where a bridge name in the text is printed in bold type, it indicates that the bridge is also illustrated.

---

* Due to the change from imperial to metric measurements, which commenced in the late 1960s, each scheme is recorded on the basis of the measurement system in use at that time.

1 The Past and the Beginning

History

From the time of the Emperor Claudius the Romans ruled Yorkshire and the North East for nearly 350 years. In A.D. 78 Governor Agricola commenced the building of a network of roads and forts to control the Brigantes. His army surveyors planned the routes; soldiers, slaves and locally recruited labour were used to build them. The skill of the legionary road builders was such that they achieved on average one mile of road every three or four days, with an estimated 650 miles constructed in the North East out of the 10,000 miles throughout Britain. Bridges were seen as vulnerable and only constructed where there was no practical alternative. It is probable that ferry services were operated across the larger rivers. Bridges were used when fording was precluded, and mostly constructed of wood such as oak and elm. Few stone arches were built in Britain and this happened long after occupation.[1]

Early stagecoach with eight-horse team.

After the withdrawal of the Romans the region was occupied in turn by Angles, Scots, Danes and Normans. The building of a bridge over the River Ure at Boroughbridge by the Normans was important in the history of the great road to the north.

It was the route to Scotland of the early Kings of England, John, Edward I and Edward II. The whole court was itinerant with its baggage train of ten to twenty carts and wagons containing everything from the Treasury to the King's wardrobe.

Drovers in charge of 600 or more head of cattle walked this route from Scotland to London, up to 20 miles a day, resting at night at the numerous hostelries. In those days it was largely an unmade road, which, following the Dissolution of the Monasteries in the 15th and 16th centuries, continued to suffer neglect. The packhorse and horseback was still the chief means of transport. Country roads were often impassable and the state of bridges declined.[2]

To remedy the situation Henry VIII's Statute of Bridges of 1531 placed responsibility for bridge building and maintenance on the inhabitants of the Counties and Boroughs and was enacted through local Justices of the Peace. The act compelling parishioners to maintain and repair the highway was passed in 1555. The 17th century saw an enormous increase in wheeled traffic with stagecoaches running regular services between the more important cities in England such as from London to York and

Carlisle, as the old mile-posts and its many coaching inns in the towns and villages along the way remind us. Winter conditions often rendered roads impassable where they were unmetalled.

The poor administration of roads by parishes and the government's neglect of national roads led to a public outcry following which Turnpike Trusts were formed to build roads and collect tolls, but ignorance about construction and dishonesty of the trustees saw riots at tollgates and many of the turnpikes were destroyed.

It was Blind Jack (John Metcalf) of Knaresborough who attempted to institute a road maintenance system early in the 18th century but his efforts were not readily appreciated.[3]

The Industrial Revolution (1750-1850) brought about expansion of the iron, steel, coal and wool industries and turned the North East from its predominately agricultural past into one of the country's leading industrial regions. With the development of ports and shipbuilding and the increasing density and spread of populations the need for improved communications became inevitable. The first solution was to increase the availability of waterborne transport and led to the great age of canal building.

It was not until Thomas Telford using six by nine inch pitching and Macadam using broken stone, in the first half of the 19th century, that methods of road building improved, driven by the need to facilitate the transport of goods to and from the industrial towns such as Leeds.

During the 19th century these forms of construction were adopted with improvements in the methods of consolidation with rollers and binding, brushing the surface with clay. The first tar-bound macadam road was that laid outside Nottingham on the Lincoln Road in 1848. Other developments followed.[4]

The last of the Turnpike Trusts disappeared in 1895 – the passing of the Trusts was a slow process and many became insolvent with increasing competition from the railways. The purpose of the road had declined as the railways developed and restrictive legislation prevented the development of mechanical transport. Nevertheless, the first British-built petrol-driven car appeared on the roads in 1896.

The road, known from early days as the Great North Road, gradually improved with the advent of the motor car and the lorry, although much of it remained a single carriageway for the next fifty years.

A new body called the Road Board was constituted in 1909 with powers to increase taxation on cars and to assist local highway authorities in the construction of new roads. Unfortunately in 1914 the War broke out to restrict developments to those mainly of a military nature. At the end of The Great War a Ministry of Transport was formed in 1919 to replace the Road Board but found its proposals limited too much by the difficult financial position.[5]

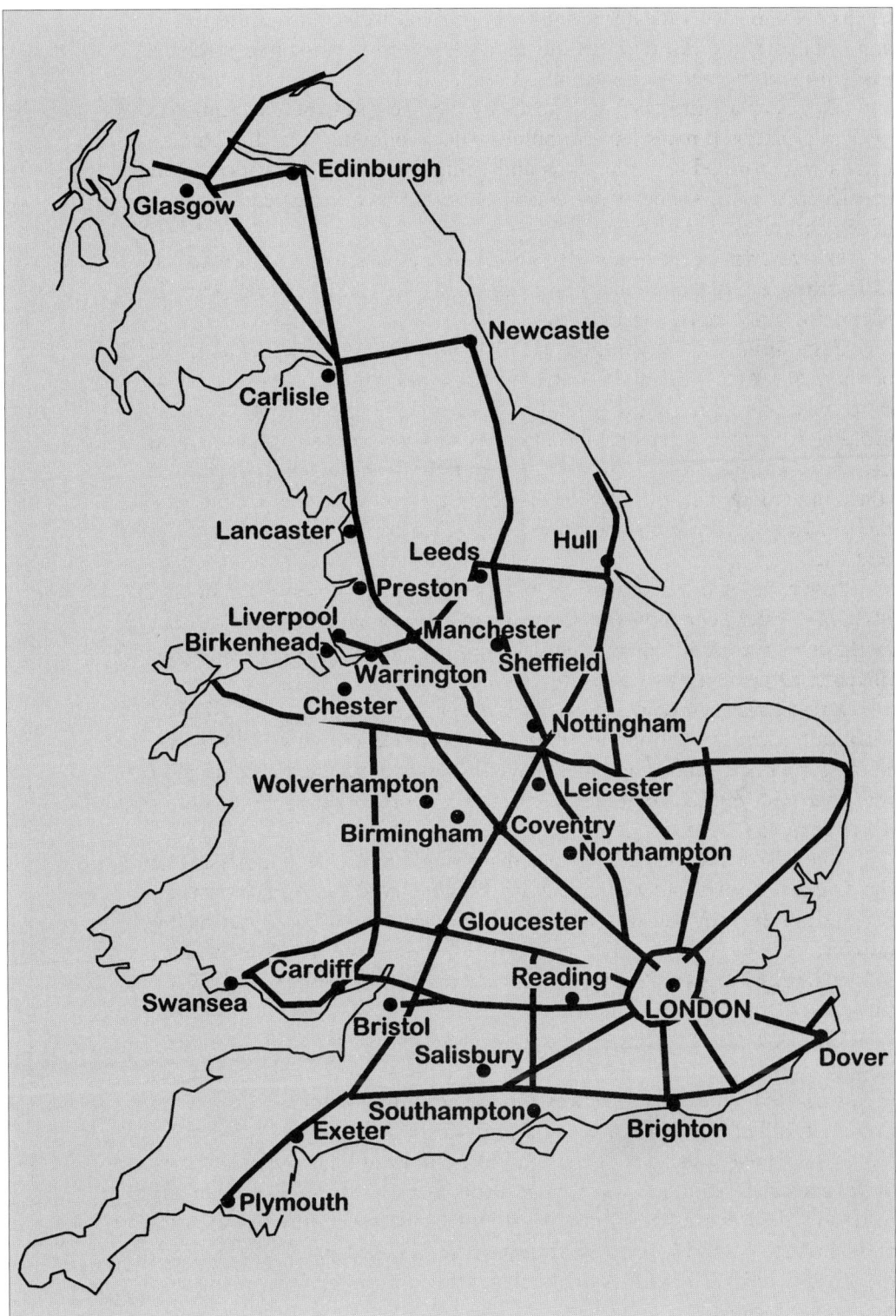

IHE proposals, 1936.

4 / Building the Network: The North East of England

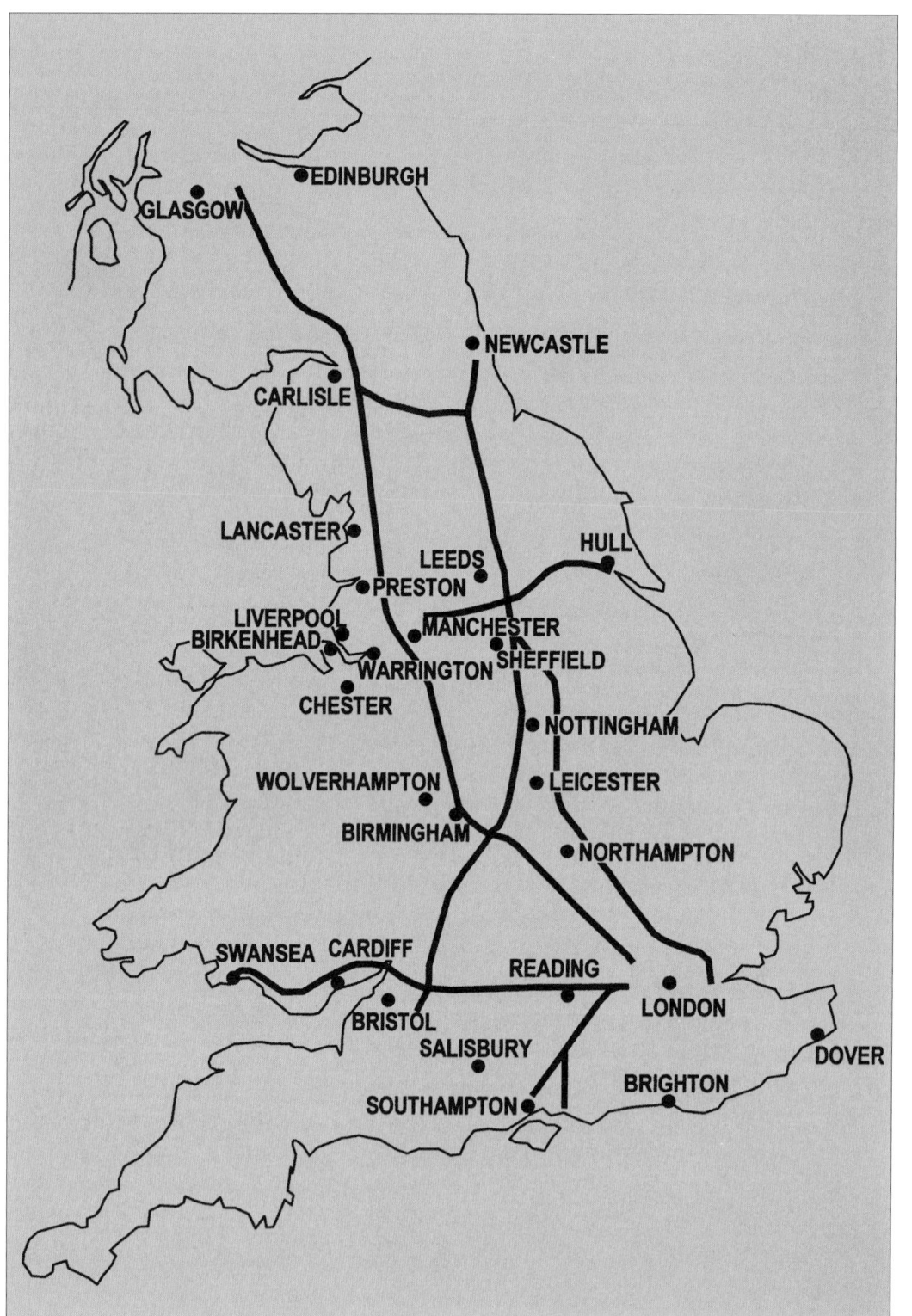

CSS proposals, 1938.

The Great North Road becomes a Trunk Road.

Following the Local Government Act of 1929, the County Councils became responsible for all Rural District Roads and Urban Districts, where the population was less than 20,000. The Trunk Roads Act of 1936 provided for the Minister of Transport to be the Highway Authority for the principal roads in Great Britain, which constituted the national system of routes for through-traffic. The A1 became a Trunk Road.

Some unemployment relief schemes were put in hand in the 1930s including the dualling of the A1 at Darrington and other work further north. The programme was again to suffer as the war clouds formed. Schemes were suspended and normal maintenance to meet military demands now had priority.[6]

It is difficult to believe that the A1, as a major industrial artery of Britain, was tolerated for so long by the road user, and incredible that local and through-traffic, together with traffic from the industrial centres of Yorkshire, could squeeze through one narrow junction in the centre of Doncaster. There were similar problems for the cities, towns and villages to the north.

Early Planning

The first strategic plan for motorways in the North East is to be found in the Institution of Highway Engineers proposed system of motorways submitted to the Minister of Transport in 1936. The plans, which included cross-country motorways from Liverpool to Hull and Carlisle to Newcastle together with a London to Newcastle Motorway via Sheffield and Leeds, failed to get the 'green light' to go ahead from the Minister of Transport at the time, the Rt Hon. Leslie Hore-Belisha.

The County Surveyors Society prepared a less ambitious plan in 1938 for a motorway system linking the main industrial centres of the country. So far as the North East was concerned, the former strategic links were retained. Again this plan failed to find favour with the Minister.

The next plan to emerge followed the ending of hostilities in 1945 and differed from the previous submissions in that the existing route from London to Newcastle (via Doncaster) was to be improved generally on its present alignment, as was the road from Darlington to Carlisle. The proposals for motorways from Manchester via Leeds to Hull and from Sheffield to Leeds were still retained, together with links from Doncaster to Hull as part of a new motorway from Bristol to Hull, via Birmingham.

It was in the early 1950s under Alan Baker as Director of Highways Engineering that the first motorways were planned and brought to fruition. In the North East the work of upgrading Trunk Road A1 and preparing plans for the construction of the proposed new motorways was largely undertaken by the County Surveyors of West Riding, North Riding and Durham County Councils.

It was these County Surveyors, Col. Stuart Lovell, Ronald Sawtell and Basil Cotton, who took the lead in this new era of road-building in the region. The City Engineers of Leeds and Newcastle, Geoffrey Thirwell and Derek Bradshaw, also became involved with the early planning of the urban links to the main strategic network. Since the 1950s the several County Surveyors of Northumberland, George Garnett, Cyril Girven and Basil Arthur, were involved in eighteen or so by-pass schemes to upgrade the Trunk Road A1 through Northumberland to the Scottish Border, although much of it was still a single carriageway.

During the immediate post-war years, whilst there was considerable design activity in the highway and bridge design offices, there was little outside work other than repairs to war-damaged roads and the normal maintenance to keep the highways 'in a commodious state'. By the mid-'50s a few small improvement schemes were being undertaken by the Counties' direct labour workforces in accordance the criteria that had been produced by the Minister of Transport in the war years.

Memorandum 575, published in 1943, set out recommendations in relation to highways in open country and those parts of urban areas where building development had not yet imposed serious restrictions upon road planning. The *Design and Layout of Roads in Built-up Areas*, published in 1946, in addition to laying down technical standards further promoted the view that the best results could only be maintained by wholehearted co-operation from the earliest stages between the Planner, the Engineer and the Architect.

The following extract from Lovell's Annual Report for 1953/54 to the West Riding County Council reflects the early financial constraints imposed by the Minister of Transport and Civil Aviation on improvement schemes and the limited work allowed to be undertaken to progress the motorways:

> The continued policy of restricting expenditure on Major Improvement Schemes to the minimum has resulted in very few schemes reaching the construction stage during the year ... However, on the instructions of the Ministry of Transport and Civil Aviation, some work has been carried out on the re-design of the junction of the Ashby St Ledgers–Sheffield–Leeds Motor Road with Rotherham Southern By-pass and also the junction and approaches of the Ashby St Ledgers–Sheffield–Leeds and Lancashire–Hull Motorways. Draft improvement Lines have now been laid down on all trunk roads in the County Area and sent to the Divisional Road Engineer for approval. These draft lines have now been approved in respect of 48 per cent of the total length of trunk roads and work on the preparation of the final drawings is proceeding.

The 1954/55 Report was more encouraging:

> The position with regard to Motorways generally remains the same as at the beginning of the financial year with the exception of the Doncaster

Western By-pass. Preliminary plans and relevant information required for the purpose of making an Order under the Special Roads Act, 1949 were forwarded to the Ministry of Transport and Civil Aviation during the year. It is hoped to proceed with the preparation of the detail plans for the new road as soon as the Order has been confirmed.

There is little doubt that the old rivalries between Lancashire and Yorkshire surfaced again in the race to build the first motorway in Britain. This honour was to fall to James Drake (later knighted), County Surveyor and Bridgemaster of Lancashire County Council with the Preston By-pass motorway on which work started in 1956 and was completed in 1958.

However, the Yorkshire engineers were entirely sympathetic when their Lancashire colleagues became involved in problems of frost damage shortly after the road was opened and thankful for the lessons learned on drainage, hard shoulders and temporary surfacings.

A boost to Yorkshire's endeavours came in 1956 when Harold Watkinson, then Minister of Transport and Civil Aviation, in a written answer in the House of Commons, gave notice of five schemes to which over-riding priority was to be given in the next few years. The first project was the improvement of the Great North Road from London to the North East which was to involve the great Counties of that region.

It was in July 1957 that the County Engineer and Surveyor, Col S. Maynard Lovell, announced that the County Council had accepted the Minister's invitation to prepare improvement schemes that would result in 50 miles of the Trunk Road A1 in the West Riding being raised to motorway or modern dual carriageway standards.

The Highways Act of 1959 consolidated the bulk of law relating to highways and streets into one comprehensive Act. This proved more convenient for local government officers concerned with the administration of highway legislation. It was estimated that some 39 steps were necessary from concept to implementation of a new scheme.

By this time Sawtell in the North Riding was already undertaking work on the A1 by direct labour at Sinderby, Londonderry and Catterick Village. He and Cotton in County Durham had also undertaken investigations and consultations for a by-pass of Barton and the Darlington By-pass Motorway, which crossed the County boundaries, and Orders were made.

Following the Minister's announcement of work on the Great North Road, programmes were drawn up and recruitment of staff commenced. The commentary by Hutchinson,[7] summarised below, is of relevance in the way work was being undertaken by the Counties at the time.

The highways and bridges departments now had a roads section and a bridge section – in the larger Counties a number of the roads sections were sub-divided under major works and general highway works and, with an imminent motorway programme to be completed, motorways sections were created.

The role of the individual engineer in fitting into one or other of the sections identified him as a specialist – no longer was a roads design engineer involved in bridge design and vice-versa, and, with the increasing significance of traffic management and forecasting, the sections of the highways and bridges departments multiplied when planning, traffic and safety sections appeared. No longer was the site investigation entrusted to the design engineer and a further section appeared under a laboratory engineer.

In the course of time the construction role became one of supervision with a contracts section to advise on the finer points of the Conditions of Contract, save in the highway maintenance field where direct labour still predominated.

The Ministry of Transport had by now produced a memorandum summarising the practice to be adopted in the design of motorways in rural areas of England and Wales. This embodied many of the principles developed by enlightened engineers of the day practising in both the public and private sectors. Technical details included treatment of central reserves and hard shoulders on the nearside of carriageways with light-coloured surface contrasting with the carriageways in texture.

Among the wider aspects, the need to recognise and protect agricultural interests was important and, indeed, the re-grouping of holdings to avoid expensive accommodation works. An Advisory Committee on the 'Landscape Treatment of Trunk Roads' was set up by the Minister to advise on the fitting of new highways into the surrounding countryside.[8]

In pioneering the new motorways, the design and construction of bridges was to offer a special challenge and excitement all of its own. The basic requirements governing the design of all bridges, then as now, are safety, durability, appearance and economy.

In the mid-1950s the guide to bridge design and construction was the Ministry of Transport's Memorandum No 577. This specified an equivalent loading curve based on a standard loading train developed by the Department in 1932. In 1961, Memorandum 771 confirmed the adoption of BS 153 loadings and introduced HB loading.

It was not until 1978 that BS 5400, the most advanced Bridge Code of its time, was produced by the British Standards Institution and the Department allowed it to be used on selected schemes before agreeing to its full adoption. From its inception the Code Committee was chaired by the illustrious Dr Oleg Kerensky until his retirement; the writer succeeded him in 1982 and held office until 1999. Other engineers from the North East were involved in Code work.

The Royal Fine Arts Commission exerted its influence over the aesthetic design of many bridges submitted for its acceptance. The general principles governing the Commission's approval were that 'expression of function is the basis of good design' and of equal importance there should be 'development of character and individuality in design'.

In the North East few if any bridges submitted to the Royal Fine Arts Commission were turned back. The general public also acknowledged in the early days of motorways that the further north they travelled the greater the variety and the attractiveness of the bridges became!

The problems of mining subsidence predominated in both design and construction in the mining areas of the region.

So it was with a background of the criteria outlined for roads and bridges that the first motorway in the North East and the improvement of Trunk Road A1 began. With emphasis on safety, central reserve guard rails were later introduced and emergency telephone and emergency warning systems installed, using the technology of the time.

The Highway and Bridges Sections

Lovell wrought many changes to the traditional ways in which a County Highways Department conducted work and his voice was increasingly heard on highway matters. The emergence of trunk road reconstruction and motorway building in the late 1950s and early 1960s looked an attractive and certain route to eminence. The award by the Ministry of Transport of successive Agreements for the County to act as Minister's Agent in major highway schemes saw Lovell's prestige and standing advance nationally.[9]

In the West Riding Lovell initially divided the planning and designs of the new Schemes for the improvement of Trunk Road A1 between Norman Ellis and Eddie Williams. Ellis, an experienced municipal engineer, and an efficient, determined and well respected individual had Doncaster By-pass, Wetherby By-pass and the schemes to Ferrybridge. Williams, a likeable Welshman, known for his occasional fiery outbursts when things went wrong, was allocated the Ferrybridge By-pass to Boroughbridge schemes. Their principal assistants were Fred Scott, David Lowson, Eric Howie and Harold Williams, later joined by Jack Shelbourn, John Glanville and Stan Grocott.

The Senior Bridges Engineer was Henry Roberts who was an able administrator and his principal assistants were Gordon Race, Norman Buchi, Arthur Beevers and John Adamson; two of them later became County Surveyors and one a City Engineer. All 'heads' and team leaders took great pride in ensuring that their graduates achieved professional status and that the Technicians who came later achieved their full potential.

The offices abounded with talented young engineers, many of whom went on to higher office in both the public and private sectors. One of them, Michael Callery,[10] writes:

> We were a young enthusiastic bunch of highly motivated civil engineers, whose mission it was to create a quality motorway network to cater for

'free flow' traffic as an inevitable consequence of advancing technology, a changing economy and life style and indeed our aspiration to 'predict and provide' was, to our perception, widely shared and accepted by the community at large.

Lovell encouraged his fledgling bridge engineers to adopt a liberal and adventurous approach in seeking individualistic and aesthetically satisfying solutions to specific bridging problems.

Buchi, a man of considerable experience and technical ability, succeeded Roberts, following his promotion within the Department, and the writer was privileged to follow him in 1963 and head the Bridges Section. The post was later designated Chief Assistant County Engineer – Bridges.

Mention should also be made of Ray Forrester, the County's Chief Laboratory Engineer – a physicist by training and a talented bridge player, who was responsible for setting up one of the leading local authority laboratories of the time and recognised as a national expert in his field.

Gilbert Senior, the County Mining Engineer, was also involved in advising on the mining and mining subsidence problems associated with the new schemes. An expert in his field, he was a member of the Institution of Civil Engineers Committee, which produced the Report on Mining Subsidence in 1959.

The design offices were places of great hard work and in the early days the working week included Saturday mornings. They were also places for fun; office cricket played between desks was a popular relief from work. Often pranks were played on unsuspecting staff.

The other Counties comprising the North East also had their main players and characters of these early times. A major difference, particularly in the case of the County of North Riding, was the considerable number of schemes undertaken by direct labour, whereas in the West Riding all of the schemes under consideration were undertaken by contract, as were most of those in County Durham. The West Riding, however, as with other Counties of the North East, did have an anathema to the appointment of consulting engineers and most of the motorway and trunk-road schemes were undertaken by local authority staff even in the days of Road Construction Units, to be discussed later. Tinsley Viaduct and the Calder Bridge were among the exceptions.

This is just a glimpse of the atmosphere that existed in most highways and bridges design offices at that time. A somewhat different climate from that of today's offices, governed by the profit motive, short-term contracts and private finance, rapid advances in information technology and far less time in which to think the job through.

So, to return to those early halcyon days of the '50s, we will see how the Trunk Road A1 and various motorway schemes developed into a regional strategic network.

On the way we will examine the major contribution that the North Eastern Road Construction Unit made to the programme during its lifetime, the effects of local government reorganisation in 1974, the demise of West Yorkshire Metropolitan County Council in 1986, and how the latest additions to the network have been achieved through the 'private finance' initiative implemented by the new Highways Agency, in the late 1990s.

2 The First Motorway in the North East

Doncaster By-pass Motorway A1(M)

Doncaster has a long history, having been garrisoned by the Roman Crispinian Horse (when it was called Danum), and later became the seat of the Angle Kings, before being destroyed by the Danes in 794. It flourished under the conqueror and its Norman masters, and was destroyed again by fire in 1204. It was garrisoned and fortified by John in the Magna Carta era.

The Great North Road traversed the whole length of the town and, where it passed the racecourse, was said to be 'the finest thoroughfare between London and Edinburgh' in the old coaching days.

North Bridge, close to the Town Centre, provided the only crossing point of the River Don for the very busy A1 Great North Road, whilst the A630/A18 east–west route carried heavy industrial traffic from south Yorkshire to the east coast. The town also served as the major business and shopping centre for the mining and agricultural communities surrounding it, whilst also boasting one of the finest and nationally important racecourses in the UK. As a consequence, by the early '50s, Doncaster was extremely congested and in urgent need of a by-pass. It therefore bore very strong similarities to Preston, on the other side of the Pennines.

Also lying on the direct railway route from London to the North, Doncaster had become an important railway and industrial centre in the midst of the Yorkshire coalfields. The problems of subsidence from coal-mining activities, the number of railway crossings and the River Don were leading factors in the design and routeing of the by-pass motorway.

Race[11] records: 'The first essential in the preparation of any motorway scheme is to fix the line in plan and, having accomplished that, to fix the grade level. The main factors influencing the line are terrain, the balance of the cut and fill, bridge crossings, sub-soil conditions, agricultural and property interests.'

In the case of the Doncaster By-pass, national road planning suggested that the route was to be on the western side of the town, a decision also influenced by agricultural interests. There were then three fixed points to establish as the first steps in determining the line – the southern terminus in Nottinghamshire, the northern terminus providing a junction with the existing A1, and the crossing of the River Don.

The Motorway through Warmsworth.
W.E. Middleton & Sons Ltd.

The southern terminus, 2¼ miles south of the West Riding County Boundary on the Bawtry–Nottingham Trunk Road A614, linked with the new Blyth By-pass (opened to traffic in December 1960) and the then recently improved existing road system joining the A1 at Markham Moor. The northern terminus was chosen at the junction of the A1 and the Redhouse–Wakefield Trunk Road A638, which was clear of the urban development north of Doncaster.

The Don Crossing more or less fixed itself as the only possible crossing within reasonable distance west of the town. It was constrained by the suburban development to the east and an extensive deep quarry system on the west. Any other crossing point would have involved either major property demolition or major structural works, both of which were prohibitively expensive.

It was not possible to make this bridge straight over its full length owing to the curve of the motorway through Warmsworth; the last three spans on the south side of the river are on both a horizontal and vertical curve.[12]

Proceeding northwards, the 12½-mile by-pass runs close to the once Saxon villages of Wadworth, Sprotborough, Pickburn and Brodsworth, before rejoining the Great North road at Redhouse. At the time it was the largest single project to be undertaken by the Government to upgrade the Trunk Road A1 into a national highway suited to the needs of modern traffic.

The line of the Doncaster Motorway was confirmed in spring 1957 and in July of the same year the Minister of Transport invited the West Riding County Council to act as its Agent Authority and to prepare the scheme and contract documents to tender stage.

Work on the detailed survey and engineering design started immediately, with Lovell entrusting the roads design to Ellis and a team headed by Lowson with Race and Adamson and their teams under Roberts undertaking the bridge design. Additional staff were recruited, the advertisement for staff alluding to previous feats of the Romans in building the original highway to the North. Teams under Forrester and Senior undertook the soils investigation for the route and the mining surveys and subsidence predictions respectively.

Although most of the land was acquired by negotiation it was necessary to hold a Compulsory Purchase Order public inquiry in May 1959, presided over by the Ministry's Inspector.

In June 1959 a £5.5 million contract was signed with the Consortium of Holland Hannen and Cubitts (Great Britain) Ltd, Fitzpatrick and Son (Contractors) Ltd and Lehane, MacKenzie and Shand – the consortium to be known as Cubitts, Fitzpatrick, Shand. The project manager was 'Sam' Henry and Senior Planning Engineer R.C. Joyce.

The Engineer for the project was Lovell the County Engineer and Surveyor, Chief Resident Engineer was Race and his Deputy was Lowson. Colin Beevers, Graham Johnson, Keith Williams and Callery were Resident Engineers for roads and bridges. Bill Bailey was attached from the Royal Engineers.

With a contract time of two years, the contractor had to negotiate quickly to buy or rent the land needed for construction purposes. Although all the land required for the motorway had not been finally acquired, construction started in June 1959 on a 200,000-cubic yard embankment at Cusworth Park.

Meetings were held with the public and authorities affected by the construction and arrangements made for temporary services to ensure least interference with the use of the roads and railways affected by the Works. Side roads were diverted and at Sprotborough Road a temporary Bailey bridge was erected.

A peat bog at Tickhill some three quarters of a mile long had to be removed by two Lima 1201 draglines. A fleet of Michigan loading shovels transported the 250,000 tons of imported sand and gravel infill.

The design of the motorway was in accordance with Ministry of Transport Standards with dual 24-feet carriageways, a 15-feet-wide central reservation and nine feet hard shoulders. The curves were designed for a safe speed of 70 mph. A standard side slope to cuttings of 1 in 2 was adopted with 1 in 3 in boulder clay areas. The cutting at Warmsworth, with its many bridges, was in magnesian limestone and side slopes were increased to 1½ in 1. Gradients were no steeper than 1 in 26, with a minimum visibility distance of 800 feet being relaxed in only one or two instances.

Drainage was by means of French drains in cuttings, connected to main drains. Embankment drainage consisted of open ditches. Because of to the probability of mining subsidence, flexible jointed reinforced concrete pipes were specified for main drains and piped culverts.

The carriageway construction was also flexible, comprising an eight inch cement bound granular base and four inch asphalt wearing surface. Because excavation material was magnesian limestone, a minimum construction thickness of 18 inches was specified with 28 inches over boulder clay and the marles.

Earthworks was a very complicated element of the scheme, consisting of approximately three million cubic yards of excavation, varying from solid rock to peat bog, and embankments of varying volumes to be placed and compacted. The area of road wearing surface was 390,000 square yards.

The 28 bridges on the contract gave the West Riding engineers their first opportunity to attempt some standardisation of designs.

Excluding the major bridge over the River Don there were five types of bridge: four span bridges carrying existing roads over the motorway, single span bridges carrying the motorway over existing roads, footbridges and railway bridges. There were also a number of culverts and subways. In the congested Warmsworth area the motorway is spanned by three two-span bridges. The aesthetics of the designs were discussed and agreed with the County Architect's Department and approved by the Royal Fine Arts Commission.

Fundamental to the design concept was the choice of simply supported spans with jacking facilities to cater for mining subsidence. The four-span overbridges consisted of three piers with skeleton abutments or bankseats if on rock. The centre piers were fixed and the side piers hinged at the bottom. Generally, spread footings were adopted. Both over and under bridges used pre-stressed concrete beams.

A unique feature developed by the West Riding was the rock face texture to exposed concrete faces. This was achieved by lining the formwork with vacuum formed plastic sheets having a light filler to maintain the shape. The blockwork effect also masked construction joints, bolt holes and shutter lines.

Two of the pre-stressed concrete footbridges designed by Callery are of note for their extreme slenderness. The cantilever and suspended spans were cast *in situ* and rest on leaf piers and bank seats. When the bridge was nearing completion Lovell became concerned that soldiers 'quick' marching might create a mode of vibration in sympathy with the natural frequency of the bridge. To satisfy the Engineer on this point a platoon from the local Territorial Army was marched in step at varying pace across the bridge to test its integrity before the bridge was allowed to be open for public use. Callery gives a graphic account of how he 'sweated bricks' until the tests were completed. To crown it all a TV crew turned up to film the whole thing. That evening the daughter of the landlord of his local pub was much in admiration of their new celebrity, the first person known to her to have appeared on TV!

The **Don Bridge** carries the motorway over the Don Valley at a height of 70 feet above the river and access to the site was consequently difficult. Large quantities of rock were blasted on both approaches to form access roads. This major bridge, 760 feet long between abutments, consists of two parallel but separate structures of seven spans. The 180-feet river span

Don Bridge construction.

comprises a suspended span of 100 feet and two 40-feet-long cantilevers; the adjacent anchor spans are 100 feet long. Of the remaining spans two are 100 feet and two 90 feet long. Each carriageway is carried on five riveted steel girders and a nine-inch thick reinforced concrete deck. Provision was made for jacking to deal with mining subsidence.

The Braithwaite Foundation & Construction Company, as sub-contractors, undertook the bored cylindrical piles for the piers, together with the fabrication of steelwork at West Bromwich, and its site erection. The steel superstructure was assembled on the approach embankments and launched into position. The launching girders were made up from the approach span girders and a light lattice launching nose. Bernard Pearson, the Supervisor of Works, got a severe dressing down from Williams when he launched himself across the gap as the bridge was being closed to become 'the first man across the River Don'.

The bridge was designed in the bridges office by Adamson's team, which included Allinson, Callery, Clague and Williams. Adamson and Callery, having never previously designed a steel deck, travelled to Preston to see Bill Atherton, the designer of Salmesbury Bridge on the Preston Bypass, to get some advice and he was exceedingly helpful in giving them a day's 'grind' in the essentials of steel bridge design. Lovell usually sent his bridge engineers to site to supervise the bridges they had designed, thus gaining valuable experience.

The five railway bridges, designed by the British Railways' Chief Civil Engineer, presented a major obstacle to the completion of the contract because of the many regulations to cover working in close proximity to the line. There are three steel decked railway underbridges and two concrete decked bridges over the motorway.

The largest bridge, Warmsworth Railway Bridge, has four spans and crosses the slip roads in addition to the motorway at the junction with the A630. Construction of these bridges involved driving sheet-piled retaining walls to enable each separate pier and abutment to be excavated and built under a temporary bridge of heavy steel joists. The single-span girders of the permanent deck were assembled on suitable trestling alongside their final position, the concrete deck cast, waterproofing, ballast and the track work laid and the span was then rolled into position onto the piers and abutments.

In the case of Brodsworth Railway Bridge, which carried heavy colliery traffic, the railway embankment was excavated during a week's holiday period at the colliery and a temporary bridge constructed to carry the line until the permanent bridge was built.

The section of the Doncaster By-pass in Nottinghamshire, 2¾ miles in length, together with the Blyth By-pass, was undertaken as a separate contract. The specification for the roadworks was similar to that for the West Riding section.

The southern access to the motorway was provided by a 240-feet-diameter roundabout at the junction with the Blyth By-pass and the A614 Blyth to Bawtry trunk road. Bridges carried the motorway over the Whitewater drain, the Styrrup–Harworth road B6463, the Harworth Colliery railway line and the occupation road at Common Lane. The Styrrup–Serlby Class III road is carried over the motorway on a bridge, the design of which was approved by the Royal Fine Art Commission. The bridges are constructed in two halves to allow for differential settlements and jacking beams have been provided to allow for future raising should this prove necessary as a result of mining subsidence.

The motorway also crosses the unclassified road at Styrrup but, as the motorway here is in a 60-feet cutting and a bridge would have been very expensive, a short length of new road was built connecting it with the Class III Styrrup–Serlby road. The diversion of this minor road saved a substantial amount of money.

The motorway was designed to blend in with the surrounding countryside and additional land was acquired for tree planting.

The Highways and Bridges Department of Nottinghamshire County Council under Reginald Kidd, the County Surveyor, undertook the design of this section of the by-pass works. The contractors were Sir Robert McAlpine and Sons Ltd.

At the opening ceremony in July 1961 the Minister, the Rt Hon. Ernest Marples, said the journey from Blyth to Redhouse could now be completed in 20 minutes compared with two hours on the old route. He stressed that people should drive carefully and at a reasonable speed. 'It is not a rival to Doncaster Racecourse', he said.

Mr Shand for the contractors, supporting the toast to H.M. Ministries, is reported to have made an impassioned plea for better arrangements for fixing rates and dealing with variations under the contract. Contractors often took this very public opportunity, at an opening ceremony of motorway works, to press their claims!

3 The Improvement of the Great North Road, Trunk Road A1 in the West Riding

From the Doncaster By-pass at Redhouse the Trunk Road A1 was to be improved to dual-carriageway standards with by-passes of Wentbridge, Ferrybridge, Brotherton, Micklefield, Aberford and Bramham before coming to Wetherby By-pass. The remainder of the route mainly followed the existing road as far as the approaches to Boroughbridge, where a new by-pass was to link up with the Great North Road in the North Riding.

The improvement lines and design of the roads was undertaken by Ellis or Williams and their teams, with the bridges by the Bridges Section under Roberts, Buchi and the writer as successive heads.

The dimensions generally adopted throughout the West Riding improvement of A1 were: carriageways 24 feet, central reservation not less than 15 feet, side margins 12 inches and an eight feet-wide hard shoulder.

The list of schemes is shown below and is followed by further descriptions.

Scheme	Completed	Length	Cost/Comments
Redhouse–Wentbridge	1961	4.5 miles	£879,000
Wentbridge Viaduct and By-pass	1961	1.92 miles	£803,000
Wentbridge to Ferrybridge	1960	3.5 miles	£259,000
Ferrybridge By-pass and Aire Bridge	1967	1.24 miles	£2M
Brotherton By-pass	1962	1.01 miles	£486,000
Brotherton to Micklefield	1964	4.5 miles	£1.6M
Micklefield By-pass	1960	1.64 miles	£418,000
Aberford By-pass	1963	1.8 miles	£741,000
Aberford to Wetherby	1965	5.72 miles	£2.4M
Wetherby By-pass and Wharfe Bridge	1959	2.25 miles	£571,000
Wetherby to Allerton Station	1960	4.0 miles	£488,000
Hopperton Station diversion	1962	0.93 miles	£245,000
Allerton Park flyover scheme	1971	-	£1.0M
Allerton to Boroughbridge	1960	3.25 miles	£586,000
Schemes undertaken after Local Government reorganisation in 1974 and before 1980			
Redhouse Junction Improvement	1979	-	SYMCC £3.2M
Barnsdale Bar Grade Separated junction	1985	-	SYMCC £0.8M
Flyover at Darrington Crossroads	1978	1.8km	WYMCC £1.5M

Redhouse–Wentbridge

The contractors were George Wimpey and Co. Ltd. The start date had been agreed as 7 January. The Resident Engineer was A.T. (Hutch) Hutchinson and the Assistant RE, Reg Allenby. The contractors' Agent was Frank Archer.

The roadworks were to consist of a new carriageway alongside the existing carriageway together with its improvement in parts to form a dual carriageway for a length of approximately 4½ miles. The existing carriageway was overlaid as a second phase.

Bridge construction was supervised by Callery, which included the replacement of the existing Humber Head railway bridge carrying Trunk Road A1 over the Leeds–Doncaster line north of Redhouse by a new concrete bridge. The culvert in Hampole Dike adjacent to the railway bridge was extended on the west and east side. A mass concrete retaining wall was constructed along the east side of Trunk Road A1 from north of the Humber Head Bridge for a distance of some 400 yards. A footbridge was added much later to retain access to adjacent properties. The 107-feet Robin Hood's Well culvert was of reinforced concrete and carries the River Skell.

At Barnsdale Bar Railway Bridge, Kirk Smeaton, the railway cutting was filled in and, after the east carriageway was completed, the existing brick arch was collapsed and further filling placed there to bring the west carriageway to required levels.

Barnsdale Bar culvert, situated just north of this railway bridge, was replaced by a 54-inch-diameter Armco riveted pipe.

The drainage provided for sub-soil water and surface water run off using a porous piped french drain system laid on puddle clay (later to be changed to concrete). The catchpits at 300-feet intervals had an 18-inch depth of sump from which silt could be removed under normal maintenance.

Amongst the 250,000 cubic yards of imported fill was material from the coalfield tips. Some of this was unburnt clay, which was prevalent in the coal seams, and many a loaded truck burst into flames if the material became too hot and reacted to exposure through digging operations.

Opening was achieved within the contract period, at the same time as the completion of the Doncaster By-pass in the summer of 1961, notwithstanding the inclement weather in the winter of that year.

Hutchinson[13] has some interesting stories. A delay occurred at Skellow Cross Roads where one 'Smiler' and his masons, excavating the foundations for a wall, unearthed a pile of bones. As becoming workmen with no concern for gentlemanly etiquette, the jawbones were put on display. Clearly this was a matter for concern; the jawbones were human and questions of missing persons abounded. The area became a 'no-go' area while the police were called in. In due course they pronounced the bones to be too old to concern them but advised that the curator of the Rotherham Museum should be called in. The archaeologists found the remains to be too recent to interest them and so the bones were interred in a common grave without ceremony, covered over, and work on the stone walls proceeded.

The existing Hull to Barnsley line had recently closed to rail traffic. The railway cutting possessed a spring of clear water that remained the only supply for an elderly couple – mother and daughter who resided nearby in a tin shelter with earthen floor. Daily they visited the cutting with a bucket. They refused to be rehoused having arrived with the railway. The deceased male member of the family had been the tunnel foreman at the turn of the century, and they were reluctant to leave. An alternative supply of water was provided from the nearby Highway Café, originally with buckets carried by the inspector until a more permanent supply could be arranged. The Health Authorities were aware of their plight and eventually the two 'Victorian' ladies were taken into care and the building was demolished to avoid further occupation.

Redhouse–Wentbridge was full of folklore, and historians will continue to argue the connection with Robin Hood. An item in the 'Site Clearance' section of the Bill of Quantities stated:

> Very carefully take down, marking the position of each stone, the ancient structure known as Robin Hood's Well situate near chainage 7,400 clean all stones as directed by the Engineer and cart to store on site where directed and dispose of surplus material. Cubic content above ground 520 cubic feet approximately haulage not exceeding 2 miles.

Robin Hood's Well

The sum of £49 was inserted to cover the item.

The stones of the Well were duly numbered for re-erection and a plan was prepared showing the arrangement. Before preparations were made for its orderly removal it was inadvertently demolished. A truck delivering a load of burnt red shale for use in the road works one Saturday 'dinner' time left the existing road, and careered into the structure displacing the stones. These were removed to prevent further damage and later stored in a stable at Womersly Park, the home of the Earl of Ross, one of the defenders of the Well, whilst a decision on its rebuilding was made.

The stone canopy was erected in about 1720 over the centuries-old site of a spring about seven miles north of Doncaster on the edge of Barnsdale Forest, a known haunt of Robin Hood. The Ministry of Transport offered to remove the Well stone by stone but it was not prepared to put it up again. A public appeal fund was launched, and the Doncaster Rural District Council put the re-assembly of the heavyweight jig-saw puzzle into the hands of the contractors.

The Well, now re-erected, stands not over a spring but on six inches of concrete foundations on the line of the Old Great North Road overlooking the high-speed clearway of the new road. (Some suggest that the stone identification plan was lost and the re-erection was simply achieved by a very skilled bricklayer.)

Wentbridge Viaduct and By-pass

Wentbridge lies in the 'bonnie Vale of Went'. This is an area of high ecological value, designated as a site of special scientific interest. The River Went has Ancient Woodland on both slopes and folklore has it that this was one of the haunts of Robin Hood. When Queen Anne reigned, Tom Sagle kept the *Blue Bell Inn* in the village, claimed to be the oldest hostel on the road. Dick Turpin was on the list of wayfarers who took shelter at the inn.

The village was well known to motorists for the road's tortuous descents from both the north and the south. The poor visibility and narrowness of the road created a considerable bottleneck with queues of traffic forming behind climbing lorries.

The by-pass, which is nearly two miles long, runs to the east of the village. The central reservation was widened to 30 feet at junctions and the verges increased to 12 feet.

The **Wentbridge Viaduct** carries the by-pass at a height of 96 feet over the picturesque and steeply sided valley. At road level the crossing is some 1,000 feet long and the gap was reduced by means of short approach embankments to give a span between abutments of 470 feet. Although the Went is only a small stream, the floor of the valley is subject to flooding.

The valley strata comprises of sandstones and mudstones, overlain by

Wentbridge Viaduct

alluvium with magnesian limestone found high in the sides on the valley. The underlying coal seams in the area were not considered by the National Coal Board to be worth exploring and consequently the absence of mining subsidence permitted the use of a hyperstatic structure.

The design of the roadworks for the scheme was a continuation of the work of Ellis's team, with bridgeworks designs being undertaken by Buchi's team under Roberts.

It was in this team that the writer was privileged to play a significant part in the design of the viaduct, and a young 'Sri' Sriskandan, originally from Sri Lanka, was involved, particularly in the Brotherton By-pass bridges which were also allocated to the team. Buchi, Markham and Sims[14,15,16] cover the design and construction of the viaduct in detail in several papers. In its day, Wentbridge Viaduct was the largest viaduct of its kind in Europe, having certain unique features. Although bearing a superficial resemblance to other structures with sloping legs, it differed from them basically in its proportions and method of structural action. There are two side spans of 140 feet, a centre span of 190 feet, the span at the leg supports being 308 feet.

The roadway on both approaches slopes down towards the viaduct and crosses it on a downward vertical curve. This curve has been deliberately emphasised in the elevation of the structure.

In the planning stage the viaduct was submitted for the approval of the Royal Fine Arts Commission and received with acclaim. It also had the distinction of being selected for inclusion in the exhibition of Twentieth Century Engineering by the Museum of Modern Art, New York, in 1964. In 1998 it became one of the few bridges to be listed.

The contract was awarded to Taylor Woodrow Construction Ltd; work began in October 1959 and it opened to traffic in November 1961. The tender price was £682,000. The Director in charge was Tom Reeves; Contracts Manager Angus McLarty; Bill Mangan was the Agent. The Resident Engineer was the writer, with Frank Whitehead and later John Stothard undertaking supervision of the roadworks.

The deck of the viaduct is of concrete cellular construction comprising six cells with cantilevered footpaths on both sides. The main pre-stressing of steel cables are placed external to the webs inside the cellular structure and British Ropes Ltd at Doncaster manufactured the 18½ miles of cable. This was the first bridge in the United Kingdom to use external cables.

The tapered legs, with 'hinges' at top and bottom, are of reinforced concrete with their axis inclined at 54°. Exhaustive tests were carried out on a short specimen hinge of full-size cross-sectional dimensions at the Cement and Concrete Association's Research and Development Division at Wrexham Springs to determine the suitability of the design before it was incorporated in the structure.[17,18] The leg foundations are solid mass concrete blocks founded on sandstone rock.

The centring for the bridge structure was itself an engineering feat. Five schemes were considered. In December 1959 Taylor Woodrow put forward a scheme based on the use of Bailey bridge panels proposed by Thomas Ward. In September 1960 Taylor Woodrow dropped the scheme, because the deflections would have been excessive, in favour of a scaffolding scheme.

The proposal adopted was for a scaffold 'bird cage' on a four-feet grid using about 120 miles of three-inch and two-inch tubing, founded on a temporary reinforced concrete raft laid across the valley floor. The design and erection of the scaffolding was sub-let to the Mills Scaffolding Co. Ltd, erection taking from October 1960 until the following March. The scaffolding was designed to withstand a wind velocity of 100 mph. The traverse bracing was designed to take this wind pressure over the whole projected area of the scaffold structure together with the agreed restraint against buckling.

Notwithstanding the contractor's responsibilities under the contract, the Resident Engineer's Supervisors gave meticulous attention, as the scaffold structure was erected, to compliance with tolerances, to the installation of couplers, strappings and bolt tightness. All of these contributed to the safety of the temporary works.

The Scaffold centring

With scaffolding covering the valley and construction well underway, Trevor Philpot and his cameraman Slim Hewitt arrived on site to interview the writer for the *Tonight* programme. The fee was a good lunch at the *Wentbridge Hotel*! The following evening, Cliff Michelmore appeared before the camera handling a piece of Meccano saying that they had found some chaps from Yorkshire who had graduated from Meccano and were 'playing' with scaffolding. The uniqueness of the structure and the engineering feat of its construction were barely mentioned!

This work furthered knowledge of the behaviour of birdcage scaffolding for temporary works which was later used in the construction of the Scammonden arch bridge on the M62.

The great bulk of the 14,000 cubic yards of concrete was mixed on site. Tom England[19] the Supervisor of Works (on this and many other contracts) recalls:

> One morning work was delayed due to the mixer driver not reporting for work. It transpired his sister Viv Nicholson had won £152,000 on the Football Pools. She was notorious at the time for her 'Spend, Spend, Spend' lifestyle. The mixer driver did not return to work. He came on site a week later driving a pink American convertible car.

The major part of the abutments is buried beneath the approach embankment fill – the south abutment is 87 feet high but only 30 feet is visible. They are of reinforced concrete construction throughout except for the concrete encased steel beams supporting the bearings.

Alderman A. Dwyer cuts the tape

The north abutment is founded directly onto soft sandstone rock but the south abutment is on 3 feet 4 inch-diameter *in situ* concrete piles 50 to 65 feet long, because the strata was found to dip at 50º to 60º. Thus the whole structure is ultimately founded on sandstones of the Middle Coal Measures of varying degrees of hardness. Because the strata was very variable, provision was made for jacking the legs on the north side should any slight differential settlement occur.

Construction of the approach embankments involved the placing of 110,000 cubic yards of rock fill, much of which came from the excavation required for the roadworks construction.

A two-span bridge carries the Went Edge Road over the by-pass at its southern end. The final contract cost was £803,000, which included the additional costs of piling the south abutment.

On 11 December 1961 the by-pass, having been open to traffic for a fortnight, was closed to traffic by the police for about half an hour to enable a ribbon to be stretched across the viaduct.

Alderman A. Dwyer, chairman of the Highways Committee of the West Riding County Council, somewhat hastily, officially opened the by-pass and received the gold-plated scissors donated by the contractor.

Wentbridge to Ferrybridge

This improvement scheme passes close to Darrington and comprised the duplication of 2¾ miles of existing trunk road carriageway together with the construction of ¾ mile of new dual carriageway. It was undertaken by McLauchlan (Knottingley) Ltd, a local contractor. The Resident Engineer was Jim Coffey who had also headed the design of the roadworks.

Access to the village of Darrington remained at grade for a further twenty or so years until the Darrington Flyover and Junction scheme was carried out (see p.43).

The Ferrybridge By-pass and Aire Bridge

Ferrybridge 'is in all our histories', quotes Jackson. 'The passage over the river at this point has always been of greatest importance, certainly since the Conqueror'; he sent de Moutiers to find a ford for his army. 'Leland came here – over Ferrybridge, of seven arches, under which runneth Aire.'[20]

The first Ferrybridge improvement scheme was carried out in the late 1920s and directed through-traffic toward the centre of the old village with its coaching inns: the *Angel*, *Greyhound* and *Swan*. In the 1960s, with peak traffic of some 40,000 vehicles a day, it became a notorious bottleneck with three-mile queues at busy periods. The existing Aire Bridge, built in 1803 with single 20-feet carriageway and acute approach bends, was a major obstacle to traffic flow, and the problems were compounded by a roundabout with the Pontefract to Goole A465, a signal-controlled junction with the Knottingley to Castleford road and two narrow arches passing under 35-feet-high railway embankments.

With dual carriageways already constructed and in use to the north and south, the possible alignment was very limited. The route chosen by Williams and his team led by 'Palf' Tayler necessitated the demolition of some 15 houses, one petrol filling station, the old derelict *Angel Inn*, the fish and chip shop and the premises of the local bookmaker.

The origins of the old Aire Bridge are of interest. On 21 January 1797 an advertisement appeared in the *Leeds Mercury* seeking from 'such persons as think proper plans for building the said bridge', the decision to be taken five days later at a meeting of the General Quarter Sessions of the Peace.

John Carr of York, in conjunction with the builder Bernard Hartley, submitted the winning design for the present three-arch bridge, with two small approach arches, which was built in masonry and completed in 1803 at a cost of £24,864. The bridge is scheduled as an ancient monument and carried 40,000 vehicles a day and individual loads up to 300 tons until by-passed.

The **New Aire Bridge** was a major challenge for the Bridge section of the Highways Department. Bill Varley, Maurice Allinson and Keith Green-Armytage formed the team for the design[21,22] with Denis Taylor undertaking the railway bridge designs, which showed the confidence British Railway engineers had in the County's bridge staff.

In March 1964, tenders were submitted, which included the construction of 1.2 miles of dual carriageway Trunk Road, a new 480-feet-long bridge over the River Aire, a 190-feet-long flyover at Knottingley, a 116-feet-long North Road Bridge (an underline bridge), the 147-feet-long Doncaster Road Bridge carrying rail traffic over the A1, a footbridge and a subway.

The construction of the new Aire Bridge involved bridging the River Aire without interfering with the barge traffic, and was therefore designed for cantilevering from the piers.

The successful contractor, Martin Cowley, commenced work in May 1964, but went into liquidation during Autumn 1965, having virtually completed the Doncaster Road Bridge, one span of the North Road Bridge, and some 20-30 per cent of all other work which included the piled foundations for the Aire Bridge. During excavation the ancient timber piles of the pre-1800 bridge were revealed.

Construction having started, it had been decided that a fly ash embankment would be constructed each side of the bridge to lighten the load on the ground. The associated problems brought many complaints in a built-up area, as did the heavy piling for the Aire Bridge. This was restricted to the hours of daylight, which provided little peace for those on night shift at the nearby power station also under construction. Much liaison on sleeping hours was necessary.

A workman obeying the laws of nature against a wire fence was electrocuted and carted to hospital. Wires suspended along the fence to convey electricity to the railway bridge must have shorted.

In December 1965, tenders were invited for the completion of the contract from a few major contractors with experience of cantilever bridge construction. Christiani and Nielsen were awarded the contract and started work in April 1966, under the direction of Alister Robertson as Agent and Keith White as Contracts Manager. The Resident Engineer (Roads) for the County Council was Charles Howieson who had succeeded Hutchinson, with Taylor Resident Engineer (Bridges) and Green-Armytage Assistant Resident Engineer (Bridges) for Aire Bridge.

White[23] records:

> The construction period of the Aire Bridge was the determining factor of the overall contract period, as construction time occupied all but the last three months of the critical path. In order to complete the contract in the specified period, it was necessary for Christiani and Nielsen to pick up the proposed construction methods, utilise the partly completed temporary works and engage the consulting engineer, Mr C. Parry, to complete his temporary works design.
>
> Fortunately, Christiani and Nielsen had available staff and key-men experienced in cantilever operations, which enabled them to open the bridge to southbound traffic only three weeks later than planned. The good progress also being made by the roadworks staff enabled the contract to be completed on time.

Christiani and Nielsen also constructed other bridges. Knottingley Bridge is a four-span bridge built on a skew and to horizontal and vertical curves. The bridge, which carries four lanes of traffic, was opened 12 weeks ahead of programme.

North Road Bridge a two-span bridge, carries two main railway tracks on eight feet steel plate girders. The construction of the abutment involved removal of track and part embankment under a railway possession to install way beams over the position of the abutment during a rail possession. On completion of the 45-feet-deep excavation, the piled foundations were undertaken in conditions of limited access and headroom, and the abutment constructed. The 180-ton bridge deck, which had been constructed on adjacent trestling, was rolled in during another rail possession involving removal of track, way beams and embankment.

The dumpling of earth under the new bridge-span was removed, wing walls constructed, footbridge built, and carriageway opened to traffic. The southbound carriageway and roadworks were completed five weeks ahead of programme.

In situ cantilevering in progress

The constraints imposed on the bridging of the River Aire were many and some quite rigorous. The Rivers Board would not allow any alteration to the regime of the river and the Navigation Authority requirements were most exacting. The closeness of the existing bridge, the hazards of boats, barges and tankers entering and leaving Ferrybridge Lock downstream, required a single span without need for centring in the river. The soil survey showed the bridge site to be composed of sand and gravel overlying badly weathered magnesian limestone.

After careful comparison of costs a concrete bridge box girder bridge of varying depth was selected as being the most economical and aesthetically in keeping. The 83-feet-wide bridge was constructed as an *in situ* pre-stressed concrete, balanced cantilever structure of three spans, the centre span being 290 feet long and each side span 145 feet. It incorporates handrail crash barriers, two 24-feet carriageways, one 10-feet central reservation and 12-feet acceleration lanes. The abutments and 'V' leg piers are of reinforced concrete.

The centre span, cast in nine-feet sections, has a shear pin[*] joint at mid-span and was constructed by cantilevering out over the river from

---

[*] The shear pin joint was designed to resist vertical forces whilst accommodating most of the horizontal movements. It was the first time a joint of this type had been used on a bridge in this country.

The Aire Bridge

each pier, whereas the land spans were cast on movable shutters supported from the ground level. The land span was constructed in advance of the river span, supported by eight temporary A-frames and eight 250-ton jacks positioned 24 feet from the pier under each land span. The design enabled construction to proceed independently on the river and side spans. During the winter electric blankets were used for curing the deck to ensure that the concrete obtained the necessary early strength.

The applied longitudinal super elevation to the bridge deck was calculated with the aid of a computer for each concrete pour, to allow the bridge to creep to its true alignment in ten years' time. The maximum super elevation applied near the centre of the bridge was 3¾ inches. At the time of writing, there is no evidence of 'sagging' at the mid-span joint which has occurred on some continental bridges.

The completion of the temporary works left by the previous contractor and construction of 60 complete nine feet concrete sections of the bridge took approximately one year. The cycle time for each concrete pour varied widely from seven to 26 days. This was largely the result of having to launch into complicated cantilever construction without the opportunity of building up gangs of men on less arduous work such as the construction of foundations and piers, and was a peculiar feature of this contract.

Although the by-pass was successfully completed in 1967, the settlement of the final account occupied the contractor and the Resident Engineer's staff somewhat longer.

The final contract cost with disruption and the re-assignment was of the order of £2 million with the Aire Bridge accounting for about one quarter of this sum.

It was during the construction of the by-pass that three of the original eight cooling towers, shortly after their completion at Ferrybridge 'C' Power Station, collapsed in a vortex created by a freak wind storm, witnessed by both Howieson and the writer, who now headed the Bridge Section, during a site meeting.

This was the last major contract for the improvement of the Great North Road in the West Riding during the 1960s.

Brotherton By-pass

North of Ferrybridge lies the village of Brotherton known for its ancient manor house of the Archbishops of York.

The by-pass scheme has a length of 1.01 miles and traverses an area extensively quarried for limestone. Major features were the construction of four bridges (a railway bridge, two over-bridges and a footbridge) and the extension of three large flood culverts at the southern end, which traverse the flood plains of the River Aire. One of the footbridges, designed by Callery for the Doncaster By-pass, was, with modification, used on this scheme, but this time troops were not called upon to test it!

Sriskanden[24] writes:

> The decks of the Fox Bridge and the railway bridge consisted of Universal Beams placed side by side with steel mesh top and bottom and the whole encased in a concrete slab. The purpose of this type of deck was to reduce the construction depth to a minimum in order to take the motorway under the road at the *Brotherton Fox Inn* and then over the railway.
>
> Dish Hill Flyover was on very poor ground and very long cased piles were used. When drilling for site investigation, the auger went down 15 or 20 feet under its own weight and the wash water on one borehole was found to bubble out through another ten's of feet away.

The deck of this bridge was of steel construction despite Lovell's prejudice against steel. The studs had to be individually welded on site by a stud gun. The testing of suspect studs took the form of swinging a five pound hammer against them. The contractor felt this was not very scientific when they started to go over like ninepins. So, in collaboration with McCalls, an attachment to the Lee McCall jack was devised and used to test the pull-out strength of the weld.

The contract for construction was awarded in 1960 to Harbour and General Works Ltd in the sum of £486,000. Jim McConnell was the Agent and Howieson the Resident Engineer (Roads). Sriskandan was Resident Engineer (Bridges) and Gerry Morgan Assistant Resident Engineer. The by-pass was opened to traffic in 1962.

Howieson was a Freeman of the cities of Glasgow and Bruges in Belgium. He was a talented artist and painter.

Brotherton to Micklefield

This scheme, another designed by Williams team headed by 'Palf' Tayler, involved the dualling of the existing road between Brotherton By-pass and Micklefield By-pass, a length of 4½ miles. Grade separation of all junctions was achieved throughout together with the segregation of local traffic and pedestrians in the village of Fairburn. All junctions were provided with acceleration and deceleration lanes.

Three major interchanges occur at the southern junction with A63, B1222 and again at the northern junction of A63.

The contract, awarded to Dowsett Engineering Construction Ltd, commenced in July 1962 and was completed in November 1964. This was the first of many contracts to be undertaken by this firm, which was started by Harry Dowsett, an entrepreneur and businessman of considerable talent and a 'character' in his day.

Construction commenced and was undertaken in three sections. The first section extended from Brotherton By-pass to Selby Fork. Phase 1 included a new carriageway forming the ultimate southbound carriageway of the dualling. This section of road was opened to traffic in the July. Reconstruction of the existing carriageway was carried under Phase 2, and provided the northbound carriageway of the duals.

The third section extended to Micklefield By-pass. Mention must be made of the drainage outfall along the Sherburn in Elmet road which was dug in solid rock for some two miles by Ben Tully and his gang of Irish labourers; 'his movements could usually be traced by following discarded 6 inch nails used by Ben to insert the detonator into the sticks of gelignite. He was also to be seen on pay-day with bottles of whisky for the labourers as an added incentive.'[25]

Towton Field stretches across the Great North Road near Sherburn in Elmet and is the site of a famous battle of the Wars of the Roses. Huddleston Quarry nearby provided much of the stone for York Minster and Selby Abbey – its winning would have been appreciated by Ben and his gang.

In situ marginal haunches with white top were constructed on this scheme using the 'Parry' type road form enabling approximately 1,000 linear feet of haunch to be completed in a 10-hour shift. Base construction was designed as a flexible type of pavement because of the possibility of settlement from mining subsidence. All main drains were laid and jointed with Cornelius-type joints to ensure flexibility for the same reason.

England[26] refers to the use of Pulverised Fly Ash (PFA) as embankment fill. 'Moisture content was very critical to achieve full compaction. During the winter of 1962-3 the site was closed down for over two months due to snow, which commenced a week before Christmas, and then severe frosts until March 1963. Tests were taken and frost had penetrated the embankment fill to a depth of some 3 feet.'

During the construction of the works a disused tunnel was found near Brotherton Village. It had apparently been used years ago to transport materials from a quarry to the canal. No ownership could be found and, as the tunnel was under the carriageway, it was decided to brick wall each end at the road boundary and pump a mixture of PFA and cement in a 20 to 1 mix to fill the tunnel section between the walls.

There are several bridges of note on this contract:

The A1 passes through the centre of Fairburn Village and **Fairburn Footbridge** was constructed to provide a link between the two communities. To allow for traffic of cycles and perambulators, approach ramps at a gradient of 1 in 10 were provided in the form of an elongated spiral. The deck had a central freely supported span of 45 feet between columns.

Fairburn Footbridge

Through the Boot and Shoe Flyover to Micklefield By-pass

The vertical faces of the columns, piers and spline walls were treated with matt black 'Arpon' paint and the soffits of approach ramps and deck beams with white 'Inertol', which was considered quite novel at the time. This bridge has since been demolished when by-passed by the new A1(M) upgrading.

Rawfield Lane is a single-span overbridge and at Selby Fork two bridges of three spans carry the A1 dual carriageway over the Leeds–Selby Trunk Road. Whitecoat Lane Bridge is similar but with a reduced centre span.

Adjacent to the *Boot and Shoe Inn* a two-span bridge supports a 24-feet carriageway, which connects the Leeds Road (A63) with the southbound lanes of the A1. Staircases have been provided at the abutments for pedestrians.

During this contract the writer became acquainted with Mrs Anne Lovell. It was she who made the final choice of colours for the 'Darvic' facia panels used as an artistic feature along the edge beams and continuing across wing walls. Outside of this involvement Lovell generally left the business of bridgeworks to his engineers.

The site of the Brotherton–Micklefield Improvement overlies extensive areas of mineral deposits. In the future it was expected that these would be worked and bridges were designed to accommodate 18 inches of differential settlement with facilities for jacking.

With Hutchinson, George Walsh acted as Assistant Resident Engineer (Roads) and John Lovell oversaw the bridgeworks. Fred Hatter was the Agent and John Jeffs and John Thompson the Sub Agents. The cost of the final work was £1.6 million.

Micklefield By-pass

Derek Goldsborough and his team under Williams designed the scheme. The contractor for the £418,000 Micklefield By-pass was the Paviors Construction Co. Ltd. Work on construction started in July 1959.

The 1.64-mile dual-carriageway by-pass has similar design features to the Brotherton scheme, including surfacings, and involved some 300,000 cubic yards of cut and fill earthworks. A new railway bridge to the east of Micklefield Station carries the by-pass over the railway.

The agent for the contractors was George Crow and Harold Williams was Resident Engineer (Roads) with Trevor Stocks the Resident Engineer (Bridges) who was also the lead designer of the bridges. The by-pass was opened in Dec 1960.

Aberford By-pass

Jackson[27] describes Aberford as 'an old market town retaining historic features back to the days of Imperial Rome. Samual Hicks, the famous Wesleyan Blacksmith of Micklefield, is buried there.'

A gate boasting a carved mouse running up one of the timbers approaches the churchyard at Aberford. This is the trademark of a North Yorks carpenter and it is to be seen wherever he plied his trade.

The by-pass was routed to the east of Aberford by Williams and his team headed by Harold Williams. Amongst other requirements was the retention of large stately beech trees in the vicinity of the Cock Beck. Unfortunately, a gale in the winter of 1961 uprooted them, much to the annoyance of the conservationists. Many trees suffered the same fate further north at Hook Moor, blocking the A1.

Hutchinson[28] records: 'The night watchman left the offices to make his tour of inspection and to visit one of the workmen's huts. He found this had disappeared and returned only to find the contractors and Resident Engineer's offices blown over. The Resident Engineer's deck trays of papers and books were recovered next day from the fields towards Towton on the road to Tadcaster, some gale!'

The contract for the Aberford By-pass was awarded to Dowsett Engineering and Construction Ltd, and commenced in October 1961 and was completed in 1963 at a cost of £741,000. The Agent was Frank Deady and the Sub-Agent John Jeffs.

The Resident Engineer who succeeded Hutchinson was Geoffrey Hunter, who later took up the same duties on the M62 Scammonden Contract, but more of him later (see pp.143-9). The Resident Engineer (Bridges) was Trevor Newsom.

The construction of the carriageways was experimental, having two layers of cement bound granular sub-base (five per cent cement) laid by Blaw Knox/Barber Green pavement finishers and compacted by vibratory rollers. An on-site batching plant was used for mixing. The surfacings were two-course dense tar.

Hunter recalls how he left the site immediately the road was open to traffic. There was no ceremony – it was generally called 'kicking the barrels away'. This apparently surprised Lovell and Eddie Williams, both of whom arrived a day late to witness the opening!

Aberford to Wetherby

The Great North Road between Aberford and Wetherby passes several historic sites including that of 'the fierce battle of Bramham Moor fought in 1408 during the Wars of the Roses'.

> Bramham Park is the site of a magnificent classic style mansion built 1698–1710 by Queen Anne's Lord Chamberlain, Baron Bingley. It is superbly set in French style gardens. The park is the venue for the annual Bramham Horse Trials.[29]

This section again, designed under Williams, between Aberford By-pass and Wetherby By-pass involved dualling of the existing road for a greater part of its length and a new by-pass for the village of Bramham – a length of 5¾ miles.

The grade separated junction with the Leeds–York Trunk Road A64 also required the construction of an additional mile of dual carriageway. Grade separation of all junctions was achieved throughout.

Three major interchanges were required at the junction with the A64, Tenter Hill, Bramham, and the A659 at Boston Spa Cross Roads.

The bridges on the contract included a four-span concrete overbridge at Bramham Cross Roads carrying the A1 over the Leeds–Tadcaster Road (A64). The decks were supported on slender reinforced concrete wall-type piers and skeleton abutments concealed beneath the approach embankments.

At Bowcliffe Hall a single-span accommodation bridge was constructed to give access to this historic house. This bridge was similar to Rawfield Lane Bridge at Brotherton.

Maurice Couchman[30] recalls: 'blasting alongside the Hall caused some excitement but although we were within some 50 feet of a listed building we didn't even break a window.'

At Boston Spa the intersection between the A659 and A1 consisted of two three-span bridges on reinforced concrete abutments. These two bridges carried the A1 over the A659.

Throughout the scheme abutment finishes and artistic treatment to fascia beams were similar to those used for the Brotherton-Micklefield Improvement Scheme, again with the help of the County Surveyor's wife in choosing the colours!

The A1 passes Bowcliffe Hall

The contract, awarded to A. Monk and Co. Ltd, commenced in April 1963. The Agent was Couchman, and the Sub-Agent was Len Brown. The Resident Engineer for Roads was Howieson, with John Lovell for the bridges.

The cost of the Works completed in 1965 was in the order of £2.4 million. The whole of this section of the A1 was replaced in the upgrading to motorway status carried out in the 90's and will be returned to later (see p.215).

The Wetherby By-pass and Wharfe Bridge

The small and ancient market town of Wetherby is situated on the north bank of the River Wharfe. There has been a bridge across the river since 1233. The original three-arch hump-backed bridge was 11 feet wide.

Wetherby, on several occasions the meeting place of the Kings of England, notably John and later Edward I in the year 1300, became an important town with the coming of stage-coaches in 1658. At the *Angel* and *Swan* and *Talbot* hotels more than 100 horses could be stabled. At one time North Street was reported to be the narrowest part of the road between London and Edinburgh being only 'three paces wide'.[31]

The by-pass of Wetherby was opened to traffic in October 1959. It was the first planned improvement scheme in the country on the Great North Road. The roadworks were designed by Ellis's team, which included Fred Scott.

The Wharfe Bridge

The line and side road orders were in place and the scheme prepared to the Ministry of Transport Design Standards produced during the 1940s. Scott[32] tells of how 'he was run off site with a shotgun when setting out the last northern curve, as the landowner insisted that he had been told by one Carnegie-Smith from the Ministry that the curve finished at a certain telegraph pole. The curve was adjusted and work proceeded.'

Some 2¼ miles in length, the by-pass starts with the bridge over the River Wharfe and rejoins the Great North Road near the famous Wetherby Racecourse.

Scott continues, 'The Suez crisis broke just after the tender documents were issued and Norman and I re-priced the estimate for the Works to allow for a fuel surcharge of one shilling a gallon. The contract came in at long last under estimate'.

The contract for the by-pass was let to Crowley Russell and Co. Ltd in October 1957 for the sum of £493,000. The sub-contractors for the Wharfe Bridge were the Cementation Co. Ltd. Crowley Russell's Contract Manager was Jim Smart (who later joined the West Riding Highways Department). The Agent was Peter Maguire and the Resident Engineer was a Major De La Tour.

The **Wharfe Bridge**, designed by Race's Team in the County's Bridge Section, was the first new major bridge to be built in the West Riding. The bridge has two side spans each of 96 feet and a central span of 160 feet, the length of the cantilevers being 45 feet each with a suspended span of 70 feet. It has an angle of skew of 13° and the width between parapets is 74 feet.

The design for the elevation of the bridge was approved by the Royal Fine Art Commission who took a keen interest in its appearance, as the bridge occupies a commanding position in a setting of considerable rural beauty.

The anchor spans and cantilever arms were constructed in reinforced concrete, the deck slab being similarly constructed, and cantilevered out to carry part of each footpath and forming a feature of the elevation. The abutments and wing walls were constructed of mass concrete, taken down to a rock foundation, and faced where exposed with squared snecked rubble masonry.

The two piers are constructed of mass concrete, taken down to a rock foundation just below the level of the riverbed. The surface finish to the piers consists of a multiple needlepoint-tooled finish to the concrete, which had previously been left with a textured surface provided by means of a special plastic lining to the shuttering.

Positioning of the beams was carried out by means of a temporary launching girder. Each beam was carried out on bogies and jacked down into its final position after removing the launching girder sideways.

Concrete was made with quartzite gravels from the Doncaster area from a single source to avoid unpleasant differences of colour and to obtain an appearance after tooling which would blend with the stone of the district.

The exposed faces of the piers and bridge elevations were given a silicone treatment, used for the first time in the West Riding, to reduce the effects of grime and road dirt. The damaging effects of the use of de-icing salts had not yet been recorded!

The entire surface area of the deck slab, footpath and central reservation, was covered with a ½ inch-thick asphalt waterproofing upon which was laid a protective layer of concrete averaging three inches in thickness.

The construction of the roadworks was not without its problems. Scott[33] says:

> The ground north of Sandbeck Lane was so bad that we did not strip the turf or top soil. The area was covered with magnesian

Construction of the suspended span

limestone waste from an old quarry at Collingham that included large blocks of stone …

North of this fill area we went into cutting about 20 feet deep. When excavating the drainage trench at a depth of 6 to 7 feet we came across a strong spring that would have been 25 to 30 feet below the original surface. The outfall drain was through very bad ground and was laid on a bed of straw and brushwood as it was below the water table. We only excavated two pipe lengths at a time as the trench would not stand.

He recalls how 'the whole of the road junction marginal strips were completed when the Ministry brought out new design standards which included acceleration and deceleration lanes. So the whole lot was ripped out and rebuilt to meet the new requirements.' The by-pass opened in October 1959. The final cost of the Works was £571,000.

One other event is recorded. The railway bridge adjacent to Wetherby Racecourse was altered to provide additional clearance for electrification of the Wetherby–York line. Beeching closed the line at about the time the by-pass opened.

Wetherby to Allerton Station

Although there is little on record of this scheme, it, nevertheless, involved the improvement of the Great North Road from the Wetherby By-pass to Allerton Station. A team headed by Harold Williams under Williams designed the scheme.

The contract awarded to Crowley Russell & Co. Ltd for £488,000 started in February 1959 and was completed in August 1960. Smart was the Contracts Manager. The Resident Engineer was Trevor Wadsworth.

The construction included the provision of a second 24-feet carriageway over a distance of four miles and included the widening by some 20 feet of existing Walshford Bridge, which carried the A1 over the River Nidd.

The construction of a new bridge to carry the A1 over the Harrogate and York Railway line at Hopperton was still under design when this contract was underway. The scheme for this bridge[34,35] known as Hopperton Station Diversion was let as a separate contract being awarded to Dowsett Engineering Construction Ltd and was opened to traffic in 1962.

Allerton Park Flyover Scheme

Jackson[36] refers to Allerton Manleverer as 'the chief seat of that ancient family who is said to owe its surname to maladroitness in hare hunting. He was a member of the High Court, which tried Charles.' He 'lost a great estate in the Parliament Service in raising two regiments and a troop of horses, and became a ruined man.'

The Allerton Park scheme replaced the staggered junction of the A59 with the Trunk Road A1 some five miles north of Wetherby.

The Works were designed in the late '60s and, although the Road Construction Units were now in operation, the scheme was designed in the Highways and Bridges Department of the West Riding County Council under Lovell's successor Tony Gaffney. The bridges were designed in the Bridges section headed by Jack Milburn. The scheme consisted of re-alignment of the A59 and included the crossing of the Harrogate–York railway at Goldsborough Station and the A1 at Allerton Park.

The contract was awarded to A Monk and Co. Ltd and the total cost was approximately £1,000,000. The Resident Engineer was David Woodhead.[37] General roadworks amounted to £760,000 and the Allerton Park Flyover and Goldsborough Station Bridge accounted for the balance of £240,000, of which some £88,000 was expended on piling works. Construction started in July 1969 and was completed in 1971.

Allerton to Boroughbridge

Boroughbridge was once the place at which Edinburgh stage coaches diverted through North Allerton. The Great North Road met the old Roman road from York on the south side of the River Ure. The old arch river bridge was built by 'Blind' Jack Metcalfe, the Yorkshire road engineer who preceded Telford and Macadam in the design of road pavements. A trio of megalithic stones, 'The Devil's Arrows', adjacent to the modern highway has been ascribed to a meeting place for the celebration of Druid rites.

This was the most northerly of the West Riding major improvement schemes on the Great North Road and included several diversions. The scheme consisted basically of the duplication of the existing single carriageway by the construction of a new 24-feet wide carriageway for a length of 3¼ miles between Allerton Station and Gibbet Hill. Also included were three dual-carriageway diversions at Allerton Grange, Claro House and the White Gables Café for a length of 1¾ miles. The earthworks involved cut and fill of some 225,000 cubic yards.

The contract was awarded to A. Monk and Co. Ltd and was completed in November 1960 at a cost of £586,000. It was Couchman's first job as an Agent and Eddie Shields was his Sub-Agent. Brian Lakeman was the Resident Engineer, having headed the road design under Williams. Bob Harris was the Assistant Resident Engineer.

Couchman[38] tells an amusing story. 'We had a Ganger called Ernie Waller, an ex-sergeant in the Guards, he had worked for me for about 9 years. Brian Lakeman spoke to him about his torn trousers (possible exposure). Ernie enquired as to whether he had any old suits. The following day Brian arrived with an old dinner suit. Ernie, a fine figure of a man, donned this whilst concreting, much to the astonishment of passing motorists!' It was the like of this man who carried out the hard physical work in the building of these new roads.

With the exception of the Allerton Park Flyover Scheme, the Highways and Bridges Department of the West Riding County Council, as Agent to the Ministry of Transport, undertook all schemes described so far, amounting to some £12 million.

A1 improvements by South Yorkshire Metropolitan County Council

On Local Government re-organisation in 1974 the maintenance of the Doncaster By-pass A1(M) and the A1 to the south of Wentbridge, formerly in the West Riding, was undertaken by South Yorkshire Metropolitan County Council as successor authority. The improvement of the junctions at the northern end of the Doncaster By-pass and at Barnsdale Bar were carried out by that Authority.

Redhouse Junction Improvement

Gordon Corby,[39] the County's former Assistant Chief Engineer – Major Works Construction, says: 'The principal object of the improvement scheme was to eliminate the roundabout at the junction of the A1, at the north end of the Doncaster By-pass, and the A638 Doncaster Wakefield Road. This was achieved by dualling and realigning the A638 to the south and carrying it over the A1(M) on a four span pre-stressed concrete structure, in addition there were various adjustments to the alignment of other local roads.' 200,000 cubic metres of colliery shale was imported as filling.

The work was undertaken under the direction of the County Engineer John Kirkham, the Chief Engineer (Major Works) was Ivor Marshall, and Brian Davies was Chief Engineer (Bridges).

The roadworks design was under David Saltmarsh and for bridgeworks John Powell, both Assistant Chief Engineers.

The contract for construction was awarded to A.F. Budge Construction Ltd who commenced the works in August 1977. The scheme was opened to traffic in the early summer of 1979 and cost £3.2 million.

The Project Manager was Ian Green, and the Resident Engineer was Alan Speed.

Barnsdale Bar Grade Separated Junction

Corby[40] states the reason for the scheme. 'The construction of a two span pre-stressed concrete bridge over the A1, at its junction with the A639 at Barnsdale Bar, in 1985, eliminated a potentially dangerous at grade crossing of the Great North Road. The contract was undertaken by A. Monk & Co. at a cost of approximately £0.8 million and the works were supervised by the County on behalf of the Department – the Resident Engineer was Bill Ham.'

The County Surveyor was Marshall who had succeeded Kirkham. The design of the roadworks was by Chris Basford, and Davies, Chief Engineer (Bridges), was responsible for the bridgeworks.

A1 improvements by West Yorkshire Metropolitan County Council

With the formation of the West Yorkshire Metropolitan County Council in 1974 the maintenance of Trunk Road A1 from the south of Wentbridge became the responsibility of the Directorate of Planning, Engineering and Transportation (DOPET). Gaffney was the Director of Engineering Services and Eddie Naylor was Executive Director Traffic Transportation. The writer, as Executive Director of Engineering, was the 'Engineer' responsible for the design and construction of new works, including schemes on the A1.

Fly-over at Darrington Cross Roads

This was the only scheme undertaken on the A1 by the new authority and was designed in Williams' department under Howie, his Chief Engineer, with bridgeworks designed in Jack Milburn's Structures Department.

Howie recalls that Bob Ashworth and his section had prepared contract documents for the demolition of a house on the south east of

Darrington flyover

Darrington Cross roads on the A1. Designs for the scheme were being finalised.

It was arranged that Bob would meet the successful contractor on Monday morning to agree a start date. However, he was soon back in the office to report that the contractor had already demolished a house, on the north west of the cross roads, which had not been purchased by the Department of Transport.

The contractor's foreman had carried out work for a local farmer, and thought whilst he was in the vicinity he might as well 'do this small job' on his way home.

The contractor made his peace with the owner. The Ministry immediately purchased the vacant land. Could such an arrangement be achieved today?

The contract, completed in 1978, was awarded to A.F. Budge (Contractors) Ltd at about £1.5 million. It involved the construction of 1.8km of dual carriageway and the Darrington Fly-over, to carry the Trunk Road A1 over the Darrington to Womersley side road linked by slip roads. 60,000 cubic metres of rock and other material was excavated to form the embankments, together with associated side road construction, drainage, fencing and street lighting. Major temporary diversions and a Bailey footbridge for diversion of pedestrians were required. The Resident Engineer was Alan Bradley.

Of particular note was the use of reinforced earth techniques for the abutment wing walls to the fly-over, based on designs by Dr Colin Jones, who later went on to become Professor of Geotechnics at Newcastle University and a recognised expert in reinforced earth structures.

4 Trunk Road A1 in the North Riding of Yorkshire

Introduction

In the Highways and Bridges Department of the North Riding County Council, the construction of roads, apart from certain specialised work, e.g. steelwork fabrication, which was sub-contracted, was largely undertaken by the Council's own workforce. They worked under the control of the appropriate District Surveyor, depending on the District in which the works were located: Thirsk, Bedale or Richmond. With increased mechanisation there was a corresponding decrease in the number of highway workmen. From over 2,000 employed in the late '30s this number had been reduced to 1,000 by 1960 and 740 by 1973.

Improvement schemes on the Great North Road A1, undertaken by the County Council on an agency basis, included two short sections of motorway, constructed in the early 1960s. These were A1(M) from north of Scotch Corner to its junction with the Darlington to Bishop Auckland Road, A68, in County Durham, and the A66(M) motorway leading to Darlington as far as Blackwell Bridge.

After the war priority was given to industrial routes such as the A1, including by-passes for Catterick, Boroughbridge, Leeming and Darlington and the conversion into dual carriageway of other stretches. Eventually, under the direction of the then County Surveyor and Bridgemaster, Ronald Sawtell, the North Riding became the first in England to provide dual

Old A1 Catterick Village

carriageways on the A1 throughout the length of its County. The provision of a second carriageway was possible over long lengths of the A1 without affecting properties, but horizontal and vertical alignments were adjusted to meet minimum visibility requirements for both carriageways. Work had started on providing dual carriageways as early as 1936/37, recommencing in 1946 and continuing in stages until 1960.

Sawtell was a hard taskmaster, highly respected, a man with foresight who must surely be ranked alongside contemporary County Surveyors in the North East of England. The 'modus operandi' of design work in the drawing office at that time differed from the West Riding. Deryk Wilkinson[41] writes:

> Each Engineering Assistant was allocated a scheme or schemes to prepare, and from that point forward he was entirely responsible for all the necessary work for that scheme or schemes, without support staff, including survey, design, Line and Side Road Orders where necessary, land plans, detailing, bills of quantities, specifications and estimates.

Closely linked with the maintenance of highways were the building, maintenance and repair of bridges. The late 1950's and 1960's were notable for the building of bridges in connection with by-pass schemes. These included eight bridges on the A1 for the Catterick By-pass, six bridges on the A1 for the Leeming By-pass, and ten bridges on the same road for the Boroughbridge By-pass. Additionally a considerable number of bridges were reconstructed as part of the normal Trunk and County road improvement programme.

The highways laboratory started from very humble beginnings in 1958 and grew when sufficient apparatus to undertake the full range of testing for concrete and bituminous materials, and drilling rigs to undertake soil surveys, were acquired. It was not until the planning and design of the Catterick By-pass that an aerial survey was used by the County.

Following the provision of a second carriageway throughout the length of the A1, apart from the major by-pass schemes to be described later, work commenced on a whole series of schemes to bring the original single carriageway of the A1 up to more modern standards. The original width of 22 feet was by that time outdated. The upgrading provided for a 24-feet-wide carriageway and regrading where necessary to achieve vertical visibility requirements.[42]

The schemes

The schemes carried out are listed in the table, and described in more detail below where appropriate:

Catterick as a military base has its origins in Roman times. Under the Angles it played an important part – indeed, it was here that in 762 King Ethelwald married Etheldreda. It was later torched by the Norsemen.

In Leland's time Catterick was a 'very poore towne' and had no market. The *Angel Inn* and *George Inn* at Catterick Bridge are among the oldest of Yorkshire's posting houses. The racecourse was one of the first in the country.[43]

Scheme	Completed	Length	Cost/Comments
Catterick By-pass	1959	3.5 miles	Sub-standard central reservation and side-slopes. cost £1.06M
Leeming By-pass to Catterick	1958	4.5 miles	Carried out in sections.
Leeming By-pass	1961	3.0 miles	£1.026M
North of Scotch Corner to the boundary	1960		Overtaken by the County Darlington By-pass Scheme.
Boroughbridge by-pass	1963	4.5 miles	£1.65M
Scotch Corner diversion	1971	1.34 km	First major use of a Contractor
Catterick North and South junctions	1983	Local	£3.1M

The **Catterick By-pass** was the first major by-pass scheme to be undertaken in the post-war years and had surface level roundabout junctions at each end (grade separation was to come later), together with nine bridges. The bridge over the River Swale was a three-span structure made up of steel beam and composite concrete construction. All bridge abutments were faced in natural sandstone.

In constructing this scheme, North Riding engineers claimed the first rolling of Universal Beams from Dorman Long's Lakenby Mill and one of the earliest uses of wet-mix in road construction.

In the vicinity of the River Swale crossing, the road passed through the Roman site of Cataractonium. It became necessary for archaeologists to undertake further detailed investigation of the site before the 'go-ahead' signal was given for roadworks to proceed. The main portion of the 'bath-house' is in the eastern side slope of the by-pass. Wilkinson and Cyril Burn were involved in the road and bridge design respectively and Peter Furness was the Resident Engineer.

Leeming is famous for its Royal Air Force base. The **Leeming By-pass** was the second major scheme; construction started immediately after the completion of the Catterick By-pass and included three overbridges and three underbridges.

There was always great urgency to get on with schemes and, if it was known that there were no objections, it was quite common for the appropriate Area Surveyor to meet individual landowners, probably in the local hostelry, to do a deal giving early entry on to land. This caused serious embarrassment to one senior engineer from the DRE's office in Leeds, who came on site to sort out a potential problem with one of the landowners, only to find that the A684 road had been completely lowered and the abutment foundations laid for the bridge. After realising what had happened he turned and said, 'I haven't been to Northallerton today'.[44]

48 / Building the Network: The North East of England

The final length of the A1 in the North Riding to have dual carriageways was the **by-pass of historic Boroughbridge.** The length of by-pass south of the River Ure was in the West Riding, and it was agreed that the scheme should be designed by the North Riding County Council and constructed by its Direct Labour Organisation.

The bridge over the River Ure had a double-cantilever and suspended span design. The steelwork in the superstructure of this bridge was fabricated and erected by Dorman Long.

Prior to the construction of the by-pass, Mr Sawtell had visited the M1 and seen the use of *in situ* kerbing. On his return he demanded that a design for, and fabrication of, moveable shutters should be undertaken within the week. The design was a scissor arrangement using 10-feet-long side shutters with levelling screws at each corner, and the fabrication was undertaken in the County's Central Depot under the eagle eye of David Hunt, the Superintendent of Plant and Transport. The shutters proved to be very successful in that, by using a fairly dry concrete mix they could be moved to the next section within three to four hours.

The *Daily Mail* got hold of the story by speaking directly to David. On 15 May 1962 the story appeared under the headline 'David's new kerb laying method can save millions'. The article referred to 'Ronnie' Sawtell being 'delighted.' Mr Sawtell took exception to this liberty and as Hunt had supplied the information severely reprimanded him – he nearly got the sack.

The Roman site of Cataractonium

Leeming By-pass

Ripon Road Bridge girder erection

The length of kerbing laid in a day was phenomenal. Three times as quick as hand laying by workman and at 40 per cent of the cost. However good the result, one always had to remember who was 'the boss'.

The introduction of the recommendations of the Worboy's Report on signs coincided with the construction of the by-pass. This became the first length of the A1 in the North Riding to incorporate the larger signs with green backgrounds, although great difficulty was experienced in finding a firm capable of producing the 'new' type signs. The design of the two schemes was again undertaken by Wilkinson and Burn and the Resident Engineer was Hopkins.

1960 onwards

One of Sawtell's ambitions was to see the whole length of the A1 improved to dual carriageway standards. He had reached the retirement age of 65 shortly after construction had commenced on the Boroughbridge By-pass, but had remained in post in the hope that he would see its completion. His untimely sudden death early in 1963 prevented this. He was replaced by Reginald Gibson who himself died suddenly and was succeeded in 1970 by Colonel 'Gerry' Leech (who was the President of the County Surveyors' Society from 1979 to 1980).

The **Barton Motorway Compound** was constructed in 1965 at a cost of £60,000 primarily to deal with the maintenance of the Darlington By-pass Motorway, not only in the North Riding but the length in County Durham up to the interchange with the A68. It also became a service centre, especially during winter maintenance operations, for the northern part of the A1 and the A66.

By the '70s more use was also being made of contractors and included the **A1 Scotch Corner Diversion and grade separation**. Here, grade separation was achieved at the A1/A66 junction at Scotch Corner in 1971 by the provision of a two-level interchange including two bridges over the A1. Tony Jerred and J.A.K. Schou were the road and bridge designers. Construction was undertaken by Contractors Messrs Brims and Co. of Newcastle with Bill Harris as Resident Engineer.[45]

Other schemes on the A1 were being prepared by the County Council as Agent Authority for the Department of Environment, including four grade separated interchanges at Baldersby, Dishforth and Catterick North and South Roundabouts.

Following the 1974 Local Government Reorganisation the work on the A1 continued under the direction of the North Eastern Road Construction Unit. The administration of the old West Riding, north of Wetherby, was now within the new North Yorkshire County boundary.

The County Council assumed responsibility for the maintenance of the A1(M) Motorway from north of Scotch Corner to its junction with the Darlington–Bishop Auckland Road A68 in County Durham and also the A66(M) Motorway leading to Darlington. They operated from the Motorway Maintenance Depot.[46]

Although coming in the new era of consultancy, further 'in-house' design was undertaken by North Yorkshire County Council for schemes to provide grade separation and eliminate the roundabouts at **Catterick North and South Junctions**, together with alterations to the side roads. Construction was again undertaken by Messrs Brims and Co., with Raidar Kristiansen acting as Resident Engineer.[47]

Before leaving the North Riding of Yorkshire the writer is indebted to Mike Moore, Director of Enviromental Services and the last to hold the title of County Surveyor in Yorkshire, for help with information and to Deryk Wilkinson, former Assistant County Surveyor, for his contribution[48] to the archive which adds 'colour' to the events of the time. Moore became President of the County Surveyors' Society in 1998.

5 Trunk Road A1 in County Durham

The principle of a new route for the Trunk Road A1 through County Durham was established in the early 1930s and took a tangible form in the building of Chester-le-Street and Birtley By-passes immediately before the Second World War. At this time the order was made for the Darlington By-pass, which subsequently in May 1965 became the first section of full scale motorway to be completed in the County.

William Henry Basil Cotton[49] swept into the backwater of Durham with a ferocious enthusiasm, much to the discomfort of the existing staff. In a short time he arranged to expand his department and embraced all effective modern technology across the full spectrum of highway activity. All his young engineers were subjected to intensive training in computer programming and the like.

The accounts side of the Department was streamlined so that unit costs for Direct Labour Work were available on Monday morning for expenditure up to the previous Friday, resulting in an effective control on all work. He also set up a material and soils laboratory about a decade ahead of their general use and arranged for tradesmen and supervisors to attend day-release college courses so that they could handle the new information on road and bridge construction. A specialist was also appointed to handle Project Planning twinned with computerised Critical Path Networks.

When motorways in the Durham area became a likelihood he was determined that neither the designs nor the contract documents should repeat difficulties that had been experienced in earlier motorways constructed elsewhere in England. Therefore, he sought changes in the specification and bills of quantities. The Ministry of Transport, not surprisingly, wanted a common standard and resisted many of the changes. However, a reasonable compromise was reached and most of the Durham Motorway was constructed with only a moderate number of claims – even though the area was much affected by old coal workings.

A motorways design team was installed and headed by Wesley Samuel Hydes. Initially, bridge design was undertaken by the Bridges Section and involved George Bushall and then Jack Horsfield. Hydes took over construction of the Darlington By-pass as Chief Resident Engineer. He was suceeded by Jim Mackenzie and Arthur Jacomb took charge of the design team.[50] Both Cotton (1966-7) and Jacomb (1982-3) later became Presidents of the County Surveyors' Society.

The Darlington By-pass Motorway A1(M) and A66(M)[51]

Darlington is an early industrial town based on the former NER locomotive works, iron and brass foundries and worsted mills. A by-pass of Darlington was first considered in September 1929, when a proposal to widen and utilise Carmel Road met with strong opposition. Eventually a line was located west of the cemetery, coinciding for some of its length with Nickstream Lane. The overall highway width was then to be 60 feet and the total length 5½ miles. A new bridge crossing over the River Tees was in the vicinity of Blackwell Bridge. This scheme was shelved during the economic depression in July 1930.

Following the War, further lines were investigated, and eventually a line located west of Darlington and the Merrybent mineral railway line was adopted. However, this railway line was ultimately abandoned over the whole of its length so that in June 1950 the opportunity was taken to move the line of the by-pass slightly eastward to coincide generally with part of the abandoned railway line. Severance would thereby be minimised and the area of agricultural land required for construction purposes would be much reduced. A further Trunk Road Order was therefore made in December 1950.

After the passing of the Special Roads Act in 1949, the Ministry of Transport decided to include the Darlington By-pass in the proposed network of new Motorways. Eventually, the two County Councils of Durham and North Riding of Yorkshire and their respective County Surveyors, Basil Cotton and Ronald Sawtell, undertook the necessary investigations and consultations, with the result that the draft scheme for the Darlington By-pass Motorway and the draft Barton By-pass Trunk Road Order at its southern terminal were both published by the Ministry of Transport in 1956 and became operative in 1957. The Ministry then invited the Durham County Council to survey and design works in both Counties. The two County Councils accepted this invitation on the reciprocal basis whereby the North Riding would carry out the whole of similar work on the Thornaby Link road in the east of the two Counties.

Survey and design work, together with the necessary consultations, started in earnest in September 1957, and standards to be adopted were agreed with the Ministry of Transport for the realignment of County and other roads affected by the motorway. The design work had reached an advanced stage when, in 1959, because of a sustained objection to the line of the Barton Trunk Road By-pass, the Ministry of Transport decided to amend the alignment of the motorway at its southern end. The main alignment was swung westwards and extended further south along the line of the disused mineral railway line through Barton Quarry to join the existing Trunk Road A1 near Kneeton Corner. A two-level roundabout

The River Tees Bridge

connection was located in Barton Quarry and a motorway spur taken from the main motorway south of Cleasby to a single-level roundabout near Blackwell Bridge to form a southern connection for Darlington and Teesside traffic.

Several alternative alignments were investigated in the area of Barton Quarry and for the Spur Link to Darlington (to become the A66(M)) in order to secure the best engineering line before the amended draft motorway scheme was published by the Ministry of Transport in May 1961. The scheme was confirmed in December 1961 to become operative in January 1962.

To facilitate construction work during the main contract, it was decided to undertake advance works on three bridges.

The bridges over the **River Tees** and the Barnard Castle / Darlington Railway line were let to the Cementation Co. Ltd in 1961 and completed in June 1963.

The bridge carrying the Bishop Auckland/Darlington Railway line over the motorway was let to the Cleveland Bridge and Engineering Co. Ltd in June 1962 and completed 12 months later.

In addition, work was completed by the County Council direct labour force on the construction of two major culverts required to carry large diameter trunk water mains under the motorway. Work was also undertaken by the North Eastern Electricity Board on alterations to important high voltage electricity cables.

Certain country roads and a bridge over the Bishop Auckland/ Darlington Railway line, which it was anticipated would carry the construction traffic required for the main contractor to and from the site, were realigned, widened and/or strengthened by the respective County Highways Departments.

Three Compulsory Purchase Orders were published to which there were numerous objections and a Public Enquiry was held in September 1962. The Order was finally made in January 1963.

The contract was advertised in December 1962, and was ultimately awarded to Messrs Dowsett Engineering Ltd of Gateshead, to start in April 1963, for the sum of £5.23 million and a contract period of 24 months. In May 1963 the Right Honourable Ernest Marples MP, Minister of Transport, 'cut the first sod' at the inauguration of the work.

The Dowsett Agents were Frank Deady then Fred Hatter. The Chief Resident Engineer was 'Wes' Hydes and his deputy McKenzie who succeeded him during the contract. John Jefferson became his deputy.

Dowsetts' contract provided for the construction of 10½ miles of motorway to by-pass Darlington and Barton, with an additional two-mile spur to Darlington, A66(M). In addition 9½ miles of side roads were re-aligned and reconstructed.

The by-pass runs from just north of Kneeton Corner, in the North Riding of Yorkshire, to Crumbley Corner in County Durham. It passes through country entirely rural in character and the only properties affected were the old Station House at Barton and some glasshouses at the Merrybent Nurseries.

The geology comprised mainly glacial clay deposits with pockets of gravel, sand, peat and some alluvium. Rock also occurs as both Magnesian and Carboniferous limestone. The 3¾ million cubic yards of earthworks included importing 900,000 cubic yards of fill. Surfacing work was carried out by Constable Hart and Co. Ltd. The 34 bridges comprised a mixture of steel, pre-stressed concrete and composite construction.

Dowsett Engineering Construction Ltd divided the contract into two sections, north and south of the River Tees, each being under the direct control of a Section Agent working under the main Project Agent. The Durham County Council Resident Staff was allocated on the same basis with two Section Engineers supported by the appropriate complement of Engineering Staff, Clerks of Works and Inspectors. The separate sub-contract for bridges carried out by Brims and Co. Ltd was supervised by a separate County Council bridge engineer and staff with the overall co-ordination carried out by the Chief Resident Engineer. This breakdown worked out very well in practice.

The Contractors made the fullest possible use of local indigenous materials, utilising imported fill from borrow pits, hard well-burnt red shale from a number of old colliery heaps in Durham County, and a hard carboniferous limestone won from a new quarry opened up at Barton.

The Darlington By-pass A1(M) together with the two-mile Motorway Spur to Blackwell Bridge and Darlington A66(M), which cost in total £6½ million, was opened in May 1965 by the Rt Hon. Tom Fraser, Minister of Transport.

Durham Motorway A1(M)

Durham is described in *AA Town Walks* 1984 as 'one of the most splendidly sited medieval cities in Britain, its rocky outcrop, washed on three sides by the River Wear, was from the earliest times a secure fortress against invading Scots and Danes. The town grew up in the shelter of the towering cathedral and castle, both built by the Norman Prince Bishops who ruled Durham as a City State. The unique powers which succeeding Bishops held were not relinquished until 1836.' They did much to enhance the city we find today.

The following is abstracted from the opening brochure[52] prepared by the Durham County Council.

The route of the Durham Motorway, from Aycliffe to Chester-le-Street, was first published in the County Development Plan in 1954. In 1958 the County Council, as the Agent Authority of the Minister of Transport, was invited to carry out the detailed location work to line order stage, and subsequently to undertake the complete design in 1961.

Over its 22-miles length, the motorway crosses three Principal Roads, the A689 Bishop Auckland to Hartlepool, the A177 Durham to Stockton and the A690 Durham to Sunderland. The major interchanges planned on these roads broke the whole project into four sections of between five and six miles, each estimated to cost £3-£4 million and contracts for these were let over a period of two years from October 1965 to October 1967. In addition, new side roads totalling some 13 miles of new construction were necessary. The individual sections of the motorway were progressively opened to traffic when completed, thereby easing congestion on heavily overloaded sections of the Trunk Road A1.

It had been recognised in the earliest stages of the location of the route that ground conditions were bad, but in the event, when combined with a succession of wet summers during the construction period, they turned out to be rather worse than expected.

On the **Aycliffe–Bradbury Section, Contract 1**, let to A. Carmichael Ltd, the route crossed the site of a post-glacial lake, the Skerne Lake. Bore holes and probes proved depths of up to fifty feet of soft silty clays, with the consistency of toothpaste, underlying a crust of firm material three or four feet thick. Investigations spread over a band of several miles' width to locate an optimum narrowest crossing point of this prehistoric lake. This was found, but even so, 300,000 cubic yards of the material was removed over a length of a quarter of a mile. This was dumped on 45 acres of adjoining land and the excavation backfilled with slag and other waste material. The slag came mainly from a reclamation scheme in Spennymoor. The silty-clay after drying out for three years was levelled off and soiled over and later returned to agriculture. Dowsett Engineering carried out the main excavation works prior to the letting of Contract 1.

Ricknall Carrs was a lake of fine-grained silt, on the line of the motorway about ¾ mile across. The Durham engineers had decided that the silt should be excavated and backfilled with Colliery shale.

A lot of plant had been retained by Dowsett from open-cast mining operations amongst which was a 110 RB dragline shovel – a 'big beast' with a 90-feet jib and four-cubic yard bucket. The excavation dipped quickly to a maximum of 25 feet. The excavated material was to be tipped outside the line of the motorway. The plan was to use the 110RB and dragline load into small trucks. Because of the weight of the 110RB some large timber pontoons had been built on which it could stand. On one occasion, the

Dowsett's 110RB Dragline

machine had slid sideways off the pontoons and lay at a 45° angle with its jib on the ground, one set of tracks buried in 15 feet of silt. Initially, two Caterpillar D8 bulldozers, staying on firm ground, were roped to the 110RB's 'A' frame. Attempts to pull the 110RB out of the silt were unsuccessful.

Hatter[53] decided to use explosives to clear away the silt. He suggested a line of holes at 45° into the face of the trench beneath the track about five feet deep and five feet apart. It was, however, necessary to undertake some trials to determine how much gelignite should be used. Following the trials, eight holes were made with a long broom handle and charged with four ounce gelignite sticks.

With everyone cleared back, the D8 drivers were told to increase the tension on the cables and then with baited breath Hatter signalled the foreman to 'press the button.' 'What happened then was sheer magic', recalls Hatter. 'There was a dull boom, the 110RB moved slightly the wrong way then, like some huge prehistoric monster rising from its sleep, slowly and gracefully settled back level on its tracks as its jib lifted into the air. Everyone swarmed over the machine, tracks were cleared, fitters checked the engine, which started, the ropes and controls were checked and it was driven out of the excavation onto firm ground. There was no damage and it was ready to work.'

The **Bradbury–Bowburn Section, Contract 2**, was let to Cementation Construction Ltd. The Agents were Ken Bullock, Bill Steel and Colin Foot. On this section the outcrop of Permian geological series is criss-crossed with extensive dolomite quarries. Here the motorway was routed to sterilise a minimum amount of this valuable mineral. North and south of the Magnesian limestone ridge the usual Durham County patterns of soft laminated clays and silts were encountered which, near the interchange on the A177 at Bowburn, necessitated considerable extra land acquisition during the contract works to deal satisfactorily with a perched water-table as well as water-logged silty sand that had not been revealed by the preliminary soils investigations.

The third, two-year, contract, **Bowburn–Carrville,** started in May 1967 and was undertaken by W. & C. French Ltd. It comprised the construction of a further 4½ miles of the Durham Motorway from north of its junctions with the A177 at Bowburn to half a mile north of the two level interchanges with the A690 at Carrville. Included with the motorway works were several structures, including overbridges, underpasses, Armco culverts, and an extension to the existing railway bridge at Carrville.

The route lies through the Durham coalfield, an active mining area, and particular attention had to be paid to possible surface settlement in the future. It also crosses the recent alluvium of the Wear Valley where soil conditions were expected to be particularly difficult. At the design stage approximately one-third of the excavated material had been identified as potentially unsuitable for fill, but with an unusually wet summer during the works more than half had to be removed from the site. Because of the poor ground conditions, cutting slopes of 1 in 4 and 1 in 3½ were adopted and produced an easy blending of the motorway into the undulating countryside, which it crosses. The main problems on this section were in obtaining stability of the embankments formed from marginally suitable material, and the underlying weak sub-soils. A number of slips occurred; to contain them the embankment slopes were graded out over the adjoining land and thick drainage layers incorporated at 10- to 15-feet intervals to reduce pore water pressure building up on the high embankments.

Drainage had to be constructed often in bad ground (including running sand), with continuous pumping operations necessary for much of its length. At one time up to 40 pumps of varying diameters were employed, and dewatering equipment was necessary to enable work to proceed south of Bridge 42 for approximately 1,000 feet run of trench. To add to these problems, storms on three occasions flooded the site. In spite of these difficulties, the work was completed to programme.

Work on the bridges was given some priority to provide access for the necessary cut and fill operations. Their early completion was achieved by working long hours and most weekends.

The earthwork team excavated and stockpiled approximately 200,000 cubic yards of topsoil, 900,000 cubic yards of cut and fill to embankments and 1,250,000 cubic yards of unsuitable filling materials off site to a tip adjacent to the site. Over and above these enormous quantities,

100,000 cubic yards of rock was excavated and broken down to size for re-use as filling in the embankments.

The fourth section, **Carrville–Chester-le-Street**, awarded to A.M. Carmichael Ltd, crossed an area of generally better soil conditions than was expected but was complicated by the presence of ancient coal workings, only partly collapsed, at a depth of about 25 feet, two areas of opencast backfill, a brickyard, and a half-mile length of low-lying river flood plain with underlying compressible clays to a depth of over sixty feet. This latter section was the site of advanced earthworks carried out by the County's Direct Labour organisation, working in close association with the Opencast Coal Executive. The northernmost opencast site was worked where the motorway was to be in about twenty feet of cutting, the land was restored to this level and the surplus hauled to form the motorway embankment further north, after removal of 80,000 cubic yards of soft surface layers. The anticipated settlement of the embankment had largely taken place by the time the carriageway works were commenced under the main contract. Ameys were the surfacing contractor for this section.

There were 60 bridges on the four sections of the motorway and their overall cost was almost £4 million.

In November 1964, a contract was awarded for the advance construction of two crossings of the River Skerne, three bridges over the main London–Edinburgh railway and two other bridges, and these were completed in time to provide accesses over these obstacles for the earthmoving equipment used on the main contracts.

Possessions of the railway track were only available for periods of over seven hours early on some Sunday mornings, and the bridges were therefore designed largely for speed of erection. Two railway bridges on Contract 1 were underlain by some 30 feet of soft laminated clay, and were designed to be supported on bored piles, but the alternative of using steel H-piles was accepted. A very close watch was kept during the driving of the first piles to ensure that there was no excessive heave of the track. In fact no measurable movement was detected at any time. A speed restriction was enforced during piling operations but the foundations of these bridges, and the two bridges at Nunstainton on Contract 2, which were founded on boulder clay, were given sufficient clearance from the track to enable them to be constructed while trains were operating at full speed.

On the main motorway contract, the same type of bridge design was used for both Sections 1 and 2. North of Bradbury the motorway is built over the coal measures, and the possibility of some movement from old and fairly shallow workings could not be ignored. This consideration, together with a desire to keep obstructions on the motorway to a minimum, resulted in simply supported single-span bridges of robust appearance, which reflects the workmanlike character of the region to visitors approaching from the south, and is in keeping with the semi-industrial nature of the mid-Durham countryside. This theme was continued in the colour schemes of the bridges, where the sombre bulk of the substructures was relieved and given continuity by the lighter shades of fascias and copings.

The bridge decks in the mining areas have provision for jacking to correct the effect of subsidence movement and laminated rubber bearings were used throughout.

On Sections 3 and 4 of the motorway there was a change of emphasis on the bridge types. The possibility of mining movement was less general and rock strata nearer to the surface. Thus, although five single-span composite bridges were built on these sections in positions where visibility or subsidence requirements made them necessary, there are also six multi-span bridges. Two bridges on Section 3 under the Ferryhill and Pelaw branch railway created the usual problems of keeping rail traffic operating during construction. At Whitwell a temporary diversion of the railway was formed so that the bridge could be built *in situ*, but at Belmont Railway Bridge the problem was to add a second span to an existing bridge. This was done by carrying the railway on way-beams and troughing, erecting the deck on trestles, and rolling-in in the usual way. The design of the new span followed that of the old span as far as possible. Plans of the existing bridge dated 1890 were obtained from the Railway Board and although the substructure information was rather sparse it was quite accurate.

At the Blind Lane Interchange at Chester-le-Street, two bridges and the embankment between them were built in advance, to allow for the

Lumley Dene Bridge

River Wear Bridge

settlement of the embankment due to the considerable depth of underlying alluvial material. To avoid the problem of the bridge being left at its original level while the embankment on either side settled, an extra foot depth of filling was laid over the bridge which could be removed if it ever becomes necessary to regulate the pavement levels.[54]

Two major structures on the motorway were required at the crossings of the Lumley Dene and the River Wear. These are the only structures on the Durham Motorway designed by Consultants, and the Ministry of Transport with the full approval of the County Council appointed Messrs R. Travers Morgan and Partners.

Lumley Dene Bridge crosses 'a deep, steep-sided valley of considerable natural beauty', and, in keeping with this setting, each carriageway of the motorway is carried by a shaped steel arch, which soars some 80 feet above the valley floor. Both arches have a span of 191 feet, and the side spans, each of 70 feet, are of structural steelwork with reinforced concrete deck slabs. The foundations of the arch piers were taken down to siltstone.

The River Wear Bridge also has separate structural systems for each carriageway. The bridge is of reinforced concrete construction with a total span of 345 feet between abutments. Each pier under each carriageway consists of two V-shaped supports springing from a common base. The bridge is supported on steel H-piles driven down to rock level.

All but the southernmost section of the Motorway, Contract 1, Aycliffe to Bradbury, cross the Durham coalfield. At an early stage discussions with the National Coal Board were opened in an endeavour to relate coal extraction to the motorway construction programme.

The Coal Board was able to re-phase its work to ensure that subsidence was virtually complete under long lengths of Contracts 2 and 4. No further extraction was planned that would affect the motorway but in line with the then Ministry of Transport's policy of not sterilising coal, the structures and motorway construction were designed to withstand subsidence without serious damage should this occur in the future. A section of shallow coal workings in Contract 4 was dug out and refilled by opencast methods. Quantities of unstable coal were uncovered in the pillars between these old workings and the Board met the cost of selecting, digging, and transport.

At the River Wear Bridge site on Contract 4, boreholes penetrated old workings only 20 feet below river bed level. It is unlikely that the river was in that position at the time of the workings given the evidence of substantial movement of the channel at that point. The bridge was sited clear of the workings, built in the dry and then the river was diverted back to its original course under the new bridge.

This, however, still left the workings, but sited under a 40-feet-high approach embankment. The closeness of the River Wear, the waterlogged ground, and the likelihood of connections with current workings precluded the possibility of opening them up and it was decided that the area should be slabbed over in heavily reinforced concrete.

With the possibility of mining subsidence on Contracts 2, 3 and 4, and the extensive alluvial deposits on Contract 1 with its long-term settlement problems, a fully flexible construction for the carriageways was adopted.

A positive system of drainage was provided throughout – the carriageway draining into pre-cast concrete channels and normal road gullies. On the Durham coalfield section flexible pipe-joints were specified and the system was designed to function with a 1 in 250 change of level. French drains were provided in the verges and the central reserve.

The main Service Area, initially planned for building concurrently with Contract 2, was unable to go ahead due to difficulties in land-acquisition and was built later. Service facilities were also provided north of the Durham Motorway on Birtley By-pass.

The construction of this motorway network involved the excavation of some 5,800,000 cubic yards of material, 870,000 cubic yards imported fill, and 930,000 cubic yards granular and free-draining special fill. The road pavement was 1,140,000 square yards. The cost of the whole scheme excluding land and preparation costs was estimated at £18.33 million.

The section of the motorway from Bowburn to the two-level interchange at Carrville was opened to the public in May 1969. The opening was very informal with the traffic flowing through without ceremony of any description.

The official opening of the full Durham Motorway A1(M) was by the Rt Hon. Richard W. Marsh, PC, MP, Minister of Transport, in September 1969. This included the four sections constructed respectively by Carmichael, Cementation, French and Carmichael covering the full length from Aycliffe to Chester-le-Street, a total distance of 21 miles.

The County Engineer and Surveyor's staff unit closely associated with the project on the road side were John Petrie, George Robinson, Walter Donkin, Reg Alexander and George Lister and on bridgeworks; Peter Mead, J. Robinson and Frank Smith.

The Chief Resident Engineer and staff were: John Perkins, Jim Marsden and Dougal Brown. Resident Engineers were Don Shaw, Harry Harris, Ted Simpson and Ted Wall.

Birtley By-pass A1(M)[55]

The By-pass consisted of 2½ miles of dual three-lane carriageway with associated structures costing a total of £2.3 million. It was constructed between July 1968 and April 1970, the main contractor being Robert McGregor & Sons Ltd; the earthworks Sub-contractor was Richards and Wallington. It is thought that this was the first contract let by the Durham Sub-Unit. On completion this was the first dual three-lane motorway north of the M1 at that time.

The scheme was basically constructed on the same alignment as the existing Trunk Road A1 dual carriageway by-pass, built in the 1930s but with improvements to the horizontal and vertical alignments. The contract included the construction of five main bridges, one being over a railway. All the bridges were founded on spread footings, four of them had pre-cast pre-stressed beams. The remaining bridge had steel 'I' beams and was the longest single-span bridge to have been designed in the Durham office. The span was 150 feet and had a skew of 33° – each of the eight beams weighed 30 tons. This bridge carried the bifurcated north carriageway over the southbound carriageway of the A1(M), being the future link road to the Tyne Tunnel.

Even in the 1960s this section of the A1, adjacent to Washington New Town, carried substantial volume of traffic, particularly at peak times, being the main feeder into Newcastle from the south. Difficult traffic diversions onto existing single carriageways had to be organised in sections as the work progressed. Many traffic meetings were needed involving high police presence. One of the early meetings in July 1968 had to be postponed when the police were unable to attend – 'Public Enemy No. 1', McVicar

Erecting 30-ton girders
Huwood Ltd

had escaped from Durham Prison and all police personnel were involved to expedite his early capture!

The Contract Drawings showed 12 disused mine shafts within the site; some had been extinct for nearly a hundred years. Only two shafts were found and the NCB required proof of previous back filling by sinking boreholes. After proving, the shafts were capped by massive reinforced concrete slabs, two feet thick, 115 feet by 115 feet approximately in plan.

John Collins was the Resident Engineer, David Cole and Arthur Main the Assistant Resident Engineers (Roads and bridges). Robert McGregor's Contracts Manager was Len Taggart and John Hobbs the Site Agent.

White Mare Pool to Black Fell A194(M)

The £1.6m contract for the White Mare Pool to Black Fell improvement of the A1 to dual carriageway standard and now designated A194(M) was undertaken by Brimms & Co. Ltd. Work started on the contract in April 1968 and was completed in March 1970. The scheme included the construction of the Havannah Interchange with the B1288, the Follingsby Interchange and the A195 and Peareth Hall overbridge. The Durham County Council Sub-Unit of the NERCU designed the scheme.

Newcastle Central Motorway East

Newcastle upon Tyne the County town of Northumberland, is a city port having heavy industries including shipbuilding.

In the early 1960s proposals were put forward by the City's Chief Planning Officer, Wilfred Burns, for a system of motorways in central Newcastle and crossing the River Tyne to Gateshead. The motorway network ringed the central business district and included a link through the central area.

Burns considered that 'where the motorway could enhance the atmosphere of the area it should be designed as a piece of civic or traffic architecture'.[56]

A start was made on the Newcastle Central Motorway East in 1972 as a trial Urban Motorway running from the north side of the central area eastwards to Tyne Bridge. This motorway was opened to traffic in 1975 and became part of the Great North Road, A6157(M), later renumbered as A167(M).

A downturn in the economy and policy changes in favour of public transport resulted in the plans for the completion of the system being abandoned until the late 1980s.

Newcastle Western By-pass

The Newcastle Western By-pass was listed in the Department of Transport's *Policy for Roads, England 1980* to link the A69 to the A1(M) to the south. The County Council proposed an extension of the by-pass to the north.

The A1 Newcastle Western By-pass holds the distinction of being one of the major road schemes in the North East opened by Her Majesty the Queen, which took place in December 1990 and included the naming of Blaydon Bridge over the Tyne.[57]

One of the much later improvements of the A1, it came after the demise of the Road Construction Units and in a time when government policy brought about the transfer of work from Counties to Consulting Engineers. This scheme was awarded to Bullen and Partners; the partners involved were Keith Best and Desmond Scott.

Best[58] in his memoirs *Best Endeavours* says:

> The biggest project inherited from the Durham Sub-Unit was the Newcastle Western By-pass. When we took over in 1981 the scheme had been in preparation for about four years although the route was first suggested in 1936 and a corridor was reserved in the development plan for the area in 1945. Residential development then took place on either side of the corridor; it was a good example of a farsighted planning judgement long before the days of sophisticated traffic forecasting and cost benefit analysis. After public consultations, a preferred route had been announced in 1981 that linked the Great North Road near

The route across the
River Tyne

Gosforth to Scotswood Bridge across the Tyne. Soon after we started work on the scheme, we believed some improvements to the design would be worthwhile. In particular, Scotswood Bridge was not in very good condition and the approach roads on the south bank, connecting to the Gateshead Western By-pass, were tortuous, substandard for the expected traffic flows. We proposed a re-alignment with a new bridge crossing of the Tyne and a new length of road to the south, providing a much better connection near Gateshead. In due course, after much analysis and scrutiny, the Department accepted this proposal and thus was Blaydon Bridge conceived.

The next task was to produce final designs, drawings and contract documents so that work could be completed and the new road opened to traffic in 1990. It was a formidable task. For highway projects there were no feasible 'fast track' procedures such as contractors starting work before the design is complete. Every detail of construction had to be prepared on drawings, specified exactly, and every item of work measured in bills of quantities priced by contractors bidding for the project. Beforehand, the conditions below ground had to be explored and tested by drilling boreholes and taking samples, so that foundations could be designed and earthmoving operations predicted. Despite such lengthy procedures, I believe it is the most efficient and cost effective way of implementing large-scale civil engineering projects. But despite such precautions, there is always the unexpected, especially below ground.

The 11 km by-pass joins the present Trunk roads north and south of Newcastle and Gateshead connecting with the key radial routes from the west such as the A69 and A696. The scheme relieved the existing Tyne Bridge, removed traffic from the Town improving the environment, and assisted in the planned urban regeneration.

The alignment follows the western edge of the Newcastle/Gateshead conurbation, from the former A69 River Derwent bridge to the A1 north to Gosforth. Blaydon Bridge was the latest addition to a collection of notable Tyne bridges for which Newcastle is justly famous, and there are seven grade separated interchanges to give access to the existing road network.

The by-pass was designed to carry 50,000 vehicles per day and is dual two-lane, with a third lane on each carriageway between interchanges from Scotswood Road to Ponteland Road. All the interchanges are two-level.

It was predicted that the reduction of traffic on adjacent roads would prevent at least two fatalities and 30 serious injuries every year. Ten footbridges and subways separate pedestrians from the traffic on the by-pass and its side roads.

Before construction started, 1,200 homes were provided with noise insulation. Earth bunds and concrete screening walls were constructed to reduce traffic noise and there has been extensive planting of trees and shrubs. Although the corridor had been protected for the scheme, designing the road to modern standards required the demolition of 66 houses.

On a historic note, where the route crosses the remains of Hadrian's Wall, in conjunction with English Heritage, stone sets and a plaque were provided to mark the line of the wall.

The importance of nature conservation is also reflected in the scheme. At Derwentaugh the embankment has been founded on a two-metre layer of inert rock to prevent contamination of the adjacent Shibdon Pond Nature Reserve.

The total cost of the scheme was some £88 million, including £12 million for the diversion of major services. £23 million was provided by the European Community's Regional Development Fund.

Because the project was so large and diverse the construction of the by-pass was divided into five contracts: Contracts 1 and 3 was awarded to Balfour Beatty Construction Ltd, Project Manager Alan Cessford. Contract 1A went to Cementation Projects Ltd, Project Director Cris Howe and Site Manager Reg Tranter. Contract 2 was awarded to Edmund Nuttall Ltd, Project Manager Paul Roebuck. Contract 4, the final contract, went to Birse Construction Ltd, Area Manager Chris Haworth.

The Chief Resident Engineer for Bullens was Ian Ainsworth with Resident Engineers Ted Simpson, Wayne Rhodes, Mike Sandell and Henry Ellis.

Contract 4 was commenced by Birse in Feb 1987 as an advanced works contract in order to prepare a 1km-long long section of the Contract 3 route at Derwenthaugh, where eight-metres-high embankments were to be constructed over deep deposits of soft alluvial silts and clays. The purpose of the advanced earthworks was to squeeze the ground by surcharging and accelerate its settlement by drainage of water from the clay through vertical sand drains. During embankment construction, 24,000 vertical sand drains with a total length of 210 km were installed on a grid layout with instrumentation for monitoring ground behaviour. Best[59] records: 'Until the ground was sufficiently stabilised, the road could not properly be built and it was predicted that the process would take at least six months. In April 1987, the advance works were formally inaugurated by John Moore, the Secretary of State for Transport.'

Contract 1 – Etal Lane to North Brunton started in August 1987. It comprised of 5.6 km of dual two-lane road with interchanges at North Brunton, Kingston Park and the A696 Ponteland Road. It was opened to traffic three months early in March 1990 by Robert Atkins, MP, who was then Minister for Roads and Traffic.

Contract 1A – Fawdon Railway Bridge. Best[60] gives an account of how the decision was made to build this bridge as an underline bridge and how Cementation was awarded the contract for its construction:

> The railway bridge is an example of how democratic procedures give the public the chance of changing things. At the public enquiry, we had

Thrust boring the tunnel

proposed a scheme, which took the road over one of the busy Newcastle Metro railway lines at Fawdon. This was much cheaper than putting the road underneath but required a length of embankment through a sensitive suburb. At the Inquiry, local residents and their councillors objected to this intrusion and in his report, the Inspector recommended that despite the increased cost, the underpass arrangement should be preferred, and so it was.

The main problem with inserting a bridge in a railway line is keeping the trains running without interruption. This usually means that the new bridge has to be rolled into position sideways and the line quickly reconnected during a short period when there are no trains. During the '70s a new technique had developed, based on a system of thrust boring started by Jim Thompson and his firm, Tube Headings, who were ultimately merged with Cementation Projects Ltd. Originally intended for jacking concrete pipes and subways, the system was developed and extended to railway bridge construction. Large square or rectangular concrete boxes, with steel cutting edges were constructed in pits below the railway line and installed under the track by progressive jacking and excavation using tunnelling methods. Cementation had patented a simple but effective refinement, not hitherto spotted by their competitors. Friction was substantially reduced during the jacking process by progressively unrolling a reinforced rubber or plastic sheet (for example, conveyor belting) between the top of the box and the soil. As a result, Cementation had successfully completed a number of bridges for British Rail and with their patented system, gained a near monopoly in this small but specialised market.

We decided that the Cementation system offered the best solution for Fawdon Railway Bridge and I decided that the safest, surest and least expensive way of implementing the work would be for Cementation Projects to design and construct the bridge. The Department of Transport were vigorously opposed to the idea that a contract should be let without competition. It took a lot of verbal and written persuasion to secure the result I wanted and adopt what I knew to be the best method. Ultimately, it was agreed that Bullens would employ Cementation as sub-contractors for the design and would retain full responsibility. Cementation would be managing contractors, with a negotiated fee but would sub-contract the whole of the civil engineering work by competitive tendering. A contract was let on this basis in November 1987, the work proceeded well and the bridge was rolled in during March 1989, the programmed date, with no interruption to commuter services.[61]

Contract 2 – Blaydon Bridge and Blaydon Haughs Viaduct commenced in November 1987. **Blaydon Bridge** is a five-span pre-stressed concrete structure, constructed using the balanced cantilever technique, with a main navigation span over the Tyne of 108 metres.

Best[62] continues:

> Several possible designs were prepared, evaluated and compared. Some were discarded on account of unsatisfactory appearance and the final choice for the river bridge was between a steel cable stayed bridge and a pre-stressed concrete box structure. The concrete alternative was thought to be slightly cheaper to build and was selected.

Blaydon Bridge

A similar comparison was made of designs for the approach viaduct and the final choice was a system of welded steel plate girders with a reinforced concrete deck ... Because of the size and importance of the bridge, it was categorised by the Department for independent checking, and this exercise was carried out by Husband & Co.

When the job was put out to tender in August 1987, our expectation that alternative designs would be bid was confirmed. One firm offered a steel bridge but the purported price margin was slim, the appearance unsatisfactory and the projected costs of maintenance too high. So Edmund Nuttall Ltd was awarded the contract and commenced work in November 1987, working exactly to the contract drawings. The inevitable and unexpected happened during the excavation, in a cofferdam, for the southern main pier, whose foundation was planned to sit on sound sandstone rock below the riverbed. We found that in two corners, totalling about a quarter of the load bearing area, the rock was not good enough. It was broken up and mixed with sand and clay, probably the result of ancient glacial activity. None of the five exploratory boreholes put down in the foundation area were located in this disturbed ground. We decided that piling would strengthen the pier foundation. This involved a large number of mini-piles using small drilling rigs which could operate from the bottom of the hole, inside the cofferdam and it proved to be very successful.

The change of design resulted in a delay of about six months, prejudicing the 1990 completion date, and costs increased substantially. Edmund Nuttall Ltd suggested accelerating the work and this was ultimately agreed. Desmond Scott and Bullens' senior bridge designer,

Construction by the balanced cantilever technique

John Shelley, put a big effort into implementing the changed foundation design. The site staff, led by Wayne Rhodes, the resident engineer and Paul Roebuck, Nuttall's engineer, 'rose equally to the occasion and in due course, the bridge piers rose above water level'.[63] The work of construction of the superstructure by cantilevering followed.

Blaydon Haughs Viaduct is a 17-span steel viaduct carrying the by-pass over A695 Chainbridge Road and the Newcastle–Carlisle railway line. It is 530m long and the deck incorporates 2,100 tonnes of structural steelwork, supported on 3,500 tonnes of steel H-piles.

Contract 3 – Derwenthaugh to Etal Lane commenced in June 1988. This is the largest contract on the by-pass, extending north and south of the River Tyne with 40 per cent of its £25 million tender value for structures. These included seven road bridges, eight footbridges, eight subways and over three km of retaining walls. The wall of Scotswood slip road is 12 metres high and of 'reinforced earth' construction using compacted pulverised fuel ash reinforced with polypropylene strips. There are interchanges north of the Tyne at Stamfordham Road, the A69 West Road and Scotswood Road and south at the Tyne and Derwenthaugh Road.

Blaydon Haughs Viaduct construction

Coal mining is an important feature of Tyneside's history and extensive old mine workings were encountered along the by-pass route. Shallow seams were excavated and filled with compacted soil and deeper workings drilled and injected with cement and pulverised fuel ash grout. Old mineshafts were filled and capped with reinforced concrete.

Best[64] has one further story to tell:

> There was also one occasion when the bridge deck had to be demolished and rebuilt. It was the first of a series of the same design and a big volume of concrete had to be poured continuously over a period of about ten hours. By a typically unlucky combination of circumstances, the result was unsatisfactory and I invoked a clause in the contract, which required reconstruction. This was a serious and expensive matter for the contractor, affecting his reputation and his pocket. So there followed a month or so of pressure to rescind – offers to repair, offers of 'guarantees', expert opinions (of the usual non-committal variety) on the efficiency of proposed repairs, and so on. But I stood my ground; the deck was demolished and rebuilt. There was no further trouble with the other bridges and the contract was finished three months early.

In December 1990, Her Majesty the Queen, on her way to launch a ship at Wallsend, formally opened the Newcastle Western By-pass and unveiled a plaque, midspan over the River Tyne, at the boundary

72 / *Building the Network: The North East of England*

Her Majesty the Queen formally opens the by-pass

of Newcastle and Gateshead, to christen Blaydon Bridge. It exemplified the value of Royal visits, uplifting morale at all levels, from the school children with their small flags, through the active engineers and shipbuilders.

Christopher Chope succeeded Atkins as Minister for Roads and Transport and was in attendance at the opening by Her Majesty. He confirmed the goal set by Cecil Parkinson in 1990 'to create a continuous motorway on the line of the A1 between London and Newcastle in a further demonstration of the Government's commitment. Indeed the Department has other projects costing £200 million planned or under construction in the North East.

6 Trunk Road A1 in Northumberland County

The following has been taken from the researches by Ray Harding, notes from Len Telford and John Cockton[65] and from other documents.

The 15-span masonry arch over the River Tweed was built in 24 years 4 months and 4 days. It was opened on 24 October 1634. As traffic increased the system of parish responsibility collapsed all over the country. The Turnpike Acts were therefore passed to authorise the repair and renewal of the main roads with the costs being met by charging tolls.

In 1746 such an Act was passed to provide for the repair of the high post-road leading from Cow Causeway near Newcastle to Buckton Burn north of Belford. This Turnpike of over 200 years ago is substantially the Great North Road through Northumberland, as we know it today. An early contract in 1836 was for the **Stannington Bridge** over the River Blyth, which stands today as a monument to those masons involved.

On 14 February 1894 the Contract Journal reported that at the quarterly meeting of the Berwick Town Council the question came up of widening the old bridge spanning the Tweed at Berwick at an estimated £4,000. Letters of protest against any alteration of the historic structure were received and a petition signed by many eminent men stated that any alteration would destroy the character of this national inheritance.

The *Berwick Advertiser* reported on 23 January 1914 that the building of a new bridge across the River Tweed was likely. The Royal Tweed Bridge, when built in 1928, had one of the largest reinforced concrete arches in the UK.

The advent of the motor car brought a dramatic increase in the volume and speed of traffic. In 1936 the Great North Road through Northumberland became part of the Trunk Road A1 and the responsibility of the Ministry of Transport.

The County Surveyor's Department

Until 1965 George Garnett was the County Surveyor when he was succeeded by his Deputy, Cyril Girven. The 1970s saw the County Surveyor's Department at its peak with a healthy commitment to the maintenance and development of the highway network. It was said that once you started to work for the County Surveyor's Department of Northumberland County Council you would never leave. This proved to be the case in many instances and one notable sceptic was Basil Arthur, who in 1973 took over from Girven as County Surveyor and stayed until he took early retirement in 1992.

Deputy County Surveyors were Neville Clarkson until 1974 then Don Esson until 1988, followed by Peter Coates. In 1988 Compulsory Competitive Tendering (CCT) led to the separation of Design and Construction roles, with the DLO becoming a stand-alone division of the County Council. From 1988 to 1992 Jim Espie was the Assistant County Surveyor with responsibility for design functions.

The design service provision, including structural services, was undertaken by the newly formed Consultancy Department, which also retained responsibility for Trunk Road design and maintenance.

The Improvement Schemes

The improvement of Trunk Road A1 in Northumberland involved 18 schemes from 1956 until the 1990s. There is no knowledge of any Public Inquiries for the improvements, which were generally well received.

Wide Open to Seaton Burn Diversion

This 2.7-mile scheme by-passed the villages of Wide Open and Seaton Burn to the west. Completion in 1969 more or less coincided with that of the A108 Tyne Tunnel Approach Road (now part of the A19) and effectively provided an eastern by-pass of Newcastle upon Tyne. The new road tied in with the Shotton Edge to Stannington Bridge Diversion.

The route line had been laid down in 1939, following the passing of the Trunk Road Act of 1936, and protected from development since then as were most by-passes built in Northumberland around this time. The Diversion now links the Newcastle Western By-pass to the dual carriageway section between Shotton Edge and Stannington Bridge.

John Miller designed the scheme and Stephan McLeod was the Resident Engineer. The contractor responsible for the construction was Higgs and Hill Civil Engineering Ltd. It was opened by Alderman Sydney Pickup.

The final structure on the diversion is Fisher Lane Bridge, which forms part of the current A1/A19 junction.

In 1995, Blagdon Bridge, at the northern end of the by-pass, was opened to traffic having been constructed to remove a junction accident spot. It was one of the first integral bridges and was designed by David Laux. John Lings designed the associated highway works.

Seaton Burn to Stannington Bridge

Mott Hay and Anderson designed the Seaton Burn to Stannington Bridge Improvement. It comprised four km of dual carriageway with grade separated junctions and was completed in March 1970.

Scheme	Completed	Length	Cost/Comments
Wide Open to Seaton Burn	Jun 1971 & 1995	2.7 miles	Blagdon Br. 1995
Seaton Burn to Stannington Bridge	Mar 1970	2.5 miles	
Stannington Bridge to Clifton Diversion	Oct 1987	5.0 km	
Morpeth By-pass	Nov 1970	5.0 miles	£2.25M
Morpeth to Felton	No improvement programmed		Priest Bridge widened in 1998
Felton By-pass	Nov 1981 & Nov 1999	4.6 km	DLO of 2.19m River Coquet tender £1.7m Now mainly dualled
Newton on the Moor Diversion	1950 & 1965	5.0 km	
Hitchcroft to Cawledge	Feb 1996	2.0 km	£2.8M
Alnwick By-pass Stage 1	Oct 1970	3.0 miles	£1.2M
Alnwick By-pass Stage 2	Dec 1985	8.0 km	
Brownieside Diversion	1993		Only DC north of Alnwick
Warenford Diversion	Oct 1977	3.0 km	
Pillars to New Mouson	No improvement programmed due to substantial SU plant		
Belford By-pass	July 1983	5.0 km	
Belford to West Mains	1974		Only local improvements
Haggerston Diversion	1969		
Berwick By-pass	Nov 1983	8.7 miles	£7.425M
Conundrum to Marshall Meadows	Aug 1993		Dualled into Scotland

This scheme has no grade-separated junctions. It includes two bridges: Seven Mile House Overbridge, carrying the former A1 across the newer diversion, and Shotton Edge Bridge, which carries the A1 over a 'C' road in a single span of 42 feet.

Stannington Bridge to Clifton Diversion

This dual carriageway scheme was not based on the pre-war alignment and full order procedures had to be gone through for both Line and Side Road Orders with full Public Participation procedures carried out.

The original Stannington Bridge, a masonry two-span arch, constructed in 1836 square to the River Blyth was demolished in 1932. The replacement bridge still stands, and now carries the northbound carriageway. The southbound carriageway is carried on a new bridge of three spans parallel and east of the existing bridge.

Ian Hatton designed this scheme and Bob Copeland was responsible for the structural elements. The Resident Engineer was Gordon Messer. The main contractor was Edmund Nuttall.

The northern junction was converted to two levels using an underpass linked to roundabouts on both sides of the Trunk Road A1 and connecting to the A1 by way of slip roads. The scheme was opened in September 2004.

Morpeth By-pass

This was one of the four schemes to be constructed along the line of the pre-war Order line (c.1939).

76 / *Building the Network: The North East of England*

The New Bridge

Peter Smith designed the scheme with Gordon Forster and Peter McKeith responsible for the design of the structures. Rod Collins was the Resident Engineer and the contractor was Cementation Construction Ltd. The Projects Manager was Colin Foote, the Sub-Agents were Mike Parry who succeeded Foote and John Kelsall.

The dual carriageway by-pass is five miles long with grade separated junctions at each end and cost £2.25 million. Half of the road's foundation was made from the recycled runaways of a nearby disused airfield and the other half from colliery shale and locally quarried limestone and Whinstone. Over 1.5 million cubic yards of earth and thousands of tons of rock were moved during the construction.

Clifton Bridge carries the by-pass over the link road for the Morpeth-bound traffic. The bridge was founded on 224 No 19-inch-diameter *in situ* concrete piles.

Tranwell Bridge takes the by-pass over the Morpeth to Belsay Road A6087 and has three spans of 35 feet, 43 feet and 35 feet. Mill Farm accommodation overbridge has four spans.

Wansbeck Viaduct was the largest bridge to be constructed since the Royal Tweed Bridge and has five spans of 88 feet, 98 feet, 108 feet, 98 feet and 88 feet,

Wansbeck Viaduct

which carry the by-pass over the River Wansbeck and the Morpeth to Cambo Road B6343. The bridge is 60 feet above river level and has plate girders. Fairmoor Bridge is over the link road taking the northbound traffic from Morpeth. Warreners House Bridge comprises a single 110-feet span which carries the southbound traffic from the Wooler Road A697 over the northern end of the by-pass.

Lord Ridley opened the by-pass and with other guests was driven along it in a 1931 Dodge Country bus.

Morpeth to Felton

This length of the A1 was improved in the early 1930s to a 30-feet-wide carriageway and there has not been any major change since, other than comprehensive traffic management measures, because the original three-lane layout had a high accident rate. It has the dubious distinction of being the first section of the Great North Road, north of London, to be single carriageway.

Felton By-pass[66]

Felton was a notorious cause of delay to the free flow of traffic on the A1 because of the steep gradient through the village main street (eight per cent), but more particularly because of the approach gradient (12 per cent) on the Newcastle side of the River Coquet and the 90 degree turn over a narrow bridge. Apart from a length of the Tyne Tunnel, it was also the first 30 mph speed restriction on the A1 after leaving the London area. The planning of the by-pass started in the late 1930s, the line for which was fixed in 1938.

The by-pass, which was constructed to the west of the village along the pre-war determined alignment, is approximately 4.6 km in length and crosses the valley of the River Coquet about one km upstream of the village of Felton. It was single 7.3 metres wide carriageway except for the northern-most section where there is an existing dual carriageway.

The main feature was the new Coquet Bridge, but construction required access from the north and south of the river, and the tender for this preliminary work was won by Northumberland County Council's Direct Labour force. Work commenced in August 1977. Approximately one km of the by-pass north from West Moor was constructed as the southern approach to the bridge site, whilst the northern approach works involved the strengthening of an access route through Felton Park Estate. In addition, an underpass and culvert were constructed and overlain with overburden to induce settlement prior to the main contract being commenced.

Harris & Sutherland were the Consulting Engineers for the **River Coquet Bridge**, and awarded the contract to Balfour Beatty Construction

Ltd in June 1979 at a tender price of £1.7 million.

The River Coquet bridge, a pre-stressed concrete box girder, is of novel design having very thin reinforced concrete webs. It has a main span of 83 metres, side spans of 49 metres, an overall width of 13 metres and is 24 metres above the river level. The bridge was constructed in increments of about three metres by the balanced cantilever method, a technique used on sites such as this where it would be uneconomic to support the whole of the deck on falsework.

The idea of this form of construction, not previously used in the UK, was proposed originally by Bridle of the Department of Transport who, in 1972, commissioned Harris & Sutherland to examine the feasibility with the Department of this novel design. The Consultants reported in March 1973 that the proposed method was technically feasible and economically viable, subject to confirmatory tests, which were duly carried out and the results enabled the design to proceed.

Once the stressing of the bars was complete, the ducts were injected under pressure with cement grout. This is the first occasion when this technique was used for a cement grout in the United Kingdom although used elsewhere in Europe.

With regard to the by-pass contracts Telford[67] says, 'to this day the Department of Transport have never disclosed the actual cost of the Coquet Bridge'.

Where possible, within the new Trunk Road boundary, the ground was graded to acceptable contours so that it blends in more naturally with surrounding plantations and agricultural land with selected areas planted with trees.

In November 1978 the County Council's Direct Labour Organisation was awarded the Contract for all the remaining works north of the Park Wood Underpass, consisting of some three km of roadworks, the construction of a bridge to carry the B6345 over the by-pass, an accommodation underpass and three culverts. The B6345 overbridge was the largest structure and was built to 'High Load Route' clearances. The site supervision staff were Brian Moore, Neil Hodgson, Ralph Dickenson and David Richardson.

The programming of the works was governed to a large extent by the need to allow for some embankments, constructed earlier, to settle. The section of road north of Lanehead was to be constructed as a dual carriageway on the line of the existing road which necessitated the

River Coquet Bridge

temporary diversion of all Trunk Road traffic and the excavation and the construction of each carriageway separately.

Difficulties were also encountered when excavating the unsuitable material south of Swarland Road. The excavation of over 50,000 cubic metres of largely running sand and silty clay material proved to be a major obstacle to the construction of the works in the area.

The southern tie-in to the existing A1 at West Moor was also carried out by the Direct Labour Organisation. The work consisted of the realignment of both the C133 from the west and the superseded Trunk Road to the east to form a staggered crossroads arrangement with the by-pass. Of necessity it was desirable that this work should be carried out as late as possible to reduce to a minimum the interference with traffic using the A1.

A team led by Hatton designed the by-pass. The structures (excluding the River Coquet Bridge) were designed by Stuart Bates, Peter Woodhead, Ron Lytton and Gordon Laurie. Site Supervision was carried out at different times by Andrew (Drew) Welch and Brian Moore. Peter Woodhead supervised the construction of the structures in Stage 1.

Mr Kenneth Clarke, MP, QC, Parliamentary Under Secretary, Department of Transport, formally opened the A1 Felton by-pass.

The section north of the River Coquet to Lane Head was later upgraded to dual carriageway, opening in November 1999. Rory O'Callaghan designed this scheme, the Resident Engineer was John Appleby and Northumberland Contracting carried out the work.

Newton on the Moor Diversion

This improvement was originally built as a dual 22-feet carriageway but work was halted at the outbreak of the Second World War in 1939. Northumberland County Council's Direct Labour Organisation completed the 5km dual-carriageway section from Lane Head to Hitchcroft in 1950. The final section at Hitchcroft was built about 1965.

Hitchcroft to Cawledge

The section of the road between the north end of the Newton on the Moor Diversion and the Alnwick By-pass was improved over a number of years in separate stages. The 2km dual-carriageway scheme was constructed by Balfour Beatty at a cost of £2.8 million and was completed in February 1996. The Resident Engineer was John Appleby.

Alnwick By-pass Stage 1

There is a plan for a by-pass of Alnwick in the Duke of Northumberland's estate office prepared for the Duke in 1800 by Thomas Telford and

River Aln Bridge

the route proposed then is very similar to that which was finally adopted.

The 3-mile Alnwick By-pass was designed as a dual two-lane road but only the northbound carriageway was built in the first instance. It was designed by Len Telford with Dave Oliver, and Forster was responsible for the design of the bridges. The contract was let to A. M. Carmichael.

The bridge works included Shilbottle Interchange consisting of a three span concrete superstructure on reinforced concrete piers and abutments; Alnmouth Road Bridge was of similar construction having four spans but built to accommodate a second carriageway; **River Aln Bridge**, a single 70-feet span with superstructure of steel beams and reinforced concrete deck supported on mass concrete abutments, faced with artificial stone, on a rock foundation; Waterside House Subway, a single 15-feet span reinforced concrete boxed culvert, 145 feet long; and Denwick Overbridge of four equal spans of 42 feet of similar construction to Alnmouth Road Bridge.

A.M. Carmichael commenced the construction of the by-pass in 1968, but having completed about three-quarters of the work they got into financial difficulties. Tarmac took over all the contracts which included the Alnwick By-pass, and rates etc were negotiated with the County Surveyor.[68] The Resident Engineer for the County Council was Andrew Welch, assisted by Tom Carberry.

This scheme was completed in November 1970 and opened by His Grace the Duke of Northumberland.

Alnwick By-pass Stage II

This single carriageway scheme was designed by Ray Harding and generally followed the line of the 1936 Trunk Road Order line. Gleeson Civil

Engineering, with Gordon Wright as the Agent, constructed the scheme. The Resident Engineer was Messer. The Duke of Northumberland opened the scheme.

Brownieside Diversion

This scheme by-passes the village of Brownieside to the east and a section of the A1 which had been subject to numerous minor improvements from about 1967.

The Department of Transport awarded to the scheme to Consultants Fairhurst & Partners in 1990 and a contract was subsequently let to Balfour Beatty for its construction.

Warenford Diversion

The ancient Warenford Bridge carrying the Great North Road suffered the storms of 1948, and many other incidents, before the by-pass brought final relief.

This 3km single-carriageway scheme, with at grade junctions, was designed by Alan Whitfield and Hatton, with McKeith responsible for the structures. Welch was the Resident Engineer and the scheme was constructed by Northumberland County Council's Direct Labour Organisation.

Pillars to New Mouson

Possibly the only unimproved section of the A1 remaining in Northumberland is that between Pillars and New Mouson. This section of the road has had numerous improvements investigated but none has been carried out due mainly to relatively low traffic volumes and the cost of diverting telephone and major gas services.

Belford By-pass

This scheme by-passes the village of Belford to the east and is slightly unusual in that there are no major cuttings or embankments as it is built on the flat coastal strip.

The by-pass was designed by Ray Harding and comprises 5km of single carriageway with at grade junctions. The Resident Engineer was Brian Gray with Peter Hedley as his Assistant. The main contractor was Gleeson Civil Engineering with Graham Wright as Agent. The Earl of Caithness opened the scheme.

The section of the road north of Belford from Detchant Lodge through Smeafield to West Main, the turn off for Lindisfarne Priory, has been systematically improved to achieve the required road width and alignment.

Belford to West Mains

This section of the A1 was improved over its full length in 1974 as part of the Marshall Maintenance Programme. The road was widened to provide a 7.3-metre carriageway with one-metre-wide marginal strips.

Haggerston Diversion

This single carriageway scheme was completed in 1969 by the County's Direct Labour Organisation. The Resident Engineer was Welch with Derek Dawson as his assistant.

The *Cat Inn* Improvement between Haggerston and Berwick was completed in the mid-'70s. The Resident Engineer was Jeff Marshall.

Berwick By-pass

The Berwick By-pass was transferred to the Durham Sub-Unit by the North Eastern Road Construction Unit in 1968.

The 8.7km-long by-pass leaves the existing A1 at Doupster Bridge, to the south of Scremerston, and passes to the west of Scremerston, Tweedmouth, East Ord and Berwick on Tweed before rejoining the A1 on the northern outskirts of Berwick.

Apart from short lengths of dualling at three of the priority junctions, it is of single-carriageway construction with one-metre hardstrips, widened to three lanes where crawler lanes occur.

The major structure on the by-pass is the bridge crossing the River Tweed. It has a total length of 195 metres and has four spans, the longest of which is 56 metres. The overall deck width is 13.5 metres and the bridge is curved on plan to a radius of 4,500 metres. Two farm accommodation bridges and an agricultural underpass complete the bridgeworks.

In the 1981 privatisation of the RCUs, Bullen and Partners took over the Sub-Unit schemes, which included the Berwick By-pass. The Senior Partner was Best and the Associate responsible for the scheme George Robinson with Ken Slater as Project Engineer. The contract for the by-pass was awarded to Miller Construction Northern Ltd, in a tender sum of £7.425 million with a contract period of two years. The Civil Engineering Manager was George Patterson and Contracts Manager Bill Haggarty.

The tender was on the basis of an alternative design for the **River Tweed Bridge** submitted by Miller Construction on the basis of a design prepared by Fairfield-Mabey who were the steelwork sub-contractors.

The steelwork for the 195-metres-long plate girder deck was fabricated in South Wales at the Chepstow Works of Fairfield-Mabey and sections were brought to site in maximum lengths of 27 metres where the deck was assembled on the north bank of the river and welded together.

Trunk Road A1 in Northumberland County / 83

In a continuous 10-hour operation the 420-tonne assembly was pulled across the river on temporary rollers mounted on pier tops, using a pair of 10-ton-capacity winches situated on the south bank.

Having spanned the river in a straight line the frame was then jacked laterally 330 mm at the centre and 600 mm and 860 mm at the north and south abutments respectively to bend the girders into a 4,500-metres-radius horizontal curve before lowering the whole assembly onto its permanent bearings. This steel deck bridge launch was probably the longest and most complex carried out in the UK at the time.

The Resident Engineer for Bullen was Wayne Rhodes, with Assistant Resident Engineers Alan Wanless (Roads) and Bob Main (Bridges).

The Berwick By-pass was opened by the Rt Hon. Nicholas Ridley MP, Secretary of State for Transport.

River Tweed Bridge

The deck launch

Conundrum to Marshall Meadows

The final section of the Great North Road to be dualled within England is from the north end of the Berwick By-pass at Highfields roundabout to Marshall Meadows on the English–Scottish border and was designed by Ian Hatton of the Northumberland County Council Technical Service Consultancy. The improvement consisted of the construction of a second southbound carriageway to the east of the existing road as far as the Scottish border, a distance of 2.9 km, the existing road forming the northbound carriageway.

The widening and reconstruction of the road between Highfields Roundabout and Conundrum was included in the scheme together with realignment to current standards of the previously unimproved section north of New East Farm.

New East Farm culvert was extended eastwards, and remedial maintenance work carried out to the existing culvert under the A1. Where appropriate the central reservation was widened to avoid the need to divert existing gas and telecommunication systems.

The contract was awarded to Balfour Beatty in the sum of £2.25 million; the Resident Engineer on behalf of the County Council was Ken Bruce.

The scheme was constructed in conjunction with the Marshall Meadows Extension, a scheme designed by the Borders Regional Council's Department of Roads and Transportation on behalf of the Scottish Office. This extended the A1 1.5 km over the border into Scotland. The contract for this work was also awarded to Balfour Beatty in the sum of £7.54 million. The Official Opening was carried out by Robert Key, Minister for Roads and Traffic.

Len Telford recalls: 'My favourite anecdote relates to the farmer at Marshall Meadows, who insisted the at-grade accommodation crossing at the point where his access road crossed the A1 should not be staggered as recommended in the Design Manual.

When asked why, he explained that his tractor driver would not safely negotiate a staggered crossing (as opposed to a straight crossing). Being further pressed on the subject, he admitted that the tractor driver was registered blind, and could only see a very narrow strip forward with no sideways vision at all!'

7 Motorways in the West Riding of Yorkshire

Aston–Sheffield–Leeds Motorway M1

In October 1956 Harold Watkinson, Minister for Transport and Civil Aviation, confirmed the scheme for the first section of the London–Yorkshire Motorway M1 (Luton to Dunchurch). Construction began in March 1958 and was opened to traffic in November 1959. There was now a new sense of purpose about road building, which was reflected in the Minister's address at the Institution of Civil Engineers in 1957 – 'if we can have less verbiage and more mileage of road construction completed we shall at least make a real contribution'.

This challenge was readily taken up by the West Riding engineers with the start of the construction of the Doncaster By-pass to be followed by work on the routeing of the M1 from Aston to Leeds via Sheffield.

The invitation from the Ministry to the West Riding County Council, to undertake preparatory work leading to the publication in 1962 of a Section 11 scheme for this 35-mile length of the M1, was issued in 1959.

Lovell initially allocated the preliminary work to Ellis and his team but in 1961 Race, having completed the Doncaster By-pass, was to become Chief Motorways Engineer and responsibility for the scheme was transferred.

Ellis together with a small group of engineers had located a line, which took into account the difficult scenic urban nature of the County.

Shelbourn[69] on the route of the motorway recalls in his memoirs, 'to the north of Wakefield the landscape was one of coal mines and pit-head gear at Kirkhamgate, East Ardsley and Rothwell crossed by innumerable pylons and overhead cables, relieved only by rhubarb fields in the Middleton area on the outskirts of Leeds. According to the locals, the finest rhubarb in the whole of Europe (if not the world) was grown in this locality, thanks, it seems, to the practice of tipping night-soil from the densely-populated adjacent urban areas over many centuries!'

Southwards from Leeds the route ran through the heart of the Yorkshire coalfields, skirting Crigglestone, Wooley Edge, Darton, Dodworth, Birdwell, Tankersley, Chapeltown and Ecclesfield, much of which was still attractive wooded areas. With mountainous heaps of shale, stark pithead gear, coal and spoil conveyor belt systems and buildings, the whole length was patterned with high and low voltage overhead electricity cables for good measure.

Although a somewhat grim industrial landscape it was where the route squeezed across the Don Valley at Tinsley between Sheffield and Rotherham that routeing proved the most challenging with rivers, canals, railways and heavy industry to be negotiated. A succession of cooling towers, iron smeltings, steel rolling mills, chemical and dye works, coking plants and the like all competed to pollute the atmosphere. Fortunately, following the implementation of the Clean Air Act in 1963 this is no longer the case.

> Once past Tinsley the route swept alongside marshalling yards and industrial gas plants at Catcliffe before finally emerging into open farming country again near Whiston, and thence to join the planned M1/M18 Interchange at Thurcroft. From this point southwards, through Nottinghamshire the design of the M1 was in the hands of Consultants – Sir Owen Williams and Partners.[70]

With the agreement of the Department of Transport major traffic surveys were undertaken both for a Trans-Pennine future route (M62) and for M1 (since one had an impact on the other) to establish demand and hence design standards including the optimum location of junctions. A good deal of detailed attention was paid to the heavily congested Tinsley area in conjunction with the County Borough Councils of Sheffield and Rotherham. The concepts were produced of a three-quarter-mile-long two-level viaduct at Tinsley together with an imposing three-level motorway-to-motorway interchange at Lofthouse (the intersection of the M1 and M62).

Race's M1 design section now comprised some forty engineers and technicians. The Principal Assistants were Harold Williams, who was to be responsible for pure design, and Shelbourn who was to take on everything else.

Williams had six design teams, each with a Team Leader, plus about five staff at various levels. Shelbourn had two teams with a call on whatever temporary assistance he might need from the design teams as the occasion demanded. His team leaders were David Pinell and Jimmy Capps. The Bridges Section was headed by Buchi with his principal assistants Bridle, Milburn and the writer.

The West Riding covered a large area and population, and with the recently recruited Motorway and Trunk Road personnel the County Surveyor's Department was the largest outside the Greater London Council.

A draft Section 11 Scheme to establish the Motorway centre line had been published in December 1961 and the next priority was to try to resolve objections received. In the main these were from Local Authorities and Public Utilities anxious to protect their various installations, and a hectic period of consultation and final settlement ensued.

Surveys

Early priorities were the aerial and soil surveys, the former Williams' responsibility, the latter Shelbourn's. Some preliminary soil survey work had been undertaken and boreholes sunk using the resources of the County Laboratory based at Ossett under Forrester.

Four contracts covered the detailed soil survey for the 36 miles of the route. Forrester[71] records:

> Boreholes were taken at about 100 yard intervals and samples were tested for bearing capacity which determined the thickness of construction to be used, suitability for forming embankments, and for determining the loadings which could safely be used in the design of bridge piers and abutments.
>
> The soil survey also revealed such features as the presence of saleable coal which was to be excavated when the road was built and the existence of old shallow workings and shafts in coal seams and bell pits from iron ore mining. A great number of uncharted ancient shallow workings were revealed in the course of the M1 soil survey and failure to have them located could have had most serious consequences. Accurate fault line identification was also vital to the bridge designers.
>
> The cost of the survey work was £183,000 for the Yorkshire section of the M1, but the savings accruing from the more refined designs, made possible from the information obtained, resulted in savings which outweighed the costs many times over, as well as ensuring a safe motorway through very difficult ground.

Shelbourn continues:

> The contractors' subsequent reports and interpretation thereof posed many questions, as is commonly the case. Nowhere was this more applicable than the site of the proposed two-level viaduct at Tinsley, where problems abounded. This was an area of underlying coal measures where coal had been mined in the past, frequently on an uncharted basis. The soil survey bore holes revealed many resulting voids, and it was essential to locate at least the shallow cavities for subsequent grouting in the vicinity of structural foundations. Because of the likelihood of undiscovered cavities, the use of piled foundation for the viaduct was not a starter, nor was the possibility of wholesale grouting over a vast area. The overburden of decomposed rock, weak alluvium and industrial waste was of insufficient strength as a founding material. To use the underlying rock would involve excessive excavation, so that by the process of elimination the relatively shallow sandy gravel deposits offered the best possibilities. Plate loading tests confirmed foundations in gravel to be practicable and meeting design strength requirements.
>
> Because of limited access at the time of carrying out the soil survey it was recognised that further probes would be required to locate the full extent of shallow workings and cavities, with detailed grouting requirements, at each foundation site. The only practicable way of undertaking this exercise was to include it as geotechnical work to be carried out by the main Viaduct contractor in due course, which became the responsibility of the Bridges Section.[72]

In association with the work on soil surveys was that of the County Mining Engineer and his department. Alwyn Smith, his deputy, undertook much of the field work. Senior[73] records:

> The motorway runs through the heart of the old Yorkshire Coal field and besides those areas which were still productive from deep mining, we were confronted with a number of very shallow mine workings.
>
> The Yorkshire Coal field has approximately 22 workable seams of coal, the majority of which outcrop along the route of the motorway, and workings have taken place over many years. These workings used the pillar and stall method of extraction, whereby small pillars some two or three yards square, were left intact to support the surface. It is remarkable that such small pillars have given adequate support to this surface, in many cases, for up to 150 years.
>
> The methods employed in this new procedure for the probing of these workings involved the drilling of shallow holes down to a depth not exceeding 50 feet at varying intervals to test the stability of the overlying strata. Such a scheme, on a length of roadway such as the M1 was, in itself, a completely new departure and a task of great magnitude. Investigations occupied a period of between two and three years, and plans were prepared to ensure that the areas were probed with great accuracy.
>
> The method used is known as open hole drilling, whereby an operator drills a hole two to four inches in diameter with a compressed air driven drill. The compressed air forces up the drilling debris and the engineer in charge can tell or detect by visual inspection, feel and colour, the type of strata through which the drill is operating. From this information, together with that from the soils survey, sections of the strata along the line of the motorway and across it were plotted. This made it possible to determine the type of ground and the number of cavities that existed below.
>
> This proved to be a highly successful method and, where suspect strata was located, trenches were excavated for visual examinations and to test the stability. The accuracy of the information produced by the drilling operations was remarkable. Over 120,000 feet of drillings were carried out and all suspect ground was made safe in order that the engineer could then proceed with normal earthworks construction.
>
> Other features encountered were the presence of geological faulting systems, which could cause natural slipping of the strata and the disruption of the finished carriageway, particularly if deep mining was to take place after construction was completed.
>
> A further complication, which had to be considered, was the presence of shallow coal seams left in a state of either partial or unworked conditions. Arrangements had to be made with the NCB for the extraction of this coal and 25,000 tons of saleable fuel was recovered.
>
> Another matter requiring serious consideration was the stability of the foundations of the various bridge structures. In many cases, these had to be stabilised by the introduction of pressure grouting methods before the foundations could be constructed.

Deep mining operations were continuing along the route of the motorway at various places and these workings were taking place from 100 to 500 yards in depth. Together with the NCB it was agreed that schemes would be prepared for the working of the vulnerable areas before the actual construction of the motorway commenced.

Some 1,200 detailed plans were prepared giving all the information of past and future mining operations as far as could be ascertained. It is interesting to note that between Dodworth and Tankersley, at Rockley, the surface had subsided 10 feet since the original aerial photographs were taken in 1961.

A very interesting operation was also undertaken in respect of the bridges at Crigglestone. A coal seam, lying at a depth of 500 yards from the surface, was worked on a pre-determined method and calculations were made so that the bridge piers in themselves could be raised by the amount of lowering which would take place.

The bridges were constructed, the coal was worked and no problems arose. The bridge engineer, at the outset of his design period, was furnished with subsidence predictions, and all the relevant data of future mining operations, and he could, therefore, design his structures accordingly.

A novel feature is that throughout the length of motorway, including the M18 and Doncaster By-pass, levelling and measuring stations have been established at intervals of 98 feet and, as a result, throughout the life of the motorway, calculations can be made if any vertical and lateral movement takes place, including tension and compression and the exact position can be fully understood.

Statutory Orders

The preparation of Scheme and Order Plans under Sections 7, 9, 11, 13 and 20 of the 1959 Highways Act, defining the motorway centre line and side road diversions, together with canal crossings and Land Acquisition plans, also brought the West Riding engineers into close encounters with men from the Ministry of Transport, District Valuers, County Land Agents, Coal Board representatives, National Farmers Union representatives, Parish Councillors and many others.

Shelbourn[74] tells how he

> got into tremendous arguments with Lands Branch in London about land for access and for working space, their view being that this was the Contractor's responsibility and things had always been done this way. The fact that the concept of building Tinsley Viaduct, for example, with piers sited in congested industrial land and adjacent to railway sidings, with virtually no access for Contractor's plant, might require a new approach, did not seem to occur to them.

Fortunately, he was able to convert the Ministry engineers,

> led by a particularly helpful Arnold Fieldhouse, to the view that if rights of access and working space were not negotiated in advance by

the Employer, and also included on Compulsory Purchase Order Plans and Schedules as a form of insurance in case negotiations broke down, then chaos would result. It was easy to envisage the Contractor being 'held to ransom' by the affected landowners and industrial interests and not unreasonably having to pass on extortionate costs to the Employer. After several high-powered meetings reaching well-nigh to Permanent Secretary level, with the Ministry engineers, to their credit, arguing on the County's behalf, the day was finally won. Just how right the West Riding engineers had been to insist on this procedure became established when the Contract Works were put out to tender and subsequently constructed ... By early 1963 all the soil survey reports had been received and analysed, and major decisions taken affecting design. The six road design teams for M1 under Harold Williams, led by Geoff Cooksey, Brian Lakeman, Dennis Radcliffe, Dennis Hawes, Howard Lawrence and Derek Sargent, were getting well into their stride and it was essential to advance the procedural steps to the next stage of publication of Section 7, 9 and 13 orders covering new lengths of trunk road to be created and alterations to side roads affected, together with Section 11 Schemes for all connecting (Slip) roads at Motorway intersections.[75]

Another Team Leader, David Butler, assisted Shelbourn in this exercise, and

feverish activity led to these Orders being published in April of that year. The objections received were again primarily from Statutory Undertakers, Drainage and similar Authorities all anxious to establish a 'fall back' position should negotiations in respect of their affected apparatus and installations fail ... In all cases an intense round of consultations with all parties concerned achieved the withdrawal of objections.

The consultations were not only essential in removing objections, but they also pin-pointed cases where alterations could and should be executed in advance of the main works, as at Stourton, where it was agreed that the preferred solution would be to provide a large diameter culvert to accommodate all affected cables and pipe-lines needing to be diverted under a main line railway and marshalling yards.

Without exception, all the Authorities and Undertakers with whom the team had dealings were extremely helpful, including the national concerns of British Rail, Central Electricity Generating Board, British Waterways etc., though all were understandably anxious to avoid any financial commitment and there were inevitable and protracted discussions on cases involving a degree of 'betterment'. A common betterment* formula had been established in agreement with all Undertakers at national level some years previously following the 1951 Public Utilities Street Works Act, but numerous instances were found when this was clearly inappropriate, the formula not having been devised with large-scale motorway works in mind. In such instances a degree of common sense had to prevail.

---

* Where the Highway Authority requires a Statutory Undertaker to relocate their plant, the cost of so doing is a charge on the road scheme. In determining this charge, account must be taken of the residual life of the plant concerned. This adjustment is called 'Betterment' and is determined by an agreed formula.

In the event all the negotiations were successful, and the Orders were made in October 1963, clearing the way, as soon as detailed design became sufficiently advanced, for the publication of Compulsory Purchase Orders covering land acquisition. (Concurrent procedure had been considered but not thought appropriate to the target dates achievable.)

In the Tinsley Viaduct area 270 houses were affected and in order that Sheffield County Borough Council might legally undertake re-housing of tenants (the Ministry of Transport having no power to do so) a Compulsory Purchase Order was published in August 1963 and, after a Public Inquiry, was duly made in January 1964. Compulsory Purchase Orders for the remainder of the motorway followed in sequence during the latter part of 1963 and into 1964.[76]

The account of the 'Shelbourn Team' has been included to show the immense amount of effort and detailed work that had to be undertaken in the planning and the route of just one length of motorway, by one team of engineers, before detailed design and preparation of contract documents could be finalised. The aggregate of all work undertaken by the authorities involved in completing the whole network in the region can only be described as phenomenal.

Of equal importance was the aerial survey commissioned by Harold Williams and his team and carried out concurrently with the ground investigations. This was based upon a technique involving a large number of very accurate ground markers which would remain throughout construction work and which would enable the whole design of the motorway in line and level to be compatible for design by computer.

Planning and Design

The planning and design of the motorway followed a most careful and thorough appraisal of a host of detail, based first upon a large survey which would determine how much traffic would use this new road and the optimum position for the ten £300,000 junctions.

The basic design also took into account the minimum effect of severance of agricultural land and the least harmful effect on industrial premises and housing. Nevertheless, the fundamental element was the need to ensure safe use of the road, by maintaining the highest possible standards of design.[77]

A positive piped drainage system was provided for the disposal of surface water and the design had to cater for the effects of subsidence, in that final levels would still accommodate adequate hydraulic gradients. High-strength flexible jointed pipes were used for carrier drains. The danger of mining subsidence also meant that a flexible type of construction had to be used.

Vertical separation of the carriageways at Birdwell

From draft plans prepared at design stage and consideration of the scheme as construction proceeded it was possible to remould the land in some areas adjoining the motorway and also at interchanges with the object of blending it with the landscape. Where sound rock has been found in cuttings its permanent exposure has been used as a feature in rugged contrast with grass slopes.[78]

The County Council in conjunction with the Ministry of Transport prepared a comprehensive scheme for landscape treatment of the Motorway and the County Planning Officer also provided landscape schemes for the 'visual corridor' of the Motorway. An excellent and attractive scheme in reshaping and planting a very unsightly colliery shale tip adjoining the Motorway at Roundwood, Wakefield, together with further schemes in reclamation and treatment of shale tips, was later completed by the County Council and its successor Authorities.

The Construction Contracts

With the exception of the Tinsley Viaduct and Calder Bridge, which will be referred to separately, for construction purposes the M1 in Yorkshire was divided into the following contracts:

Aston to Tinsley

This contract for the most southerly section of the M1 in the West Riding was 6.5 miles in length, cost £6 million and commenced in July 1965, just three months after the start of works at the Leeds end. It was completed in July 1967. The contractor was Dowsett Engineering Construction Ltd.

In the knowledge that contracts for motorways were sometimes subject to 'stop and go' government policies, there was some justification in the thinking of the West Riding engineers that if they started at both ends they were sure to complete the middle. That wasn't quite the case as we shall see.

This contract started at, and included part of, the M1/M18 Interchange at Thurcroft, being constructed by Tarmac and French, and joined with the lengths of M1 and M18 designed by Sir Owen Williams and Partners.

The route enters a cutting, then an embankment down to the crossing of the River Rother, passing through the Catcliffe Interchange. The motorway is carried on embankment to the Tinsley Interchange which links with the two-level Tinsley Viaduct.

Heavy earthworks were involved, including the removal of steel slag from Firth Brown's tip. This was difficult material, often extremely hot with clouds of smoke and dust on excavation. The material was used in the base of the embankments on either side of the River Rother.

Fourteen bridges including a railway overbridge, three underpasses and three subways were constructed; much of the work was sub-contracted. Dowmac's of Tallington provided the pre-cast pre-stressed beams.

Hatter was Dowsett's Contracts Manager, the Agent was John Thompson and his Deputy Jeffs. Bridge Sub-Contractors were Wilson Lovatt, W. & C. French and Thomas Fletcher of Mansfield. The Resident Engineer was Corby, the Assistant Resident Engineer Roads Bernard Clay and for Bridges John Powell.

Meadowhall to Blackburn

The contract for this 1.6-mile section cost £2.4 million, commenced in June 1966 and was completed in June 1968. The contractors were Holland & Hannen & Cubitts Ltd.

The works included Meadowhall Interchange, which gave access to the upper and lower decks of Tinsley Viaduct, two major retaining walls and a complex of interchange bridges including crossing a double-track railway line in three places within 20 yards. There was one other underbridge and an arch footbridge (p.101). Extensive traffic management measures were required in this industrial area.

A noteworthy aspect at Meadowhall was the extent to which pulverised fuel ash (pfa) was used, with 120,000 cubic yards imported from Thorpe Marsh power station at a rate of 60 lorry loads per day. The use of pfa, a low density material, has been a feature of many contracts where settlement due to existing ground conditions is possible but it can rarely have accounted for such a large proportion of the total earthmoving – nearly one quarter of the total with a further 500,000 cubic yards of conventional cut and fill.

Moisture in pfa reduces dust problems which can be acute in hot weather, but it has to be maintained at 24 per cent for optimum compaction. To check the behaviour of the ground, the West Riding engineers installed pressure gauges throughout the fill areas and in Grange Mill Retaining Wall. The nature of the material meant that only pedestrian-operated rollers could be used, but satisfactory compaction was achieved.

On such a short length of motorway it was not always possible to maintain continuity of road construction, which depended on completion of the numerous structures throughout the site with interruptions tending to occur more often than would normally be the case with a longer contract.

The Agent for Cubitts was Edwards followed by 'Biggles' Jackson. The Resident Engineer was Bill Spencer and the Assistant Resident Engineers Walsh and Colin Jones.

Blackburn to Tankersley

This scheme, 3.9 miles in length, extended from the B6086 at Blackburn to half a mile south-east of Tankersley. The contract was let to A. Monk & Co. Ltd and cost £3.6 million; it commenced in June 1966 and was completed in June 1968.

The motorway here runs through tree-lined countryside, including a golf course, and heavily wooded areas beneath which were hidden nearly 300 bell-pit mines. These ironstone workings continued for almost 150 years and are believed to have been started by monks in the 17th century. There were also large areas of pillar and stall shallow coal mining, largely carried out during the 1926 strike period. Faced with large areas of motorway crossing a honeycomb of mines, the contractors carried out 30,000 feet of four-inch-diameter investigation drilling, over a period of 10 weeks, to decide the extra excavation necessary and the additional support by cement pressure grouting required for bridgeworks.

Four more overbridges, two underpasses and a retaining wall were included in the contract as well as some provision for a probable Chapeltown service area at some future date. It was never in fact built but an interchange, 35A, was built at a later date to connect the M1 with the A616 to Stocksbridge. Most of the bridges were designed to cater for mining subsidence. Hood Hill Bridge, which carries the B6135, is a four-span simply supported bridge. The uniquely designed Smithy Wood Footbridge is referred to on p.102.

The Contracts Manager for Monks was Couchman, the Agent Gordon Cartwright. The Resident Engineer was John Andrew and the Assistant Resident Engineer John Moglia.

Tankersley to Darton

This contract, 7.1 miles in length, cost £6.75 million and commenced in August 1966 and was completed in September 1968. The contractor was Dowsett Engineering Construction Ltd. This was the longest contract on the Aston to Leeds section of M1 and includes the A61 Tankersley and the A635 Dodworth Interchanges. Including the interchanges there are 16 bridges on this section, two of which carry railway lines over the Motorway and were designed by British Railways.

Leaving Tankersley the motorway passes through a side long cutting at Birdwell onto embankment with split-level carriageways before climbing through a deep cutting at Needle Eye to Dodworth Interchange. The motorway continues to climb before descending over a curved embankment, again carrying split-level carriageways. This section finished at Darton where it joined the next contract.

The need to provide an accommodation bridge crossing the massive cutting at Needle Eye gave rise to a three-pin reinforced concrete arch with 80 feet long side spans. The span of the arch is 285 feet and has an overall length of 434 feet at road level.

Other notable bridges are two 'Wichert' (see p.102) footbridges and Cock Inn Bridge, which carries a road on a gradient of 1 in 10 over the motorway in a single span.

The Contracts Manager for Dowsett was Hatter, and the Agent was Frank Simpson who was replaced by Jeffs. Clugstons undertook the remaining bridges under a Sub-Contract. Glugston's Agent was Gordon Headley. The Resident Engineer was Eric Cooksey and the Assistant Resident Engineer Bridges Alan Pollock.

Needle Eye Bridge

Darton to Wakefield

The contract for this 6.6-mile section cost £7.25 million, commenced in August 1966 and was completed in October 1968. The contractor was Costain Civil Engineering Ltd.

The works involved the construction of two interchanges at Crigglestone and Low Swithen; diversion and improvement of the A637

96 / Building the Network: The North East of England

and the re-alignment and reconstruction of seven existing roads, as well as preparatory work for the Woolley Edge service area.

In addition to the 400-feet-long bridge over the River Calder, bridgeworks included 18 overbridges, underbridges and culverts.

At Crigglestone work was stopped for over five months to enable the Coal Board to win coal seams that lay under the route of the motorway. The West Riding engineers then allowed for the calculated settlement. In one instance a forecast of a 12-inch settlement at a bridge site proved to be correct to within an inch. The West Riding engineers were able to show that the degree of subsidence was predictable where the 'Longwall' system of mining was used.

On this section of motorway, advantage was taken of sidelong ground to introduce split-level carriageways in the interest of economy of earthworks and also to increase the visual interest of the motorist.

The collapse of the Calder Bridge cast a shadow over the contract and is dealt with later (see pp.114-16).

Constain's Agent was Maurice Jackson. The Resident Engineer was Colin Pothecary and the Assistant Resident Engineer Roads, Don Carruthers. The Resident Engineer for the Calder Bridge was Malcolm Wooley of Giffords.

Costain's Contract

Wakefield to East Ardsley

This contract, 4.6 miles in length, cost £4 million, commenced in August 1965 and was completed in April 1967. The contractor was the Sir Alfred McAlpine/Leonard Fairclough Consortium.

The contract extended from south of the A650 Ardsley Interchange on embankment into cutting at Kirkhamgate, over deep embankment adjacent to Wrenthorpe Golf Course rising to the A638 Dewsbury Road Interchange, then crossing Queen Drive and terminating at the Horbury Road Bridge.

For a glimpse into the kinds of problems that were faced in the supervision of construction of the M1 a few of the recollections of Denis Bradley,[79] the Resident Engineer for this contract during the period August 1965 to December 1966, have been included.

The extent of the contract was increased to provide a rock blanket at the base of the embankment between the Horbury–Wakefield railway line and the Horbury Road, and across the old water-filled gravel workings immediately north of the River Calder. The work included the erection of the motorway fencing, the provision of a boat to take soundings in the old gravel workings and the strengthening of the floor of an archway under the railway, which provided the lorry access to the flooded gravel workings. The work was completed before the start of the adjacent Contract. The rock came by road from a quarry in Morley. The Contract was extended because the earthworks balance went seriously wrong when the predicted unsuitable material in the Snapethorpe cutting turned out to be suitable.

Colliery Shale from the tip east of the M1 and south of Queens Drive was used in the works. When excavated it was hot and caused clouds of dust to drift across the site towards Ossett. The specification did not include the use of colliery shale and, when 'Hutch' was asked for a specification, he told us, 'If it jingles when discharged from a lorry it is okay'.

Near to Queens Drive Bridge, an existing concrete retaining wall three to four metres high, supporting the south side of Queens Drive, one day slowly rotated and collapsed in textbook fashion because the support at the front of the wall had been removed.

The McAlpine/Fairclough Contract
M.T. Walters & Associates

On Dewsbury Road Interchange Bridges, some of the spans were jacked up and down two or three times because the pre-cast concrete bearings kept on cracking. The design had failed to take account the inaccuracies in the manufacture of the pre-cast units, and resulted in the point loading of the bearings. Eventually layers of lead were used to spread the loading over the appropriate area of the bearings.

The original contract included the provision of a single-span underbridge to carry the M1 over the Wakefield–Ossett railway line, but, early in the contract period, British Rail indicated that they were going to close the line. The Resident Engineer got a 'rocket' from Fred Oliver for phoning British Rail at York and trying to speed up the decision. The bridge was deleted from the Contract and an embankment for the motorway was constructed in the railway cutting. This cutting also provided an endless source of sample carpet squares, which had been tipped, for the homes of the site staff.

At Bushy Beck, the National Coal Board removed all the coal from under the motorway embankment before the contract started. County engineers supervised the replacement of material up to original ground level. One morning, after a period of continuous rain, when the embankment, carriageway drainage and pavement were complete, water was found to be pouring out of the side of the embankment one to two metres below carriageway level. It was found that a number of gully connections had not been correctly made. This event led to the use of CCTV cameras to check the construction of the drainage on other sections of the M1.

All the coal from the shallow workings under the Batley Road bridge and the surrounding area was removed to an NCB depot. The collapsed old workings and the supporting pillars of coal could be clearly seen in the temporary diversion of the road. Entry into the Supervisor of Works' office on the Batley Road was sometimes impossible. It was blocked by plastic sacks full of coal.

As soon as the motorway was complete, the ends of the accommodation underpass south of Bradford Road were blocked up and it was used to force rhubarb.

One day Jim Smart (from the contract section) rang up and said did I realise I had signed the largest interim certificate to date – £1,000,000 plus – on the M1. I'll never sign a blank interim certificate again, without the figures being in place! Jim was always helpful.

McAlpine's agent was Maurice Sutherland and Sub-Agent Ivan Abbot. Harold Genders was the Agent for Faircloughs. The Resident Engineer was Bradley and the Assistant Resident Engineer John Armitage.

East Ardsley to Stourton

This was the first M1 contract to start in Yorkshire. It was 4.5 miles in length and cost £5.4 million. It commenced in May 1965 and was completed in October 1967. The contractor was A. Monk & Co.

The contract included the construction of three interchanges. The first of these was the Wakefield–Bradford Trunk Road (A650) at Ardsley,

Urn Farm Bridge
M.T. Walters & Associates

the second is the three-level interchange at Lofthouse with the Lancashire–Yorkshire Motorway (M62) and the third with the Wakefield–Leeds Trunk Road (A61) at Stourton.

The area through which this length of motorway passes is semi-urban in character and considerable works on roads crossed by the motorway were undertaken. The total length involved, including interchange slip roads, was of the order of seven miles.

The earthworks comprised approximately two million cubic yards of excavation, about half of which was in rock. The majority of this material was used to form embankments, unsuitable material being carted to tip. It was not necessary to use any imported filling material.

Over 1,500 tons of workable coal was excavated and carted to the National Coal Board's Depot at Calder Grove from the cutting at Ardsley Interchange.

All main drainage was in heavy-duty concrete pipes having Cornelius rubber joints and laid on a granular bed, to allow for mining subsidence. The total length of drainage in the Contract was over 40 miles.

Twenty-one major structures were constructed, eight of them being associated with the interchange of Lofthouse. Special methods of design were employed for a number of them to allow for the effects of future mining subsidence. Whilst the majority of bridges have concrete deck beams, those on the curved roundabout bridges at Lofthouse were steel box girders. A notable structure is Urn Farm Accommodation Bridge, a three-pin arch structure in reinforced concrete.

The Agent for Monks was Ted Rowlands. The Resident Engineer was Howard Lawrence, the Assistant Resident Engineer Ron Denis.

Hutchinson in his memoirs[80] gives impressive statistics about the construction of the M1 Motorway in the West Riding with final costs being of the order of £36.8 million excluding Tinsley Viaduct and the River Calder Bridge. Perhaps the most impressive statistic is that settlement of claims by contractors amounted to only 2.1 per cent of total expenditure.

Bridgeworks

We now come to bridgeworks on the M1. Under the direction of the writer,[81] who had succeeded Buchi, a vast amount of design work was undertaken by the M1 bridge teams led by Bridle, Milburn and Varley.

Many outstanding bridges and important innovative techniques were developed. Friston[82] recalls 'one pioneering aspect was the use of a computer in engineering design – the 'Stantec Zebra' at Bradford Institute of Technology. The engineers devised their own programs, punched the paper tape input, fed it into the computer and retrieved the output on a teleprinter.'

Rainstorth Bridge

A standard overbridge

Motorways in the West Riding of Yorkshire / 101

A total of 120 bridges and subways were constructed on this length of motorway. This represented approximately one quarter of the construction cost. Ten contractors and sub-contractors had been directly concerned with the construction of these bridges.

Five of these bridges formed part of the Lofthouse Interchange and two railway bridges, constructed in advance of the roadworks, had decks incorporating steel beams. All the remaining structures were constructed in reinforced and/or pre-stressed concrete. Over 4,000 reinforced and pre-stressed concrete beams were used and these were manufactured as far afield as Scotland, Teesside, Nottinghamshire, Stamford and Norfolk, and involved Costain, Dowmac, Kingsbury Concrete, Ferro Concrete & Stone and Anglian Building Products.

The largest beams manufactured off-site were used on Morthern Hall Bridge which carries the northbound carriageway of the Thurcroft Link over the motorway. These beams were 116 feet 6 inches long and weighed approximately 75 tons. For this bridge 44 beams were brought from Stamford to Sheffield by special train and then transported out to site by road.

Almost the entire length of this motorway passes over land subject to mining subsidence, and this gave the bridge designers special problems in dealing with differential settlement and ground strains, which can be particularly severe where the mining is shallow. The structures have, in general, been designed to accommodate a differential settlement of 18 inches. Special techniques incorporated in the structures, therefore, include jacking pockets, elaborate expansion joints, and bearings which incorporated a layer of polytetrafluoroethylene (PTFE) sliding on a stainless steel plate.[83]

The first concrete tri-hinges used in the 'Wichert' footbridges

Dropping Well Footbridge

102 / Building the Network: The North East of England

To simplify and cut the costs of both design and construction, a series of standard pre-stressed concrete beams were produced for the motorway for use in conjunction with standard bridges. The large amount of design calculation undertaken by computer assisted in reducing design time.

The road users have been in mind throughout the design stages and the aesthetics of all structures carefully examined. Every opportunity was taken to relieve driver monotony by providing where possible variety in the type of structures, relieving large areas of concrete with features, and by giving further variety through the various coloured plastic fascias. The majority of the bridge types were submitted to the Royal Fine Arts Commission for approval. Notwithstanding the standard of aesthetics obtained, the bridgeworks costs compare favourably with those of any motorway bridges built in this country to date.

The standard overbridges have four spans, whilst the underbridges generally have three spans but in certain cases single-span bridges have been adopted. Where the road to be carried over the motorway has a steep gradient it was found that the standard overbridge was not aesthetically satisfactory due to the extremely unbalanced side spans and the lack of parallelism between the deck soffit and the motorway.

To overcome these objections **Rainstorth Bridge** (p.100) was evolved by Corby. This bridge is constructed entirely of reinforced concrete and consists of a series of simply supported spans of varying depth and each having a short cantilever at the piers. This design, which provides a soffit (under surface) line parallel with the motorway, has been partially copied for three other bridges. A manufacturer's load test[84] confirmed the design method and detailing of the half joint as a sound basis for future joints of this type. Similarly Cock Inn Bridge, a product of Varley's team, carries Pilley Lane over the motorway (at a 1 in 10 gradient) at Birdwell.

The three-span footbridges, Smithy Wood, Birdwell Quarry and Stainborough, which incorporate the principles of the 'Wichert' Truss, are the first bridges of their type to be constructed in concrete in this country, and the first use of concrete tri-hinges.[85] The principles permit differential settlement and accommodate the movements associated with mining subsidence.

Considerably adding to the aesthetics of the motorway, three concrete arches built over the motorway are notable. Approaching from the south the motorist is presented with a panoramic view of Leeds City framed by Urn Farm (320 feet overall length), located just to the south of Stourton

Lofthouse Interchange M1/M62

Interchange. Needle Eye Bridge (290 feet between springings and 434 feet overall length), is immediately south of Dodworth Interchange.

Dropping Well Footbridge (p.101), a reinforced concrete three-pin arch (169 feet between springings) is particularly interesting as the approach on the west side is by means of a spiral ramp. The east springing is sited behind the top of an attractive retaining wall and is 26 feet above the western springings, which have split legs at motorway level. On each side of the arch there are two suspended spans. Sriskanden and his team designed these arches and the 'Wichert' footbridges.

The density of property also required the construction of a 1,500-feet-long retaining wall, over 40 feet above the road at its highest point, adjacent to Grange Mill Lane. This wall together with others was used by West Riding engineers in their studies of earth pressures.[86] A second wall at Meadowhall was built to retain a housing estate and enabled the cutting to be taken out for the motorway. The wall comprised 120 bored piles, 48 inches in diameter sunk to depths of up to 60 feet. Following excavation in front of the piles an L-shaped wall was constructed. This wall has a striking appearance having a face of 12-inch-deep tapering corrugations. The above footbridge springs from this wall.

Bramley Lane Viaduct, which carries a local road over the motorway and the slip roads leading to the Wooley Edge service area, is a pleasing simple eight-span structure.[87]

Lofthouse Interchange[88,89,90] is a three-level roundabout-type interchange at the junction with the Lancashire–Yorkshire Motorway M62. Considerations of traffic loading and cost dictated its adoption and hence the high-level curved bridges, which are now familiar to users of the M1 between Wakefield and Leeds. The M62 Motorway is carried over the M1 Motorway by a four span bridge having a reinforced concrete deck. The interchange was initially conceived as a complete ring structure, but was modified to four bridges, by the writer, to reduce costs.

The north and south bridges, carrying the roundabout over the M1, have four spans of 91 feet 6 inches average length at a mean radius of 420 feet. The smaller east and west bridges, crossing the M62 motorway, have four spans of about 70 feet. All the spans are simply supported because there was a slight risk of differential settlements of the foundations from old mine workings in the area.

Three other bridges form part of the interchange complex. The first carries Longthorpe Lane B6135 over the M1 immediately adjacent to the north roundabout bridges. The other two bridges are three-span concrete

The 'banana'-shaped piers

structures, which carry the two northernmost slip roads over Longthorpe Lane.

The decks consist of curved box beams. The inner beams are rectangular in section four feet deep by two feet wide. The edge beams are trapezoidal with the outer web sloped to enhance the appearance of the structure. A nine-inch-thick concrete deck slab connects the beams.

Mild steel is used throughout as the savings in weight, which could have been achieved with a high yield steel, were largely cancelled out by extra width and labour costs in cutting the curved plates. This would have been necessary to remove local hardening caused by the cutting process. Leslie Deuce (who later headed the Ministry's Standards Division) played a prominent role in the design of the interchange.

At the time of the preliminary Merrison Report (see p.153) these structures were thoroughly checked and found to be entirely satisfactory.

Although Haddon Adams at the Ministry refused to entertain the West Riding design with its 'banana'-shaped piers, and resisted all persuasions, Lovell saw that Adams could be out flanked. 'Adams', he said, 'is retiring in a few months.' Holland, Adams' successor, did not wish to take a stance and referred the design to the Royal Fine Arts Commission, who gave wholehearted approval. So the detailed design proceeded.

Varley records,[91]

All was not over. Just before inviting the tenders for the East Ardsley–Stourton Contract the Treasury Solicitors alarmed the Ministry of Transport with advice that a start on construction of the Interchange might be legally challengeable as an action prejudging the Public Inquiry into the line of the M62, an Inquiry the Minister had decided to hold.

This was an alarming 11th hour development. The argument for pre-empting the Inspector's Report was tenuous; the Treasury was, once again, looking for every opportunity to cut back on public expenditure and, coming so soon after the loss of the Tinsley Viaduct [see pp.107-11], there was immediate mistrust of the Ministry and suspicion of its motives ...

Our Engineering counterparts at the Ministry were as surprised by, as we were suspicious of, this late development and were able to point to the political embarrassment to the Minister that would result if tender invitations were withdrawn and the much heralded start of the north end of M1 was postponed. As a consequence the contract was let on time with the interchange included as a mammoth Provisional Item, work on it to be started only 'on further instruction'.

We were confident that the Inspector would, in his Report, accept the proposed siting of the Interchange but it looked folly for us to simply sit back and await his Report. For the next 12 months whilst the Inquiry ran its course Sims and I watched the Ministry like hawks. Every letter or word that we received from the Ministry, which referred directly or indirectly or involved the Interchange, we held up to the light. Every question was answered in a way that prevented any opening

Erection of curved beams

up of an excuse to delay or change the scheme. Those Engineers who had developed Lofthouse Interchange were now out on site supervising construction of the motorway work but wondering what was going to happen to their contribution. Sims and I were determined there was not going to be a second Tinsley in our office. And so whilst the M1 was being built and the Inquiry ran its course we did much pre-planning with the Contractor (Monks) and the nominated steel works fabricator (Watsons) so that work could start immediately we had the release.

The Inspector's Report to the Minister gave us the clearance we needed, but we did not wait for the Ministry to inform us we could start. Sims wrote to the Ministry stating our intention to commence work immediately. By chance the same day I ran across Lovell whilst in his anteroom on another matter and apprised him of what we had done. 'Sims shouldn't have written to the Ministry. He should have started the job and then told them!' Returning to the Bridges office thinking that Lovell would have phoned Sims (he hadn't) I told him what had occurred. It was plain that Lovell feared the Ministry would regard our stated intent as a request and we might get a 'now hold on a minute whilst we consult Treasury Solicitor' type reply. We planned to consolidate our intent. Sims spoke to Muirhead Watson, Managing Director of Robert Watson's the steel fabricator at Bolton, apprised him of the position and the need for haste. He understood perfectly and suggested a meeting with the Contract Director of the steel plate supplier at the rolling mill in Scotland, but he needed written authority to start fabrication.

I carried Lovell's letter to Glasgow on the night sleeper and gave it to Muirhead Watson over breakfast at the *Central Hotel*. We repaired to the rolling mill – busy with producing plate for the QE2 – and the following morning I returned, travelling over that wonderful line from Carlisle–Leeds, with confirmation that orders had been placed and metal was being cut. Sims had got the motorway contractor to commence excavation to the bridge footings and place reinforcement orders.

The days passed. The Ministry did not display any discontent with our precipitate action.[92]

There was much celebration in the office and on site now that construction had started.

The piers are believed to be unique and consist of an inverted 'L' shaped member which is supported on the outer face by a cruciform shaped column.

Bridle[93] recalls: 'In order to display the erection process, how the legs may be restrained and how all was finally released, we built a model and erected it in stages at a progress meeting with the contractor while I commented on the process. When the erection was complete I hit the table in emphasis and the model collapsed. Couchmann, the Contracts Manager for Monks, leaned across the table and said, 'Ron that fills me with absolute ****** confidence.'

The 'banana' piers, as they became known, also presented a problem to the contractor in the placing of the concrete because of the heavy concentration of steel reinforcement. Couchmann approached the writer with a proposal to pre-stress these structures using strand cables to overcome their problems. This was accepted.

One other reminiscence is that of the writer's concern over the production of pre-stressed beams at various manufacturers. Sub-contracts for beams were always placed after the main contract had been let. Usually there were considerable delays between ordering, casting and delivery to site, abutments to receive the beams often standing completed many weeks before their arrival. Additionally some beams, because of the rate of production and despite deploying inspectors to the production factories, were found to have repaired honeycombed areas, often being rejected on site.

On a site visit by William Harris (the Chief Highway Engineer) with Lovell, the writer put to them the concept of a 'bulk beam contract' with beams produced, on the shelf, to be available when the main contracts were let. This idea found favour with the Ministry and West Riding Engineers later produced such a contract for the supply of the beams for many of the contracts on the M62. (See pp.134-6)

With the opening of the motorway, the West Riding bridge engineers, with their contractor colleagues, could feel justly proud of the M1 bridges built in just over three years and of a job well done.[94]

Two structures initially included in the brief of the West Riding engineers, Tinsley Viaduct and the Calder Bridge, did not have such a happy story and were designed by consulting engineers.

Tinsley Viaduct – M1

Friston[95] gives an account in some detail of the 'Saga' of Tinsley Viaduct from 1961 through to 1981.

> The site at Tinsley presented an extraordinary challenge: a structure had to carry a six-lane motorway and a four-lane trunk road over the congested and heavily industrialised Don Valley, crossing the Sheffield–Keadby Canal, the River Don and three railways; a method of erection had to be devised which would permit industrial activity to continue below the structure; the line had to be S-curved to thread a way through industrial complexes such as the power station cooling towers; condensation from these towers and the proximity of the river and canal generally kept relative humidity above the corrosion threshold of 80 per cent; with this humidity, the precipitation of over 29 tons of sulphur dioxide each day from the power station and the fumes from a nearby sulphuric acid plant gave what was regarded as the most corrosive atmosphere in Britain; the Don geological fault system crosses the site; the soil survey gave evidence of ancient uncharted 'pillar and stall' mine-working, entailing a risk of sudden subsidence; benchmark levelling had revealed settlements of up to 15 inches since 1935.
>
> The solution agreed with the Ministry of Transport after examining a range of options was for a 3,400-feet-long two-level viaduct substantially in pre-stressed concrete, with some structural steel members, which had an especially high specification from corrosion.

The viaduct designed had 20 simply-supported spans of up to 163-feet length, allowing for thermal and subsidence movement at each span end, and incorporating jacking facilities at each support for rectifying gross settlements ...

The design (carried out under Bridle's direction) involved 4,500 sheets of calculations, the writing of three computer programs, five structural analyses by computer, 176 drawings and 239 pages of specification and bills of quantities. A 12-feet-long detailed model of the viaduct and surrounding roads and buildings was commissioned ...

Pre-tender drawings were issued nine months before the tender period to enable prospective contractors to view the design and assess requirements, and to give the opportunity to comment or make suggestions during the design stage; no amendments to the basic form of the viaduct were suggested.

Drawings and contract amendments were issued to five selected contractors in February 1964, inviting tenders at the end of April. Following queries from some of the contractors about possible alternative methods of construction, Colonel Lovell wrote to all the contractors in March, '... it is inevitable that the Engineer designing the scheme must know best the details of the total problem that has to be solved. The Tinsley Viaduct project has been under active design consideration for several years and during that period many alternative solutions were studied, examined and finally rejected. It can be said that the final solution evolved and even resolved itself out of these many considerations ...

Meanwhile, plans were made for the site staffing of this and the other M1 contracts, and many of the design engineers were notified of their forthcoming appointments; I was to be the Deputy Resident Engineer on Tinsley Viaduct.

When the five tenders were opened, that from the Cleveland Bridge and Engineering Company was accompanied by a separate lump sum quotation for an alternative steel box-girder viaduct; the quotation was just over £1 million cheaper than the lowest tender of about £6 million, and was accompanied by eight pages of description with welding and painting specifications and five outline drawings prepared by consulting engineers Freeman, Fox and Partners.

The alternative design was for the upper and lower levels to be carried independently of each other by steel twin box-girders running continuously throughout the two-thirds of a mile, 20-span length of the viaduct.

A small group of us was cloistered to examine this alternative within two weeks and a detailed analysis was made, based on member sizes shown on the five drawings. Our critique formed the bulk of a 117-page *Report to the Ministry of Transport on the Examination of Tenders for Tinsley Viaduct.*

The report recommended acceptance of the lowest tender for the West Riding design and rejection of the alternative, setting out that the alternative:

- was based on a draft design without knowledge of the soil survey results or the full loading and geometric requirements;
- encroached on headroom requirements to the extent that the lower deck needed to be nearly three feet higher and the upper deck to be five feet higher, entailing the raising of the interchange roads, retaining walls, footpaths and services on this contract, and raising the motorway on the already designed adjacent contracts;
- showed piers which were four feet too wide for agreed rail track diversions;
- showed arbitrarily reduced sums for dayworks, testing and contingencies;
- reduced the welding and steel protection specifications;
- did not include allowance for the inevitable increase in capitalised maintenance costs for this type of structure;
- was significantly overstressed (even without the effects of any differential settlement) and would need at least another 2,979 tons of steel in the structure – an increase of nearly 30 per cent;
- did not show how large differential settlement would be rectified;
- was not of an appropriate structural form for this site – '... It is considered that the adoption of a continuous structure would be imprudent because the magnitude of differential settlement cannot be assessed ...'

The Report set out the conservatively calculated extra costs of the various aspects, which amounted to over £1.6 million – bringing the cost of the alternative to £323,000 more than the lowest tender for the West Riding design. The programming implications of adopting the alternative were also spelt out at length; the contract could be delayed for as much as 18 months – '... Any delay in the completion of the viaduct would have considerable financial and programming repercussions on at least the adjoining two contracts, if not over a wider field. Indeed, the loss to the national economy by unnecessary delays in this heavily industrialised area cannot be overlooked ... '

We received the news of the Ministry's rejection of the recommendations in the Report with incredulity. Disagreement persisted throughout consultations over the succeeding months, principally over steel protection, the assessment of capitalised maintenance and settlement; the Ministry accepted Freeman Fox's view that 'a continuous form of structure rather than simple supports or other form of articulation should be adopted for this structure', and was convinced that there was still about half a million pounds' advantage in adopting the alternative.

West Riding Councillors stood by Lovell's findings, and the Chairman and Vice-Chairman accompanied him and his Deputy, Colonel Oliver, to a meeting with the Minister, Ernest Marples, and his officials. We were told that the meeting ended with Marples banging the table in expressing his exasperation with the procrastination and saying he was prepared to defend his position at the Despatch Box (this was three days before Parliament rose prior to the election which brought in the Wilson Government).

The Council resigned their Agency for Tinsley Viaduct on behalf of the Ministry; the other M1 contracts were necessarily postponed; the notified site staff appointments were nullified. Colonel Oliver called the design staff together and in an impassioned speech assured us that we would leave this debacle with honour and that '...the chickens will come home to roost ... '

The Ministry invited re-tenders on contractor's own designs based on changed requirements: the degree of live load to be allowed for was reduced; the viaduct was to be five feet narrower; construction operations would be easier because of the Ministry's purchase of land under and around five of the spans.

The lowest tender received was for £4,344,000 for a simply supported pre-stressed concrete viaduct similar to the West Riding design (two of the other three tenders were also for simply supported structures). Nevertheless, the Ministry awarded the contract to Cleveland Bridge and Engineering Company, whose tender for their continuous steel structure was £272,000 higher. The Ministry appointed Freeman Fox and Partners as Engineer to supervise the contract.

One could only speculate on the reasons for the outcome. It is hard to believe that it was to save money; if it was important to have a steel structure at Sheffield or that such a prestigious structure should be designed in the private sector, then such matters should have been resolved earlier.'[96]

Varley[97] in an archive paper, 'The Loss of Tinsley Viaduct', delves more deeply into the reasons for the outcome.

> To the Ministry the alternative presented an opportunity and a problem; to Lovell it represented a threat to his influence, and by failing to appreciate the Ministry's position he allowed that threat to develop into a rebuff to his aspirations and a rejection to his Engineers who had worked so long on the project.
>
> The Ministry of Transport was accountable for the conduct and public expenditure on trunk road and motorway schemes. Control was no mean task given the amorphous nature of the embryo road programme and that a major part of the current activity was centred in certain local government areas overseen by strong County Surveyors who acted as the Ministry's agents. Lovell's increasingly autocratic and independent attitude was giving cause for concern ... Finally, *Construction Steelwork* reported in December at 1971 'Tinsley fails test'. The Department of Environment confirmed the need for strengthening to meet 'Merrison box girder safety standards.'
>
> Mr A.E.P. Duffy MP in June 1973 raised questions in the House of Commons in an attempt to discover 'what was wrong with the bridge that had kept two of the six lanes of the M1 on the upper deck and two of the four carriageways on the lower deck closed for the past three years'.

The *Sheffield Star* of 24 April 1980, on the re-opening of the viaduct after strengthening, led with an article 'The scandal of Tinsley Viaduct' and gave a blow-by-blow account of the whole episode.

Finally, the *Daily Telegraph* of 22 January 1981 heads an article '10 years saga of 'cheap' bridge ends in double the cost'. The final bill took the cost to more than £10 million!

A brief record is included of the design and construction of Tinsley Viaduct, one of the first instances of a motorway being carried through a densely populated urban area and also the first steel structure in Britain to carry road traffic on two tiers.

Tinsley Viaduct Construction

Some 12,500 tons of mainly high tensile steel and about 80,000 tons of concrete were used in the construction of this 3,400-feet viaduct. Gas, electricity and water supplies were carried in service bays on the lower deck.

The factors most affecting the design were the two-tier requirement, the S-shape alignment (only five of the 22 spans of the upper deck are straight) and possible mining subsidence due to uncharted mine workings. The viaduct is flexible enough to take settlement, and provision is made for jacking at the main bearings.

Each deck is continuous and of composite construction – a reinforced concrete slab on two main longitudinal box girders with cross girders and cantilevers transversely at about 10 feet centres carried on 17 pairs of steel columns spaced across the Don Valley. *The Surveyor* of 22 June 1968 gives an account[98] of the construction of the viaduct.

Work on the site began in Spring 1965, the first task was to drill a pattern of 65 feet bore holes over the full area of the bases of all the piers and abutments, no undue settlement due to subsidence was expected.

Underground services caused complications in the construction of the concrete piers: two large sewers had to be temporarily supported across 30-feet-wide excavations while the pier footings were constructed underneath, and the footings of several piers were altered in shape to clear other services and to avoid any major diversion works. The 17 piers and four abutments are simple reinforced concrete structures on spread footing founded at depths varying between 15 to 30 feet. Coal or seat earth at foundation level was removed.

The erection of the steelwork was arranged to minimise use of the land and to avoid interruption of operation of the railways and factories. From its position on the upper deck steelwork over the last pier, a 35-ton derrick lifted into position the next four boxes of the lower deck, each of which was brought to the working end by a diesel locomotive running along the lower deck that had already been built, and the upper deck was completed to the end of that stage. The derrick then moved forwards to the leading edge of the upper deck and completed the next stage, which brought it within reach of the next pier. When the boxes for the last but one section of the lower deck were in position, it extended

Tinsley Viaduct construction
W.J. Harper

165 feet from the last vertical support and the end deflection was four feet. To position the last two longitudinal boxes of the section, the weight of the derrick was transferred to jacking beams and the free end of the lower deck was jacked into position: the upper deck was then completed by propping up the boxes from the completed lower deck. Each span was completed in about 11 days.

Concreting of the 8½-inch deck was begun before the steel erection was completed. To maintain operations clear of the ground, the central service duct under the lower deck was used as a channel through which all shutters were moved. The formwork was designed to be rolled out between the cross girders into position and, after stripping, rolled back into the central duct and forwarded to the next position. Concreting was started in the middle of the viaduct moving both ways so that there were four working faces, and was not placed in areas that would become subject to dead load tensile forces until that dead load had been added, thus minimising cracking.

Electric Heating cables were built into the road surface of the top deck because of the viaduct's exposed position, and to counteract the possible effects of ice formation as a result of condensation from the nearby cooling towers. The whole system is controlled automatically.

The exterior painting system was micacious iron ore and the interior of the sealed box units given red lead only. This was to prove a costly system to maintain.[99]

The lower deck of the viaduct was opened to local traffic on 25 March 1968. But the viaduct was not given a complete 'bill of health' until 1980 after further strengthening works.

The Strengthening of Tinsley Viaduct

The Merrison design check revealed the need for strengthening, particularly in the bottom flanges, the columns, the diaphragms in both longitudinal boxes and the supports.

Mike Walker[100] in *New Civil Engineer* 26 June 1975 refers to the 'hard slog' of the designers Freeman Fox in achieving a solution. 'Propping and plate doubling ideas were dropped because of technical difficulties and cost. What became known as the 'coat hanger scheme', based on new cross boxes between the main girders, on either side of the main cross boxes, with a system of tension rods and compression bars, although relieving loading within the main spans, did nothing for the loading in the cross box diaphragms or the columns themselves and was quietly dropped.'

Bill O'Neil[101] in *New Civil Engineer* of 2 November 1978 reports on the final solution adopted and undertaken by Cleveland Bridge at a cost of £5 million. Alec Connelly was a Project Engineer and Alan Treacher the Resident Engineer.

> Piers of the upper deck were indirectly strengthened by having an inverted triangular truss built around each one. The trusses spring from

Strengthening viewed from lower deck

each pier's foundations to new cross-boxes positioned within a quarter span length of the main cross-box ...

They comprise two raking steel box struts that each generated a 165 tonne nominal uplift, and a horizontal tension member to connect the strut heads. Generally eight 40 mm diameter Macalloy bars form this member, but, for the extreme north and south pairs of motorway deck piers where greater uplift is required, this number has been increased to 10 and 12 respectively.

Lower deck piers are relieved by steel links between the strut heads above and more new cross boxes under the carriageway. The links develop a nominal 125-tonne tension.

Shear and bending between the new support points are reduced to a level that is sufficient to bring the compressive working stresses within the Merrison limits. By achieving this system at the critical section, bending stresses are automatically reduced over the remaining span length, so that this too meets the Committee's requirements.[102]

The diagram on page 114, based on one from *New Civil Engineer* of 2 November 1978, shows the strengthening scheme.

The penultimate columns supported at each end of the viaduct on the lower deck abutments have special trusses, of which there are four. The 15 main piers of columns have the truss system described, i.e. 30 trusses in all.

The viaduct was re-opened to full traffic in 1980, some fifteen years after construction started.

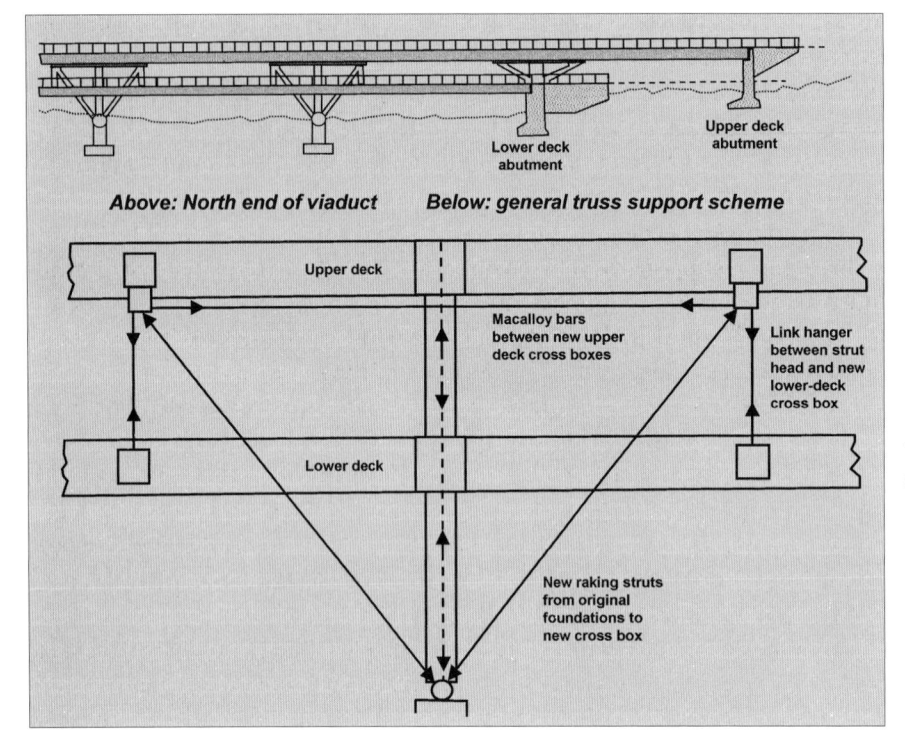

The strengthening scheme

An ironic twist in events was that Bridle, then Chief Highway Engineer with the Ministry, had become involved again. Sriskanden was to succeed him in due course.

The Calder Bridge – M1

Although Tinsley Viaduct involved considerable extra costs following its construction, the construction of the River Calder Bridge and its collapse during construction with loss of life was a more tragic affair.

The design of the Calder Bridge was the product of a competition organised by the Ministry of Transport. The competition produced about 110 entries in which the County Bridges Section was involved in drawing up the competition rules and the technical assessment of the 12 entries selected by the judges under the chairmanship of Sir Herbert Manzoni. It is estimated that something like 150-man years of effort went into the competition.

The competition was partly in response to criticisms that the younger generation of engineers were not getting an opportunity to apply their talents to design and partly in answer to pressure from the House of Commons following the controversies over the Staines Bridge and Chiswick Flyover.

The joint winning design submitted by A.A.W. Butler and M.V. Wooley in association with E.W.H. Gifford was chosen for construction.

Subsequently E.W.H. Gifford and Partners were appointed consulting engineers to the Ministry of Transport for the bridge.

The Ministry took the view at the time that the overall result did not justify them departing from their existing policy of giving bridge design commissions to firms of consulting engineers and the County highway departments.

The bridge was designed to accept ground movements due to mining. A three-point support system ensured a statically determinate structure under all conditions of ground movement.

The bridge built of twin decks has a 240-feet main span and 60-feet-long cantilevered side spans. The piers cast integral at the top and sit on a simple steel spherical bearing at the north side and at the south on two single steel roller bearings 22 feet apart.

During construction by Costains two of the 220-ton, 30-feet-long deck units and supporting falsework collapsed and four workmen were killed.

Although the disaster produced shock movements throughout the structure, no movement was found to have occurred at the piers, which were propped and stabilised.

The design and construction of the Calder Bridge is covered in the Institution of Civil Engineers Proceedings of August 1969 in Paper 7192 by Gifford, Woolley and Butler[103] where the full technical details of the collapse may be found.

The 'temporary works', i.e. those that are designed to support the structure during its construction, required temporary staging in the river. The skew at which these had to be placed, and their make-up, represented a situation where the calculation of their load-carrying capacity was very complex. In addition, the supporting structure was designed to use 18 inches x 6 inches x 55 pound high tensile steel joists, but unfortunately there was also a stock of second-hand 18 inches x 6 inches x 44 pound mild steel beams on site. Because of the close similarity in dimension and the lack of identification marking, some of these weaker beams were erroneously used in the work. The structure was built using beams which appeared correct, but were in fact weaker.

This, combined with the underestimate of the loads imposed through the skew framework, led to the collapse of one span of the temporary staging, which caused two of the concrete units each weighing 220 tons to fall into the river.

The completed Calder Bridge Gifford

Once again lessons were to be learnt about temporary works design, the importance of which was equal to that of the bridge itself.

Although the Darton to Wakefield contract was delayed, the bridge was finally completed and opened to traffic in October 1968, at a cost of £440,000. This graceful bridge crossing over the River Calder now stands as a monument to those who gave their all to its building.

M1 – Completed to Leeds

The M1 Motorway by now was completed to the outskirts of Leeds at Stourton. The continuation of the motorway into the city centre came later and is covered under urban motorways in this account.

The last section of the M1 in the West Riding was completed in October 1968 following which it was formally opened by the Rt Hon. Richard Marsh MP, who drove the full length from Aston to Leeds.

Before moving across to the most westerly borders of the West Riding to the Pennines and the M62, we have to return to the southern end of the M1 where Sir Owen Williams and Partners had completed their section of M1 through Nottinghamshire and had progressed the M18 from M1 to the Doncaster By-pass A1(M).

Barlborough to Thurcroft Motorway M1 and Thurcroft to Wadworth M18

These two sections of motorway, at the southern extremity of the North Eastern Region, have been included together as they formed part of the consultancy commission awarded to Sir Owen Williams and Partners[104] by the Ministry of Transport in 1957.

> In 1960, the year following the completion of the southern section, the Consulting Engineers were asked by the Ministry of Transport to proceed with the scheme preparation and detailed design for the remaining 87 miles of the London to Yorkshire Motorway from Crick in Northamptonshire to Doncaster in Yorkshire. Tenders for the first 15-mile length of this section were invited in May 1962 and construction was commenced in August of that year. Contracts were let successively for the remainder of the route and by December 1967 construction of this further length of the motorway had been completed …
>
> In locating the route of a motorway many factors were taken into account, not least of these was the necessity to minimise the dislocation of industry and agriculture and the effects on the general public.
>
> In 1951, when the consultants were briefed, the general location of the London to Yorkshire Motorway had already been defined in the national motorway plan. Many possible solutions had to be considered and before the 140-mile length of route was finally fixed some 600 route-miles had been surveyed. This survey covered not only topographical detail but also general considerations of drainage, soil conditions, land

use, and property boundaries. For the selection of the preferred route detailed studies were made of such factors as free-flowing horizontal alignment, ineffective rise in the vertical alignment, acceptable limits by which route mileage may exceed straight line distances between major population centres, and cost benefit analysis. From examination of these factors criteria were established governing the co-ordination between horizontal and vertical curves to give free-flowing alignment commensurate with acceptable costs of earthworks, and dictating route distance compatible with the pattern of existing roads between major population centres. It emerged from these early considerations that the introduction of horizontal curvature to avoid monotony has very little relevance to route selection in this country, where alignment is generally dictated by the location of suitable crossing of existing roads, railways, and rivers, and the minimising of adverse effects on property.[105]

Leaving Nottinghamshire, the M1 motorway passes to the east of Aston to the interchange with the A57 Worksop–Sheffield Trunk Road and then joins the M18 at Thurcroft where the motorway interchange provides an east-west link between the M18 and the 'West Riding' length of M1 to the north.

The M18 interchanges with the A631 Gainsborough – Rotherham Trunk Road and then turns eastwards, passing under some five bridges to join with A1(M) Doncaster By-pass at Wadworth. Extensive use was made of aerial survey throughout the route, both for the provision of 1/2500-scale

Interchange M1/M18 (south)

ordnance plans and 1/500-scale surveys of individual areas. Basic ground control for the aerial survey was utilised from the setting-out.

Geological investigations and soil surveys were undertaken. With this section of the route being predominantly in the coal measures, problems of dealing with abandoned mine workings at shallow depth and the subsidence to be expected from deep mining largely affected the design detail.

The effects of mining subsidence mitigated against a concrete or composite road construction and a fully bituminous paving was adopted. A single main sewer system under one verge, wider than normal, was used with high strength pipes and flexible joints. The widened verge permitted easier maintenance.

The structures vary from those in the south on account of mining subsidence. Throughout the M1, however, the bridges have been designed in a series of types adaptable to meet variations in span, skew, width and height. The possibility of subsidence necessitated the introduction of the centre pier on all overbridges. In general, all bridges are of reinforced concrete, those over railways and some roads being pre-cast. Retaining walls are, in general, of mass concrete, faced with pre-cast concrete block facing.

The Barlborough to Wadworth Contracts

The M1 Barlborough to Thurcroft Contract of some 6½ miles was awarded to Tarmac Civil Engineering Ltd in November 1965 and the 8½-mile M18 Thurcroft to Wadworth Contract to W. & C. French.

The contracts were under the overall supervision of the Resident Engineer, Ray Hartwell, operating from a Site Control Office at Leicester Forest East. A Deputy Resident Engineer was appointed to each contract and was responsible to the Resident Engineer for the day-to-day matters concerning the construction of the contract length. Each Deputy Resident Engineer was supported by a staff of engineers, surveyors, inspectors and laboratory assistants.

On all contracts, when the measurement and valuation had been completed and claims settled, final accounts were prepared, signed by the Contractor and the Engineer, and a final payment certificate issued.[106]

The final cost of the contract work done by Tarmac Civil Engineering Ltd was £4.56 million and that by W. & C. French, £5.2 million. Trevor Green was the Resident Engineer on the French Contract.

John Baxter[107] provides the following observations:

'The contract, which included the service area at Woodall, was carried out by Tarmac Civil Engineering Ltd, who sublet three of the bridges to W. & C. French Ltd, carrying out the remaining 11 themselves. Earthmoving was sublet to Dick Hampton. Tarmac's Project Manager was John Lea, and the work was divided into a Roads Section under Vince Green and a Bridges Section under John Baxter, both as Agents. The Resident Engineer for the Consultants was Maurice Fay.

The ground was coal measures throughout, so the whole motorway was designed to cater for mining subsidence, with a flexible roadway and hot rolled asphalt surfacing. Sir Owen Williams were renowned for their dislike and avoidance of pre-cast and pre-stressed concrete, so all of the bridges were fully cast *in situ*. This, together with the design for subsidence, meant that they were slow to construct, with massive reinforcement, which made placing and vibrating the concrete very difficult. Four of the bridges had decks of reinforced concrete supported by a row of reinforced concrete 'rockers' on each abutment. These were about six feet high and 15 inches square in plan, all cast *in situ*.

At Wales Bar the motorway was in deep cutting, which was expected to be rock, capable of self-support for the excavations for the bridge foundations, which were massive. In reality the rock was extremely unstable, and the proximity of dwellings at ground level plus the road diversion to enable bridge construction meant that it was imperative to excavate, rock bolt with mesh, and concrete on the same day.

This was agreed upon, and it was also decided to dispense with the 'normal' Owen Williams split faced blocks, which were standard for facing abutment walls, to allow them to be poured in one lift ...

Bridge deck pours were always times of high pressure, and a great deal of planning and preparation was involved, with extra teams of men and machinery being laid on. An innovation (for this contract and I believe for possibly the industry) was the attempt to place the bridge deck concrete by use of a mobile pump sited on the carriageway below, fed by a stream of truck mixers. It was only attempted after some misgivings, which turned out to be totally justified, as the pump was quite unable to cope with the high strength for workability concrete mix specified by Owen Williams. A disaster was averted as our customary belt and braces approach meant we had a back up monorail system fully installed and ready for use – it just took a bit longer!

Re-use of formwork was planned so as to reduce costs, but with hindsight it might have been better to go for adjacent bridges in parallel rather than in series, which blocked the carriageway for twice the time. This was especially relevant to the A57 interchange bridges, both being of heavy rocker support type, which also featured a cantilevered footway/duct bay on each side, which could not be started until the *in situ* deck had been fully stripped out and deflected under its own weight.

The service area at Woodall consisted of earthworks, drainage, footbridge, retaining wall and car parking.[108]

Construction of the 300ft-long underbridge at the M1/M18 Interchange

The following is abstracted from *Friendship*,[109] a W. & C. French's 'in-house' magazine.

> Many formidable obstacles have had to be overcome, not least of all the very hard rock. No doubt a geologist would be in complete paradise with the assortment of rocks etc, encountered – limestone, sandstone, shale, coal, mudstone – to say nothing of our old faithful, clay.
>
> Out of 16 structures, which have to be built, two have been completed. A further ten are in progress and work on the remaining four is about to commence.
>
> Drainage for the M18 has provided a hell of a problem. Excavating 60 miles of drain trench 8 inches wide by 12 inches deep to 4 feet 6 inches wide and 10 feet deep in solid rock is, we can assure all readers, no joke. However, with our good team on the M18 plus the support received from all at H.Q., this task – with many others – is steadily being overcome.[110]

To assist construction, French purchased a modern Rahco road machine from America which is shown here carrying out final trimming of the sub-base. The machine is wire-guided for the finished level.

The next issue adds

> ... Following up our first article we can now report good progress, with a clearer picture emerging. Our 'rocky' problem is still with us, but we are now calling the tune and, in fact, consider ourselves future experts in this field. Some 150,000 pounds of explosives have been used to date. Earthworks are running at 2,050,000 cubic yards with approximately 20,000 cubic yards of concrete having been placed.
>
> Various other problems have been encountered, where bridge construction takes place in areas liable to mining subsidence and in one case, after commencing work to bridge abutments, we were instructed – just in time – to extend the height of the walls by two feet. We all hope that the calculations of the expected settlement are correct; otherwise, somebody is likely to get a headache. Subsidence, as a result of shallow mine workings, also has its effect on drainage. Before commencing new lengths of drain, a survey along the route has to be carried out to allow the necessary adjustments to be made ...
>
> On 14 October 1967 it was agreed that we would attempt to complete the M18 in time to allow traffic to flow on 21 December and from that moment on the lives of the staff at M18 became completely saturated with work, work and more work. It was soon obvious to all that it would be utterly impossible for anyone to make private or personal arrangements. Christmas shopping, celebrations etc, would all have to go. And by the board, they all went.
>
> With over half a million pounds of work to do and only 58 days left it was clear that we had a very formidable task on our hands. To cope with our challenge we decided to have daily meetings and discussions continued well into the evenings. By this approach problems were solved and miracles bloomed.
>
> During this period we had an assortment of weather: rain, frost and bitterly cold winds – bringing with them a covering of snow. Heaters were used to permit surfacing and lane markings to continue. The team

The Rahco Road Machine

spirit throughout was magnificent, as was the hot soup provided by our canteen ladies. What better reward to us all than to see completion of this major motorway contract ahead of schedule and to witness the opening ceremony (which took place in December 1967) and was performed by Mr Stephen Swingler, MP, Minister of State.[111]

The Government did pay additional money to French to accelerate the works to ensure completion by Christmas, thus enabling the opening of the M1 to Doncaster to be claimed as a 'present to the nation'.

The interchange between the A1(M) and the M18 was designed by West Riding engineers.

The Wadworth Interchange Bridges

Tony Dawson[112] recalls: 'This was an advanced contract to make possible the interchange between the Doncaster By-pass A1(M) and the M18.

The contract was let to Dowsett Engineering Construction Ltd in mid-July 1965 for the sum of £169,000. The work involved the building of four bridges as part of the roundabout over the Doncaster By-pass; two bridges over the A1(M) and two to the west allowing a minor road, White Cross Lane, to pass beneath the roundabout. Completion of the White Cross Lane bridges was required within 10 months and the two A1(M) bridges within 12 months.'

The Contracts Manager was Hatter, and the Agent Tony Dawson. The Resident Engineer was John Lovell, and Assistant Resident Engineer was Roger Weatherall.

> The Concrete Foreman was Jim Conlan, an Irishman who had settled in Doncaster. In his gang was Albert Fogg, a local man, unique in that he brought his own shovel to work. At the end of each day he cleaned his shovel until shining bright, wrapped it in a sack, and strapped it to the cross bar of his bike and rode off home. Both of these men were from an agricultural background, and perhaps this was why they had many

The Wadworth Interchange M18/A1(M)

manual skills and the awesome ability to work steadily throughout a long day in any weather ...

The White Cross Lane bridge decks were single spans having pre-stressed pre-cast beams with concrete infill. The drawing showed stainless steel dowels 20 inches long and 1¾ inches diameter in the fixed end bearing shelf at 24-inch spacing. The only explanation as to why six dowels were still in store at the end of the contract had to be that they were put in at 2 feet 4 inch centres! [A fact not revealed until now!]

The construction of the two bridges over the Doncaster By-pass entailed Dowsett's having possession of the north and south bound carriageways for six weeks each. Over Easter 1966 possession of the northbound carriageway had to be relinquished from Good Friday until Easter Monday because of holiday traffic. The work closed down from the Friday to the Monday, the statutory holiday for the industry. At about 8.15 am in the morning of Easter Tuesday a labourer returning to work climbed over the boundary fence and walked straight under a car travelling north. The coroner's court returned a verdict of accidental death.

The Wadworth Viaduct, to carry the M18 over the A1(M) Doncaster By-pass, was not built until 1979 (see p.194).

8 The North Eastern Road Construction Unit and the West Riding and Durham Sub-Units

The part played by the County Surveyors of the North East, and their staffs, in the creation of this new organisation was of considerable significance; no more so than in the West Riding and Durham County Councils.

From the Ministry of Transport's standpoint the Lofthouse Committee report produced in 1966 had recommended a reduction in the number of design and construction organisations in the interest of efficiency. The Minister, the Rt Hon. Barbara Castle, was considering the setting up of a National Roads Board. Such an organisation was required to carry out the Government's burgeoning road programme and ensure that the large amounts of public money required were kept under direct management, contractual and financial control of the Minister. The concerns of the Counties were great.

When Bill (later Sir William) Harris was asked by Barbara Castle to look at a new organisation he was well aware of the Counties' concerns, as Agent Authorities for motorway and trunk road construction, that their role might be eliminated and seriously weaken their function as highway authorities. He was also aware of the difficulties that would arise if Counties, such as the West Riding, Durham and Lancashire, were not allowed to participate, having built up large departments for the agency work, already being undertaken, and also in anticipation of a roads programme well into the future. The fees generated could be considerable and helped to meet the cost of running their Highways departments.

It was Lovell, as the then President of the County Surveyors Society, and his successor Cotton, together with Hetherington of the Association of County Councils, who were asked by Harris to open discussions on a new organisation.

There were many concerns among the staff in both the Counties and the Civil Service. NALGO and the Civil Service Union became deeply involved.

Eventually a compromise partnership arrangement was agreed with the County Councils Association. There would be winners and losers. Two of the major Counties in the North East, the West Riding and Durham County Councils, agreed to set up Sub-Units with the West Riding acting as host County for the provision of staff to the North Eastern Road Construction Unit Headquarters, to be centred on Harrogate under the control of a Director. The Director would have direct responsibility to the Ministry in London, and became the Engineer under all contracts, a position up to then jealously guarded by the County Surveyors.

In the West Riding many of the staff thought, somewhat unfairly in the writer's view, that Lovell had 'sold out' when invited to become 'General Manager' over the RCUs with an office in the Ministry in London. Although he had set his cap on high office in the Ministry of Transport with the setting up of the RCUs, he found he would not have the say over staff or the completeness of power and communication that he had achieved in local government. He eventually declined the post but before doing so undertook all of the consultations with the County Councils to bring the new organisation to fruition and spent many months away from Yorkshire in the Ministry's Headquarters. He also assisted in the appointment of the RCU Directors.

Having served both the army and politicians for most of his life, perhaps Lovell had foreseen that the political will for change could not be stopped and it was better to join 'them' than face being beaten.

With a seven-year agreement for participating Counties, Lovell and Cotton had played their part in securing work for their departments for that time ahead. In fact, these agreements lasted for almost fourteen years and what a record of achievement that became. The first Road Construction Unit to be set up was in the North West in April 1968. Within a year all six regional units had been established. The first Director to the North Eastern RCU was Gilbert Norris, the Deputy Director Jim MacKenzie and the Controller of Administration Bill Rogers.

With the formation of the Sub-Units much work had to be done in setting up the new organisations in both West Riding and Durham. In West Yorkshire this responsibility was taken over by 'Hutch' Hutchinson and the writer as Superintending Engineers Roads and Bridges respectively, with the County Surveyor, Lovell (who was shortly to retire) having a dual role as Chief Engineer of the Sub-Unit. He was succeeded by Gaffney. He was to become President of the County Surveyors' Society, the Institution of Highway Engineers and the Institution of Civil Engineers, the latter being the greatest distinction for any Civil Engineer.

In Durham similar roles were filled by Cotton as Chief Engineer and John Petrie and Peter Mead as Superintending Engineers.

The West Riding as the host County was required to provide staff to supplement the Civil Service staff in the Headquarters at Harrogate and also to provide an adequate establishment to undertake the work in the Sub-Unit, which included 20 per cent of Civil Servants. Two West Riding engineers, Sargent and Deuce, were appointed to Harrogate as Superintending Engineers for Projects and Bridges. Varley was to succeed Deuce on his appointment the following year as Assistant Chief Engineer with the Ministry in London. In 1969 Denis Hall suceeded Norris until 1971, when MacKenzie became the Director.

The majority of motorway and major trunk road schemes were undertaken under this arrangement, with the exception of those carried out by consulting engineers whose role was similar to that of the Sub-Units. This arrangement lasted until the 1974 local government re-organisation and the change in County Council boundaries.

In Durham the Sub-Unit arrangements continued under the Durham County Council with John Tully, the then County Surveyor, also having the dual role as Chief Engineer of the Sub-Unit. With the formation of the West Yorkshire Metropolitan County Council the Sub-Unit became part of the Engineering Directorate within the Directorate of Planning, Engineering and Transportation (DOPET). Gaffney, the Director of Engineering Services, continued to fulfil his dual role.

For administrative purposes the Sub-Unit under Hutchinson, as Assistant Director, was part of the Engineering Directorate headed by the writer as Executive Director of Engineering. Denis Taylor became Superintending Engineer (Bridges), with Hawes Chief Group Engineer (Roads).

The North Eastern Road Construction Unit operated into the early 1980s and accomplished a great many schemes.

9 The Lancashire–Yorkshire Motorway M62

Prologue
A View of the M62 in the 1990s

Rosie Millard[113] gives a reporter's view of this motorway in the *Observer* magazine of 9 June 1991, some 17 years after its completion:

> June 1976. The M62, England's only cross-country motorway, stretching from Kingston upon Hull to Liverpool, from the North Sea to the Irish Sea, is complete. It serves six major cities and a population equivalent in size to that of Australia.
>
> Since 1975, in the face of some of the worst weather in the country, the M62 has closed only twice. It keeps open thanks to an aerodynamic snow-attack design. Moorside fences designed by the Royal College of Art keep out lambs. It has endured suicides, a shoot-out and an aeroplane landing. Cargoes of goods, from turnips to Jacuzzis, have scattered across it.
>
> The M62 connects all the major national routes. At night the country's vertical arms – M6, M1/A1, A19 – are strung out in glittering filaments from their axis, the M62.
>
> To appreciate the M62 fully, follow the track of the sun from Hull to Liverpool. The start is framed by the Humber Bridge (A10), the only way ahead is west. The supreme moment: a blue sign MOTORWAY AHEAD, 120 miles to go. A roll call of Cities begins and the tarmac changes from grey to gold.
>
> Along the M62, the Victorian cityscapes are a parade of wildly ambitious constructions. From Hull's City Hall topped by a mounted Boadicea, the M62 sweeps past the garlanded and circular Leeds Corn Exchange and arrives at the Liver Building, its Chicago-inspired design looking further west, America bound.
>
> The supreme feat of engineering that this road across the Pennines represents becomes clear as soon as you are on top of the mountains and the road scales the heights, to avoid fog. The road was blasted out of solid rock, the mountain peat proving so glutinous that it was useless for recycling, and had to be removed in lorry loads.
>
> Surrounded by Pennine glory in Hebden Bridge, David Fletcher, head of the Transpennine Pressure Group, recites the wonder of the M62. Transpennine is the M62's official fan club – an organisation aiming for national recognition of this 'linear city' as an alternative to London. Fletcher sees the M62 as part of a line linking New York to Moscow, a corridor that could make the North hugely powerful. Already the M62 is easily the Country's biggest trade route, and the Hull docks handle 10 times more cargo than the Channel Tunnel ever will.

History is embraced by the M62, the Pennine Way allowed to continue over a special footbridge, and the service stations ringing with Wars of the Roses names: Ferrybridge, Hartshead Moor, Birch, Burtonwood. Committed during the week to freight, the road's weekend traffic is devoted to sport: carloads of supporters from Grimsby Town to Everton, scarves streaming out, the service stations ready with extra food …

As Liverpool and the Irish Sea approach, the sun sets directly in front of you, casting the road into long shadow. Swooping into Liverpool on a roller-coaster slope, the M62 runs out at the Rocket Roundabout. Its future?

There are rumours of a private road scheme, a second Trans Pennine crossing. But will any substitute boast the endeavour and devotion that the M62, conqueror of the Pennines, has commanded for more than 15 years?[114]

Background

In the late 1930s, as part of a national plan, it had been envisaged that a new road would be constructed from Liverpool to Hull, linking these ports with the industrial areas of South Lancashire and the West Riding of Yorkshire.

The war prevented any progress, but in 1947 the Minister of Transport appointed Engineers to undertake an investigation for a new road to motorway standards between the Trunk Road A580, at Swinton, in Lancashire, and the Trunk Road A1 at Selby Fork in the West Riding of Yorkshire. The A580 in Lancashire and the A63 in Yorkshire were considered satisfactory to provide links to the two ports. This early reconnaissance work was completed in 1952, but the national economic situation would not allow action to be taken to develop the scheme further. The route, however, was incorporated in the County Development Plan to protect it from future development.

Following a review by the West Riding County Council towards the end of 1960 it became evident, in the light of the experience gained on motorways in operation at that time, that the line of the Lancashire–Yorkshire Motorway laid down in 1952 was unsatisfactory. In particular, it did not cater for the industrial traffic of the heavy woollen and mining areas.

A primary need in the conurbation area was for a motorway, which could tap its major industrial potential to the benefit of the whole country, and also provide the backbone of an inter-urban traffic system. The original line for the motorway did not do this. Additional problems with the route were the crossing of the Pennines at a very high altitude, which would have created severe difficulties under winter weather conditions, and the distance between junctions which could not achieve the high safety standards required.

In June 1960 an origin and destination survey, with 27 survey points, was carried out and the information linked to other available data to model the traffic needs of the West Riding conurbation.

A case for re-appraisal of the Lancashire–Yorkshire Motorway line was put to the Ministry of Transport for consideration, who, after consultation, decided to review the whole route. In 1961 the West Riding and Lancashire County Councils accepted an invitation to act as Agent Authorities in the location of a new route for the Lancashire–Yorkshire Motorway and work commenced in August 1961.

Hunter recalls how the County Surveyors Drake and Lovell met near Windy Hill and on the flip of a coin (lent by Hunter for the occasion and never returned) decided which County should lead in the naming of the M62. Lovell lost and it became the Lancashire–Yorkshire Motorway.

This account only covers the M62 in the North East Region from the Pennines eastward.[115,116,117,118]

At the outset of the investigation it was clear that the currently available Ordnance Survey maps did not meet the designers' requirements and an aerial survey was proposed. With Ministry of Transport approval this work was put in hand in December 1961.

In order to limit the areas for full aerial survey a model to a scale of 6 inches to 1 mile, with 2 to 1 vertical exaggeration was constructed from the available Ordnance Survey detail. This enabled an appreciation to be readily made of the routes, which were to be investigated more fully.

As the choice of lines was narrowed down by design criteria and other considerations, planning restrictions previously imposed on building development were lifted on the routes, which had been eliminated, and the 'zones' of restrictions reduced to the minimum necessary.

Considerable problems were presented in the routeing and design of the Pennine Section of the motorway by features of geology, geography and climate.

The weather in the Pennines provides hazardous conditions for the motorist with ice and snow in the winter. Fog, poor visibility, torrential rain and gales are also common throughout the year. It was obviously of great importance to minimise the effect of these hazards by careful selection of the route. A network of ten weather stations was set up in January 1962 along the alternative 'high' and 'low' level routes to provide

The hazardous conditions of the Pennines

comparative recordings of temperature, visibility and snowfall. From the data obtained it was estimated that the higher route would have 30 per cent to 40 per cent more fog; a 10 per cent greater frequency of frost and 20 per cent more significant snow. For these reasons the low level route was adopted.

This route crossed the County boundary at Windy Hill at a level of 1,220 feet, quickly falling to 850 feet before crossing the Dean Head Valley to join a common route at Pole Moor. Through the Heavy Woollen Area between Brighouse and Morley a northern route was chosen of the two investigated.

Through the mining area between Lofthouse and the Great North Road the route to Selby Fork was found not to be practical and that to Ferrybridge was selected.

The problems of crossing the Pennines were unique and further specialised studies were undertaken after consultation with the Ministry and the Road Research Laboratory, namely:

- The construction of two trial embankments close to the line of the motorway at Moselden Height to study the effects of wind and snow on an exposed section of the motorway.
- Field trials using various types of fencing on the Pennines to ascertain the extent to which they cause snow drifts and their efficiency as barrier fencing against sheep.
- Wind tunnel experiments to observe the airflow in major cuttings and over high embankments.
- Field trials to ascertain the best way of growing grass, trees and other plant life on the moors of the Pennines, which are subject to a high degree of air pollution.
- Blasting and compaction trials to find the best methods of dealing with the large quantities of rock involved (some seven million cubic yards) over the whole length of the motorway.

Investigations were also made into the existing use of land, which showed the overall location of mining, other industry, and agriculture. Consultations with the County Mining Engineer gave information on subsidence in the area of the motorway and on the general geology. This was further supplemented by a preliminary soil survey with trial boreholes along the alternative lines. The Pennine crossing posed major structural engineering problems and special studies were made into tunnels and ventilation, two-level structures, canopies and road heating.

The M62 Lancashire–Yorkshire Motorway Section headed by Ellis included design teams under John Glanville, and Shelbourn having teams 'to deal with everything else'. Construction of two trial embankments was undertaken in autumn 1962 using low cost materials, fly-ash, shale and a skimming of fine cold asphalt as a surfacing. Each embankment, of ranging heights and side slopes, was 100 yards long and to full motorway width.

'Will' Shakespear was appointed as a full-time observer with a Land Rover to take daily measurements of snow depths and to record drift patterns. A dedicated observer, only on one day did he fail to reach the site in the winters of 1962 (one of the coldest on record) and 1963. Shelbourn[119] says 'one had only to experience being 'up on the top' in snow, the bitter cold catching your breath and the wind forcing you double, to appreciate the dangers of prolonged exposure'. Continuous recordings were made at the site of temperature and wind speed and direction.

The results of these trials showed that side slope was more critical than height and that a slope of 1 in 5 was found to be the critical slope where snow was swept away. When roads in the locality were experiencing drifts of eight to 12 feet the trial embankments were generally blown clear.

Two very deep cuttings at Windy Hill and Dean Head up to 150 feet deep required careful consideration and arrangements were made with the National Physical Laboratory to undertake wind tunnel tests. The simple conclusion drawn was that in deep cuttings, space was the key factor. As a consequence the width of formation was increased for storage of prolonged snow, and to avoid avalanche conditions, side slopes no steeper than 1 in 1, with berms for increased storage, were adopted. It was also found that at cut/fill lines snow fences should be erected.

Shelbourn[120] takes up the story:

> Consultations with Huddersfield Water Undertaking established that they had been seeking to build a dam in this locality for some time, to supplement the Booth Wood reservoir. Huddersfield had engaged A.H. Waters and Partners as Consultants, with Professor Nash as geology specialist, and some fascinating technical meetings took place.
>
> At this early stage both authorities saw the advantages of a joint scheme and a sound working partnership was founded. In a co-operative exercise that is unique in this country, and possibly in the world; many legal, political and administrative, as well as engineering problems had to be overcome.
>
> Having reached an initial agreement on a combined dam and motorway embankment each authority then progressed with its own planning – the Corporation with detailed design of a comprehensive water supply scheme, including tunnels, treatment works, pumping stations, catchwaters and aqueducts; and the County Council with the motorway. For design and supervision of the dam the Corporation appointed Rofe, Kennard and Lapworth as their Consulting Engineers.
>
> This was the first time that a dam has been designed to carry a motorway on its crest and inevitably a number of novel problems had to be solved. On the legal side, Huddersfield Corporation had to promote a Private Bill in Parliament to obtain the necessary powers for the work, which were eventually granted in the Huddersfield Corporation Act 1965. No less a problem was the sharing of costs between the water and motorway authorities. Then because safety was paramount the Minister appointed the Corporation as his agents for the section of

motorway across the dam together with full and complete responsibility for all aspects of the structure. In addition, it was necessary to acquire several farms and houses which gave rise to numerous individual human problems.[121]

Shelbourn[122] continues:

At this stage the basic design had proceeded to the stage where centreline levels had been established to achieve an approximate balance in mass haul quantities. It had been calculated that about seven million cubic yards of rock – mainly Kinderscout Grit – would need to be excavated over the length, the most spectacular section of earthworks being at Dean Head and Scammonden where the road would need to pass from cutting about 150 feet deep to cross a steep-sided valley on embankment 200 feet high or thereabouts. The main difficulty to be overcome was that while we as highway engineers were seeking a stable embankment in which adequate compaction to avoid settlement was combined with free-draining characteristics, the Water Authority's target was a water-tight (earth) structure incorporating clay core, sealed foundations, armoured (rip-rap) face, and so on.

Added to this conundrum there was the whole question of how to excavate seven million cubic yards of rock and place it in embankment in a reasonable time at a reasonable cost. There were many characteristics of the Kinderscout and other local gritstones that we were not familiar with in this context, and would be literally breaking new ground. One thing for sure, the prospect of placing such material in the traditional nine-inch layers, required in the standard MOT Specification, was not on! It was, therefore, evident we should have to undertake fairly large-scale field trials, in which the Water Authority and their Consultants would be invited to participate. A site at Dean Head was chosen (where some preliminary snow accumulation measurements had already been undertaken), and a contract let to John Laing, primarily on a Dayworks Basis, in the sum of £150,000. John Stothard was the Resident Engineer on site. Site offices were set up at Dean Head that spring of 1964 and the whole of the summer months devoted to the tasks of establishing:

- The optimum blasting pattern to produce rock capable of being placed in, say, a three feet layer depth, and having graded particles to produce satisfactory interlocking, filling of interstices and mechanical stability. (Sieve analysis of two-ton samples in this context proved somewhat tedious!)
- The plant required to achieve satisfactory consolidation.
- The most practicable compaction specification, whether by method or end result.
- The weathering characteristics, porosity, and frost susceptibility.
- Embankment side slopes and long term stability of cut faces.
- Acceptable working tolerances for formation levels and sides slopes in cutting.
- The timescale likely to be involved, having regard to overall programming requirements.
- Anything else relevant to the overall requirements, including separate studies initiated by Professor Nash in relation

to specification for the Dam, and the forming of sections of shallow embankment of varying side slopes to enable snow accumulation to be compared in the coming winter.

Our initial approach to the task was to seek the advice of ICI Explosives Division regarding drilling pattern and depth, amount of explosive per hole and stemming details. We told them our overall objective and they duly responded. This recipe was given to the Contractor, who duly complied.

The result was quite fascinating, really. Had we been in the business of producing the largest possible gritstone monoliths for incorporation in some mammoth ceremonial temple, we should have been on a winner! As prospective fill for a motorway embankment, however, the product was absolutely useless. We thanked ICI very much for their trouble and decided to proceed on our own. To be fair, I suppose it was expecting rather a lot to get it right first time! Over the ensuing weeks we had great fun shattering the peace of the moorlands with numerous explosions associated with all possible permutations of the variants, no doubt much to the bewilderment of any indigenous inhabitants within earshot. As these were for the most part non-discriminating hill sheep of Pennine stolidity, however, no great harm was done.

We persevered in our search for the optimum combination, attracting the interest of civil engineers from far and wide with our pioneering efforts. By July we had sufficient information to be able to advise Norman Ellis of the practical timescale for incorporation of the earthworks element in the overall programme for the whole 39 miles of the M62 under design, which he was anxious to complete and present to the County Council and the Ministry of Transport. It was decided that the earthworks from the Lancashire boundary to Pole Moor (six miles) could be realistically undertaken from April 1966 to September 1968, primarily in the two summers of 1966 and 1967, given reasonable weather. This would lead to an overall target completion date of June 1970, and a detailed programme for the various sections of the motorway was formulated on this basis.

This was not the end of the matter, however, by a long chalk. The trials continued, both to fine-tune the blasting and excavation details. Various types and combinations of compaction equipment were tried on different layer depths, the assessment of results by digging trial pits, with attendant sampling and density testing being particularly tedious. Further sampling and laboratory testing were also undertaken to meet Professor Nash's strict control requirements for dam construction.

Much effort was put into harmonising the objectives in this respect, until the fairly obvious compromise was reached – the design of the dam would incorporate a thick layer of clay to act as a seal on the upstream side, brought up with the embankment as tipping proceeded, the face to have rip-rap protection, the base to include a curtain wall and the sides benched in with additional clay sealing ...

As the rock trials were coming to an end we treated ourselves to a final lunch at a pub on the A62 at Mirfield renowned for oversized and succulent Angus steaks, then decided as a last experiment to ask the Contractor to set a pattern of closely-drilled holes filled to the top with explosive, without stemming. We wanted to see if this would shatter Kinderscout Grit into small particles.

When the charges were all set, the Contractor's Foreman advised we should 'retreat some distance for this one'. We took up station about 100 yards distant. Not good enough, he said, and refused to set things off until we were at least 200 yards away behind a stone wall, hard helmets pulled down firmly over skulls.

How right he was! A spectacular explosion was hotly pursued by large pieces of Kinderscout sailing over our heads to disappear in the general direction of Huddersfield like so many meteorites, fortunately returning to earth before penetrating any inhabited areas.

The rock trials were not the only experimental work undertaken on the top of the Pennines that summer. One of the things we needed to know for fence design was just how high your average hill sheep could jump, since the prospect of mobile mutton meandering across the motorway was not a happy one. Estimates varied, even from experienced hill farmers. Finally, one of their number offered to help us mount a practical test. He had some ewes in season, which he put into a sheep pen, enclosed by a barrier of adjustable height, and his prize ram on the outside. This noble animal finally cleared 5 feet 6inches in his eagerness to get to his harem. Very reluctant he was, too, once having entered the sheep pen, to be forced to return outside to have another go as we gradually raised the barrier. Allowing for appropriate exhaustion factor, we concluded the design height for the motorway fence across the moors should be six feet. An environmentally-friendly type of fence to this height strung between slender pylons was duly selected.[123]

Following the detailed investigations on the route, the draft Section 11 Scheme for the length between the County Boundary and Outlane was published in October 1963 and the Scheme made in October 1964 with the proviso that the Minister would consider objections between Pole Moor and Outlane when the draft scheme for the next length was considered.

The length between Outlane and Lofthouse was published in February 1964. Objections led to a Public Inquiry in May 1965, at which Sir Fredrick Armer was the Inspector. Following a positive report, the Minister made the Scheme in August 1965 on the draft line, some 18 months having lapsed between publication and making the Scheme.

The draft Section 11 Scheme between Sheffield–Leeds Motorway M1 at Lofthouse and the A1 at Ferrybridge was published in October 1965. Draft side road orders followed.

In due time, all tasks were completed, contracts prepared and tenders could be invited. Eleven major contracts were required to take the M62 Motorway from Lancashire County boundary, in the west, to Ferrybridge Interchange on the A1 London–Edinburgh Trunk Road and then extend eastwards to Goole and subsequently to Hull.

Two lengths of motorway connect the M62 to the major cities of Leeds and Bradford – the M621 and M606.

From the initial invitation to the West Riding County Council in January 1962 it was to take until May 1976 to complete the M62 and involved the North Eastern Road Construction Unit, the Sub-Units of the

West Riding and Durham County Councils, and the consulting engineers, Scott Wilson Kirkpatrick & Partners.

The M62 Contracts Undertaken by the West Riding County Council and its Sub-Unit

The Bulk Beam Contract

The history of Yorkshire Motorways and the M62 would not be complete without a record of this contract. Mention has already been made of the writer's discussions with (Sir) William Harris, at the time of the Ardsley–Stourton Contract for M1, and of the need for improvement in the procurement of pre-cast beams and the proposition of an advanced beam contract.

A report is included in the Archive of *An Investigation into the Advisability of Letting a Contract for the Bulk Supply of Beams*[124] together with a note[125] of the first meeting in July 1966 with the Ministry Bridge Engineers to discuss the proposal. Frank Rush, Phil Lee and Peter Grant were present together with the writer and Les Deuce.

With the support of Rush and Lee agreement was reached to go ahead with the Bulk Beam Contract.

The erection of the bridges was the responsibility of the main contractors. Many are of a standard type, having pre-cast, pre-stressed concrete I-section beams with *in situ* reinforced concrete diaphragms and deck slab, reinforced/mass concrete abutments with forward sloping front faces and reinforced concrete slab piers.

In 1966, prior to the design of bridges, a study of beam types was undertaken by the West Riding County Council, together with an investigation into the economic advantages of letting a bulk beam contract for the supply of bridge beams for this motorway in Yorkshire.

An I-beam with a wide bottom flange, which had been developed for use on the M1 Sheffield–Leeds Motorway, was considered to be the least complicated, most adaptable and economic beam for the project. It had no projecting reinforcement, permitted different beam spacings, and in conjunction with the composite top slab could be constructed at any skew, camber, or crossfall.

It was found that, for spans over 50 feet, beams could be grouped into standard spans of 61 feet, 75 feet, 85 feet or 92 feet and four sections were designed to suit these spans for a variety of deck arrangements.

Contractors, as well as pre-cast concrete manufacturers, were interested in tendering for a large beam contract and three were selected of each. In 1967 the then Ministry of Transport approved the letting of the bulk beam contract which was awarded to Leonard Fairclough Ltd.

At the time the contract was signed, John Porter, Fairclough's entrepreneurial Director, had thought that railway sidings adjacent to

Fairclough's deflected tendon system

their offices at Adlington would provide the site for new beds. The writer's view was that this would give little scope for the future should the company wish to expand its activities in beam manufacture. Porter then investigated further sites, and proposed a site in Accrington. The writer agreed with this site as preferable, having good road access to the sites on M62 and, equally important, scope for future expansion.

During detailed discussions before the factory was built, it became clear that the contractor, in putting down new beds, would wish to standardise in the most up-to-date methods of manufacture, particularly in view of long line stressing.

Joe Thompson, Fairclough's chief engineer, undertook a study of beam production in the United States. On his return, slides were shown on the writer's office wall, deflected tendon techniques discussed and decisions reached. One problem had 'bugged' Thompson – most of the beams in the States had exhibited horizontal cracks in the ends. 'No problem', said the writer, 'it's a matter of steel reinforcement' – and so it was.

These early discussions culminated in the re-design of the post-tensioned I-beams for manufacture by a pre-tensioned deflected tendon system which resulted in a further financial saving on the contract.

The pre-cast concrete factory at Accrington was built and equipped for making and handling these I-beam and other heavy pre-cast units. The factory had two sections, the first section mainly dealing with the long-line production of the pre-tensioned units and the second section dealing with heavy pre-cast reinforced concrete and post-tensioned units. Both sections had integral cranage capable of handling units of up to 60 tons weight.

With the emphasis on production, steam curing was used to ensure a rapid turn-round of components (three 98-feet or 63-feet beams were produced a day), whilst a fully equipped factory-based laboratory covered all testing operations.

The Fairclough system, in which the West Riding County Council co-operated, consisted of 300-feet-long beds. These lines were specially designed to allow for deflecting the strands to any pattern dictated by the structural requirements of a particular member. A further advantage of the system with the standard beam types was that it permitted an easy change in the lengths of any of the four preferred types.

With rising costs of construction it is by improvements in techniques of manufacture that design and construction teams can keep prices to a minimum. This is an example of the best system having been developed out of very close co-operation between designer and constructor.

Production of the beams commenced at the new factory in October 1968, and beams were manufactured at the rate of up to 24 per week. The contract period for the manufacture of some 1,400 pre-stressed concrete beams for the M62 motorway was spread over a five-year period, and produced some of the lowest cost beams in the whole of the history of motorway construction.

As each main contract came 'on stream', the associated beams were assigned from the bulk beam contract to the contractors concerned. Although there was some anxiety that the first beams might not be ready from this new 'green field' factory, delivery dates were met on the first and subsequent contracts.

Design, preparation of contract and supervision of the manufacture of the beams was carried out by the West Riding Bridges Department. The Principal Engineers concerned were Deuce, Denis Taylor and Green-Armitage. The Supervisor of works at the factory was Cyril Nutter. The Works Manager, a former Director of Fairclough's, was Bill Warmsley, a tremendous character 'who lived concrete' and who has provided a history of the factory for the Archive; he was supported by Roger Billington, an equal enthusiast for pre-cast concrete.

The inauguration of the factory, on Lancashire's 'patch', was undertaken by Sir James Drake after his retirement.

The Construction Contracts

Commencing at the County boundary the M62 motorway crosses the millstone grit area, much overlain by peat, which extends eastwards to a major faulting system to the north-east of Outlane, near Huddersfield.

The motorway then crosses the Lower and Middle Coal Measure strata of Carboniferous age, the top few feet of which are generally weathered to sandy or silty clay. The high ground is topped with sandstone. Beneath this and in the valleys there are the whole range of Coal Measure strata from sandstones, siltstones and mudstones to carboniferous mudstone and coals. Through this area the contracts were generally balanced cut to fill, i.e. the amount of material excavated balanced the amount required to fill embankments.

East of Ferrybridge after leaving the magnesian limestone escarpment both the M62 and M18 motorways run out over flat agricultural land which is generally only two to three metres above ordnance datum (OD) and consists of superficial deposits of mainly glacial laminated clays, sands and gravels with some alluvial deposits along old river beds. These deposits, which are up to 20 metres in depth, overlay Triassic rocks, which are represented by Bunter Sandstone. In this area the motorways are formed on embankment throughout, with the height maintained at two metres minimum above original ground level, with the majority of fill imported – including the granular drainage blanket to the base of the embankments.

West of Ferrybridge, with the exception of the Pennine Area, where the surface water run off was contained by continuous channels incorporated in the depth of pavement construction, a combined system of drainage was developed using a single porous concrete pipe with an impermeable invert and gulleys in the marginal strip. Where the design capacity exceeded that of a 12-inch-diameter pipe, separate carrier pipes were provided. Throughout the mining areas gradients of drains were designed to allow for future subsidence and high strength pipes selected to withstand the associated stresses of ground movements due to settlement.

In the past, in the lowlands, east of Ferrybridge, a close network of artificial channels had been constructed in order to drain the land. The slow moving water in these channels was below the level of the water in the canal or the enclosed river flood plain except at low tide and gravity outfall gates, were used, coupled with pumping stations to provide controlled discharge into the river or canal. Additional surface water run-off from the paved motorway was taken into the existing drainage system of the area, which had been provided by the local Internal Drainage Boards with the aid of grants from the Department of Transport.

Side ditches dug along both sides of the motorway and intersected by culverts picked up carriageway and embankment drainage. Fully flexible construction was adopted for the road pavement throughout with an asphalt wearing course. Hard shoulders were generally surface dressed to provide a colour contrast to the traffic lanes.[*]

Bridgeworks were standardised so that the majority of bridges are simply supported, the overbridges being two-spans and the underbridges a single span. The standard overbridge used pre-stressed deck beams of I-section supported on raking abutments. The majority of the beams for the standard motorway bridges were produced under the bulk beam contract.

Subways were carried under the motorway in standard reinforced concrete box section structures. Footbridges and accommodation bridges were designed as special structures of multiple span and provided variety to the standard bridgeworks. At sites with difficult sight lines, bridges were designed to span the motorway in a single span and have both concrete and steel decks.

Between Lofthouse and Whitley Bridge all structures were designed to accommodate the ground movements associated with mining subsidence.

Two Service Areas were provided on the length of the M62, one of which was sited at Hartshead Moor Top midway between the Clifton and

---

[*] Hard shoulders were originally conceived simply as a place for vehicles to pull onto should they break down. For this purpose, a contrasting coloured surface was advantageous. Latterly, the hard shoulder has become increasingly important as a running lane during lane closures, and the surface characteristics must therefore match those of the normal motorway lanes. The current practice is therefore to construct and surface hard shoulders as if they were carriageway.

Chain Bar Interchanges. The other is located at the Ferrybridge interchange with the Trunk Road A1.

The Pennine Contract, Lancashire County Boundary to Pole Moor Incorporating Scammonden Dam

In both its design and construction this contract from the Lancashire County boundary to Pole Moor was unique. It presented the West Riding Engineers and the contractors with the greatest of challenges in working under extreme climatic conditions and of overcoming unparalleled physical problems. In motorway history it must rank as one of the great feats of engineering and worthy of a more detailed record than can be given here.

Sir Alfred McAlpine & Son Ltd were awarded the £10.5 million, three-year, contract in November 1966. Tony Gray[126] in his account of the company from 1935 to 1985 *Road to Success* records:

> Stewart McVey and Maurice Sutherland elected to tender for Scammonden as Alfred McAlpine, rather than in consortium with Fairclough, a practice they tended to follow on future Yorkshire motorways and commonly but not invariably in Cheshire and North Wales.

The advantages and disadvantages continue to be debated but the decision to build their own bridges had at least one major merit – it enabled them to bring into the road building team their skilled tradesmen. There was also the advantage that, because McAlpines were in control of the bridge building, they could dictate its pace according to what was required in the best interests of the progress of the motorway as a whole.

This was the first motorway contract in this country to involve large-scale rock shifting and, at that time, probably entailed the most impressive concentration of large excavators assembled on one project in the UK.

By the late '60s, three different road-building teams operated in the company, two from the Northern Company, and one from the Southern Company. Considerable rivalry existed between the teams, though, as the necessity to provide the right personnel was paramount, exchanges between the three teams were frequent.

The following account has been taken from various documents[127] including the brochure prepared for the inaugural visit by Her Majesty the Queen in 1971 entitled *Motorway across the Pennines*:[128]

Where the M62 passes from Lancashire into Yorkshire the County boundary is marked by the Pennine Way footpath. The westernmost structure in the West Riding contract is the slender concrete arch that carries the ancient path over the six-lane motorway at a height of 65 feet. At this point the M62 is at its highest elevation and deep in the Pennine hills. The next seven miles, across the moors to the edge of Huddersfield,

Rockingstone Moss Interchange

presented the motorway builders with their greatest challenges – five major rock cuttings, the removal of impassable peat bogs, a major dam, as well as some of the worst weather in the country.

Just east of the Windy Hill Cutting the M62 crosses the Halifax–Oldham Road A672 at the Rockingstone Moss Interchange – the first on the Yorkshire side and the only one on the actual Pennine section.

This interchange is also used for access to the maintenance depot, which was sited nearby. Because the existing road is unfenced across the moors it was necessary to provide 'cattle' grids to prevent the sheep, which freely graze on the moor, from wandering onto the motorway which is bounded by the specially designed stock fences already referred to.

From Rockingstone the motorway strikes out across the high open peat-covered hills of Moss Moor, over 1,000 feet above sea-level. The motorway consists of a series of embankments and cuttings levelling out the very irregular landscape it has to cross, and the embankments are built of the material excavated from the cuttings.

Some 12 million cubic yards of material, eight million cubic yards of it solid rock – had to be handled over nearly seven miles of very inhospitable terrain to prepare the way for the carriageways which, when built, could be traversed in just under six minutes.

Because of the scarcity of solid stable features such as buildings to act as reference points for the original survey, a comprehensive system of monuments had been positioned over the whole site by three-dimensional co-ordinates to an accuracy of less than one inch. These monuments were located in places unlikely to be disturbed by the construction and were used as bases from which to set out accurately the construction of the motorway.

In October 1966 the contractors started in the usual way by erecting huts for site offices, stores, messing, workshops and other facilities, but nature was quick to impart her first lesson. There was a high wind one night and when the men arrived in the morning they found the crumpled wreckage of some of the huts in the valley bottom. The cables placed over the roofs and anchored to the ground had cut through the huts as a knife through butter! Next time the cables were made to bear against substantial timber packings.

Access to the parts of the site where the contractor wanted to start working was the major headache. On Moss Moor the first job was the removal of some 650,000 cubic yards of peat on the line of the motorway. The average depth of peat was five feet but pockets of up to 20 feet depth were met and this sort of terrain presented a major obstacle to the job of simply getting about the site. Once the vegetation was stripped from the surface of the moor the peat had virtually no bearing weight capacity and could hardly support the weight of a man. Conventional vehicles, even tracklayers, simply could not negotiate it.

In these early stages access for setting out and control purposes was by the special Muskeg tracked vehicle which was sufficiently light and mobile to negotiate the rough, waterlogged ground and the deep gullies which criss-cross the moor.

Because of the remoteness, the site complex carried emergency rations and maintained fuel storage for generators. Emergency measures were activated three times during the contract.

After coming close to losing a couple of excavators to the bog, the contractor eventually evolved a satisfactory method for digging out the peat. This involved cutting straight through it and running the plant and equipment on the underlying, more solid strata, then excavating the peat from the exposed vertical face.

The peat itself had no agricultural, horticultural or other commercial value and was stacked in specially selected disposal areas on the hillsides adjacent to the motorway and later landscaped to blend in with the surrounding countryside. It was so glutinous that dump-trucks with heated bodies had to be used to ensure a clean discharge and thus a full payload each trip. After lime fertilising and seeding, the only way the disposal

Massive earthworks required to construct the dam

sites can now be identified is from an aircraft.

The motorway dam was the biggest single job and its rate of progress determined the time of completion for the whole scheme; therefore, access to the dam area was a first priority. To operate vehicles and heavy plant into and out of the steep-sided valley, over 400 feet deep, haul roads were built, which zig-zagged down the hillside with a maximum 1 in 5 gradient.

The main cuttings and the quantities yielded were Windy Hill 120 feet deep, 2,500 feet long, 1.2 million cubic yards, Deanhead 150 feet deep, 2,600 feet long, 4.65 million cubic yards, Croft House 90 feet deep, 1,700 feet long, 1.3 million cubic yards and Wholestone 50 feet deep, 5,000 feet long, 1.2 million cubic yards.

The material from Windy Hill formed the embankment over Moss Moor. Most of the material from Deanhead went eastwards to form Scammonden embankment/dam, as did Low Platt, Croft House and Wholestone cuttings.

Scammonden embankment/dam is 240 feet high, 2,100 feet long, 1,220 feet wide between toes, and consists of some 4.5 million cubic yards of rockfill, in addition to the filter material and clay core.

During the winter of 1968/69 some 52,000 tons of clay from Dowsett's Gildersome to Lofthouse Contract was transported to Scammonden and used in the construction of the Dam.

Mention has already been made of the rock excavation and specification trials, which established the most suitable method of producing the rockfill of the required grading for construction of the high embankments. The micro delay blasting techniques and borehole patterns established in these trials, which produced the maximum fragmentation with little need for secondary treatment, proved to be very successful on the actual contract.

The optimum quantity of rock to be blasted out in any single operation was up to 40,000 tons. Rockfill was compacted by large vibrating rollers, the largest of which weighed 11½ tons dead weight. They were developed on site especially for the contract.

The following is based on a paper on Scammonden Dam by Mitchell and Maguire[129] of Herbert Lapworth Partners.

One of the first tasks in connection with the dam was to prepare the foundations for the grouting sub-contractors, Foundation Engineering Ltd, and to drive the tunnels in order to divert the stream in readiness for placing fill as soon as the grouting was completed.

The reservoir overflow was designed with a six feet internal diameter concrete lined shaft leading to a lined tunnel which discharges downstream of the dam. A 'diversion' tunnel runs from upstream of the dam to join the overflow tunnel. Its purpose was to serve as a means of diverting the stream during construction and of drawing down the reservoir later. Two draw-off pipes run beneath the invert of the tunnel to take the raw water from the reservoir to the pumping station. The contractor commenced tunnelling operations in January 1967 and the stream was diverted through the tunnel in July.

When the dam foundations were being excavated it was found that the depth of weathered shale was more extensive than expected and a decision was made to remove it. This material was of no value as a construction material and it was decided to place it on the lower part of the upstream slope. This not only disposed of the material, but increased the stability of the upstream slope under drawdown conditions. As a result of this decision, the diversion tunnel had to be extended further upstream.

Before construction of the dam itself could commence, it was necessary to waterproof and seal off the reservoir area using 'grouting' – the injection of a fluidised (usually cement rich) material into the soil or rock to strengthen it, or reduce its permeability. The grouting at Scammonden dam was probably the most extensive operation of this type ever carried out in the British Isles.

It was intended originally to have a single line grout curtain, extending in the centre of the valley to the shale below the Upper Kinderscout Grit. However, as the test holes had shown that the Lower Kinderscout Grit was badly fissured, it was decided to have a three-line curtain down through the Lower Grit to the shale beneath at depths of up to 220 feet.

Grout holes in the central and upstream lines were at five feet centres, the downstream line being at 10-feet centres. Blanket grouting was carried out under the whole of the dam's core area to strengthen the foundations. The grouting sub-contractor commenced work in April 1967, and this involved drilling over 25 miles of holes and injecting about 3,350 tons of cement.

In July 1967, nine months after commencing work on the site, McAlpine's placed the first layer of rockfill in the dam. Before commencing the construction of the dam's clay core, compaction trials were carried out by the contractor in order to find the best method and equipment to use to achieve the density required. The trials showed that the normal plant used by the contractor for placing clay gave adequate compaction when the moisture content of the clay was high.

When the contractor started to excavate the foundations, clay of very variable thickness and quality was found, so that not only was the quantity eventually much less than the total required, but some of it did not satisfy the specification. However, further quantities were obtained from local borrow areas and from the Gildersome to Lofthouse section of the M62, which was under construction at the time.

Scammonden dam is unique in Britain in height, top width, cubic content, in the crest forming vertical curve and in having a motorway crossing the top. It was thus important that a constant check should be kept on settlement, horizontal movement and pore pressures, both during and following construction. A detailed scheme for the instrumentation of the dam was drawn up which would ensure that these measurements could be taken accurately and as early as possible during the course of construction. The instruments installed include 89 piezometers, four electrical settlement gauges, 11 water overflow settlement gauges, 18 total pressure cells, four horizontal movement gauges, six vibrating wire strain gauges, three water overflow steam gauges, three inverted pendulums and one mekometer (a kind of range finder). These instruments for earth dams were developed by the Geotechnical Division of the Building Research Station in association with the Soil Mechanics Section of Imperial College.

The upstream slope of the dam is protected by rip-rap consisting of uniformly graded rock. None of the indigenous sandstone satisfied the specification and it was found necessary to import it from Lancashire where a very hard sandstone from a quarry in the Upper Haslingden Flags was available. The contractor developed the quarry himself and the stone was used for the filter material as well as the rip-rap.[130]

The opening brochure[131] records: 'Construction of the dam embankment took just over three years. It was a massive task. Material excavated for the foundations totalled some 4,700,000 cubic yards – an average of over 38,000 cubic yards a day, with the record at over 113,000 cubic yards. The 420,000 cubic yards clay core was completed in about 18 months ... The reservoir has a catchment area of 1,291 acres, with additional indirect catchment areas in the neighbouring Colne Valley totalling 3,997 acres, together with 373 acres downstream of the dam.'

The holding capacity of the reservoir increased the storage within the undertaking to 4,100 million gallons and contributed almost six million gallons towards the area's daily demand, which was at the time about 13 million gallons.

In dealing with the engineering problems the contractor also had to contend with the weather. Hunter,[132] the Resident Engineer, recalls:

> ... the appalling physical conditions that men and machines had to overcome in bringing the plans to reality. At one time 650 men worked on site. It was so remote that many were recruited from Ireland and lived on the job.

144 / *Building the Network: The North East of England*

Construction of the dam, bridge and embankment

    The exposed conditions cause materials to deteriorate rapidly and the contractor developed techniques of working in conjunction with the weather rather than in spite of it. Embankments were built on a stop-go basis: work ceasing during wet weather and afterwards the graders flicking off the top half inch and construction continued.
    The whole of this area, not only the peat bogs, is amongst the wettest in the country. Snow has been recorded on seven months of the year.
    For two of the three summers worked on this contract the Pennines were lashed by some of the heaviest rains on record, with 66 inches falling during the first year, twice the national average – and as much as four inches in two days on at least one occasion. Moreover, the cloud here is often down to around 1,000 feet and much of the site was frequently lost in cloud which at times reduced visibility almost to nil.[133]
    A continuous safety guide line with red and white 'bunting' was erected throughout the job on the downhill side, with instructions issued to all site personnel to head for this if the weather closed in to get back to the rescue points – a site hut with a telephone.

This amount of rainfall, over the large areas of the motorway site, amounts to a huge volume of water. Really effective drainage was one of the main priorities of the contract, not only for the carriageways themselves but also for all the surrounding hillsides. Carriageway drainage is by continuous channels built into the marginal haunch and covered with pre-cast slotted concrete slabs. At intervals the channels are intercepted by catchpits from which water is piped into adjacent streams and ditches. Where the motorway embankments have to be protected from heavy run-off from the hillsides paved cut-off ditches have been built, which channel the water under the carriageways via culverts.

These moors are a major water catchment area for the Wakefield and District Water Board and it was necessary to ensure minimal interference with the existing catchwater system during construction of the motorway. Running the full length of Moss Moor and Moselden Pasture is an open catchwater, which is crossed by the M62 in two places, once on embankment and once in cutting. In the cutting, at Deanhead, the catchment water is taken under the motorway through an inverted syphon consisting of twin concrete pipes, three feet in diameter, tested to a head of 200 feet.

On the embankment, in the middle of the Moss Moor stretch, the building of the motorway caused a constriction in the catchwater. This made necessary the construction of a further outflow weir and spillway just upstream of the crossing. At times of heavy rain the weirs discharge water from the catchwater into the adjacent valley, which already contains a reservoir, so that it is retained in the Wakefield collecting system.

The extrusion machines used to lay the marginal haunch and the drainage channel were improved by the manufacturer in the course of this contract. The carriageway sub-base was spread and laid to a fine tolerance by a Rahco finishing machine handling 2,000 tons of material a day. Levels and tolerances were automatically set by the

Open Catchwater in spate

machine using information fed back through a feeler in contact with a preset wire.[134]

Because of the low pH value of the moorland water, special protective treatments were given to steel corrugated culverts and steel mesh boundary fencing. High strength dense concrete and air entrainment were used in drainage works and structural concrete in contact with the ground protected by a bitumen treatment.

Hunter[135] clarifies why the carriageways were separated:

> The moorland stretch of the M62 was built on geologically creeping side long ground and each embankment had to be anchored and benched into the underlying sandstone base. This called for the separation of the carriageways over three-quarters of a mile which fortuitously enabled Wildes' Farm, and buildings, to be retained together with several acres of rough grazing. Access tunnels were provided under each carriageway for maintenance of the water authority catchwater which provides access to the farm.

Life can be difficult when four lanes of motorway separate your 1,400 sheep and 2,000 acres of land from you, and Ken admitted he did the best he could with the two tunnels. A champion sheepdog trainer, he sadly lost one of his team when it forgot to use the underpass and in answering his whistle ran across the motorway. The farm at the time belonged to the Wakefield and District Water Board.

In this area, a tensioned wire barrier was used the first time in the central reserve, to avoid snow build up. The embankments which were aerodynamically designed to minimise snow deposits have ensured that the motorway has never closed due to driven snow in the years it has been in operation. It was closed once through industrial action when salting and gritting was not carried out.

There are 11 structures on the contract. The **Pennine Way Footbridge,** which carries the 250-mile Pennine Way footpath across the motorway, consists of a reinforced concrete arch of 220-feet span. Each cantilever supports concrete approach spans each 85 feet long.

Rockingstone Interchange Underbridge, a two-span concrete bridge which carries the motorway over the Halifax–Oldham Road A672. **Scammonden Bridge**, which spans the Deadhead Cutting, carries the A6025 Elland to Buckstones County Road over the motorway. Although originally designed as a flat arch spanning the cutting, further consideration of the

Wilde's Farm between separate carriageways

The Pennine Way Footbridge

aerodynamic and vibration characteristics of the bridge led to a redesign, an important consideration being to minimise disturbances in the air flow through the cutting which would cause snow drifting. The redesign was undertaken during the early part of the contract and it did require a Variation Order! There was a saving on the original price.

Because the site afforded excellent foundation material, it was decided to build an open spandrel fixed-arch bridge. The final design of the arch was arrived at as the result of analysis by a series of computer programs and proved to be both aesthetically pleasing and economic. It has a span of 410 feet supporting eight spandrel walls, which, with four further walls on the cutting sides under the approach spans, carry a deck 660 feet long, 120 feet above the motorway. The arch, which is of twin box section, is the largest of its type in the country.

Hey Lane Underbridge carries the motorway over a district road. Redlane Dyke Bridge is a four-span steel box girder bridge over the motorway and required additional stiffening under the Merrison rules. There are also seven reinforced concrete underpasses for agricultural and Water Board use.

It was during the building of Scammonden Bridge that the effects of an exceptionally severe Pennine winter were experienced. The centring of the arch was a conventional scaffolding structure of gigantic proportions. It contained no less than 70 miles of scaffolding tube and it had to be designed for wind speeds of up to 110 miles an hour. In the sub-zero conditions that prevailed during much of the construction period the worst hazard of all was freezing fog. This left a build-up of ice on everything in its path and created unprecedented structural problems as well as almost impossible working conditions. During the first winter the ice build-up was so heavy that the scaffolding framework had an additional load on it estimated at over 1,100 tons.

This type of ice build-up, in March 1969, also brought down the nearby 1,265-feet Emley Moor television mast, as well as telephone and

148 / Building the Network: The North East of England

Scammonden Bridge

The scaffold centring

power cables, and cut off the construction site from the outside world. The site offices were left without heat or light; emergency generators were not powerful enough to combat the intense cold and the offices had to be abandoned. Construction plant and equipment, too, was brought to a standstill.[136]

The writer records:[137] 'The building of this bridge gave rise to special problems because rock had to be blasted from the cutting whilst concreting of the arch was continuing. We cast samples of concrete on a trial scaffolding and monitored the effects of vibration from blast effects. The results confirmed our specification to be a practical one showing that blasting could be carried out close to the structure without impairing its integrity.'

In addition to the suite of computer programs used to aid the engineers designing the arch, another was written to analyse the effects of various construction sequences for the spandrel walls and deck so that the Contractor's proposals could be quickly checked to guard against overstressing the structure during construction.

As the M62 passes under Scammonden Bridge and out of the eastern end of the Deanhead cutting, it starts out across the 2,000-feet rim of Scammonden Dam.

To prevent high-sided vehicles from being blown over as they emerged from the shelter of the cutting onto this exposed embankment, the ends of the cutting slopes had to be very carefully arranged. The profile of the motorway on the dam itself was also subjected to rigorous design studies and these led to the provision of simple but effective windbreaks in the form of slatted fencing on either side, below the level of the carriageways.

From Scammonden the road continues its descent towards the next interchange at Outlane, the last structure on this Pennine section of the M62, built under the adjacent contract.

Grey[138] refers to social aspects of the contract: 'The public have always taken a keen interest in works of this kind and it was likened to the Victorian feats of engineering during the railway-building age. It achieved some notoriety when featured in a television programme not only showing the men at work but also at play in the strip joints in the nearest Yorkshire flesh-pots.'

Hunter[139] says: 'Home comforts were provided for with an on site brothel. This was started by two of the hundreds of lorry drivers delivering large rip-rap rocks for use on the dam water face. Contract management, locals and the police turned a blind eye. It was closed after 2½ years' operation after a police raid because alcohol was being served. The premises became utilised by business people from Huddersfield, Rochdale, Oldham, Manchester and elsewhere. The police considered matters had got out of hand!'

A major project like the Scammonden Dam changes the whole face of the valley. Huddersfield Corporation were conscious of this and were

The completed motorway dam
Stewart Bale Ltd.

anxious not only that the engineering works should fit well into their background but also that the completed reservoir area should be a source of pleasure and recreation to the whole district. Trees were planted and picnic areas laid out, with parking and other facilities, a sailing club formed and the land immediately around the reservoir used for stock farming.

Through extreme weather it became necessary to grant an extension of the contract period of some 12 months. The motorway from Outlane was opened to traffic quite informally in the middle of December 1970. On Thursday 14 October 1971 Her Majesty the Queen[140] inaugurated the Lancashire–Yorkshire Motorway, an historic day for all those involved and said:

> I am very glad to be here this afternoon to commemorate the completion of the Scammonden Dam and Reservoir. To construct a dam on this scale is a fine achievement; to build a motorway across it at the same time is remarkable.
>
> It is and outstanding feat of engineering and also an excellent example of effective partnership between central and local government.
>
> I congratulate all those who have worked so hard to bring this outstanding project to a successful conclusion.

The Queen unveiled a plaque commemorating the inauguration of the dam. Another plaque was erected on the County boundary. Lovell and Drake had wanted their County boundary signs to be erected but this was not permitted. The writer came up with the idea of a concrete plinth made with Pennine aggregates embossed with the Lancashire and Yorkshire red and white rosettes; this was accepted and stands to this day.

The final cost of the entire scheme, which included additional contracts awarded to McAlpine, was £13.98 million – the most costly rural stretch of motorway in the United Kingdom at that time.

The Contracts Manager was McVey, the Agent Sutherland, Sub-Agent Ivan Abbott, succeeded later by Dave Garner and Works Manager Mick Creaby. The Engineer for the Dam was Peter Hirst. The Resident Engineer was Hunter, the Deputy Resident Engineer Bradley then Don Hunt. Hunt was the lead designer of the Scammonden Arch. The Resident Engineer for the Dam was John Winder and Assistant Resident Engineer Dick Evans.

The Huddersfield Corporation Waterworks Engineer and Manager was Bill Jollans, the Senior Partner of Herbert Lapworth and Partners was John Mitchell. Professors Nash and Gibson of King's College, London acted as advisors for the dam. J B Blavney was the Landscape Architect.

Pole Moor to Outlane

The 30-month contract for this 1.2-mile section of the motorway was awarded to W. & C. French in the sum of £1.375 million and commenced in June 1969.

The Outlane Interchange

It enabled the Pennine section of the motorway to be completed up to Outlane at Huddersfield and provided an interchange with the A640 Huddersfield–Rochdale Road and the A643 Brighouse–Outlane Road, giving access to Huddersfield from Manchester and the M6 motorway in the west.

By now responsibility for the design and supervision of the M62 had transferred to the West Riding Sub-Unit of the North Eastern Road Construction Unit. Tony Gaffney had succeeded Lovell and was the Sub-Unit Chief Engineer, with Hutchinson and the writer as Superintending Engineers heading the respective roads and bridges offices. Denis Hall, then the Director, was the Engineer under the Contract.

The hottest Huddersfield summer for forty years allowed an exceptionally good start on this section of the M62. After excavating unsuitable material below the proposed embankment, it was used to fill surrounding fields to replace the first and eighteenth holes of the local golf course. The pipelayers moved in to speed their way through a mile of pre-earthworks drainage and outfalls ready for the main onslaught on the earthworks.

The mile-and-a-quarter stretch of motorway consisted of one big cut to fill operation involving a million cubic yards of muck and rock and an interchange and roundabout carrying the main Huddersfield to Rochdale road over the motorway on the larger of the two structures. A 400-feet-long Armco culvert was completed early in the contract. A group of local archaeologists raced against time to uncover the remains of a Roman road and camp before they were buried forever beneath 40 feet of fill.

The Contracts Manager was Peter Stephens and the agent Jack Hollis. The Resident Engineer was Moglia and Roy Jones, Assistant Resident Engineer (Bridges). The contract was completed in November 1970.

Outlane to Hartshead

The contract for this seven mile section of the motorway was also awarded to W. & C. French in the sum of £10.125 million (the largest ever undertaken by the company) and commenced in June 1970.

The Outlane to Hartshead section soon traverses the Elland escarpment along which, because of its numerous steep cloughs, the motorway passes alternately from short deep cuts onto short high embankments, and extensive benching of the embankments into the steep hillside was required. Along this length is situated the Ainley interchange which, because of the difficult terrain, has had to be situated away from the existing roads which serve it. For this reason a dual carriageway link road was built to a new roundabout constructed on the A629 Huddersfield–Elland road.

Leaving Ainley Top, the motorway passes through a large cutting at Fixby and then drops 480 feet in elevation over the next 2½ miles before it crosses the River Calder, a canal and a railway by means of the Kirklees Viaduct. Because of the sharp drop in altitude, the carriageways are at the maximum allowable gradient and the alignment has been chosen to keep cut and fill areas to a minimum as far as possible; but even so, one of the embankments rises to a height of over 50 feet.

From the viaduct the motorway crosses an area where sand and gravel had been extensively worked and the remaining silt-filled lagoons had to be filled with rock before embankments were built over them. At this point the Clifton Interchange connects with the diverted A644 Brighouse–Dewsbury road. Immediately following the interchange, the motorway passes from high embankment to the 55-feet-deep Clifton cut. Because of its complex geological formation, which includes many old slip planes, special earth and drainage works were included in the contract.

After Clifton the motorway crosses Hartshead Moor, where 32 acres of land were acquired for the construction of a Service Area. Because this was the only suitable site between Lancashire and the M1, two high-pressure gas mains, which crossed the site, were diverted around the perimeter to allow its full utilisation. The contract for the Service Area was let to Clugston Construction Ltd in the sum of £0.49 million but not until 1971.

Kirklees Viaduct and Clifton

The 19 structures constructed on this contract included Kirklees Viaduct and Whitehaughs Arch.

Kirklees Viaduct carries the motorway over the Mirfield to Brighouse railway, the Calder and Hebble Navigation Canal, and the River Calder. The bridge has six spans and varies in width from 136 to 212 feet to accommodate the slip roads.

Whitehaughs Arch supports the motorway over the realigned Huddersfield–Elland Road A629 at a skew angle of approximately 10°. The bridge is an *in situ* reinforced concrete fixed arch with a clear span between abutment faces of approximately 88 feet at springing level and a rise from road level to the crown of approximately 37 feet. The arch is approximately 443 feet long and is constructed to a horizontal curve of 716-feet radius and carries a 20-feet embankment above the crown. The arch was designed using the West Riding Arch Design Suite of computer programs. The main problem of construction was to maintain traffic flow on the A629 which it spanned.

Blakelaw Lane Bridge is similar to Hunsworth Lane Bridge on the next contract and has three continuous spans and crosses the motorway at a skew of 30°. The Kirklees Viaduct and Blakelaw Bridge were both steel box girder structures, and their construction coincided with a problem which had been encountered with this particular type of bridge. The background was that, following the collapse during erection of two large bridges designed on these principles, one in Melbourne over the Yarra River and the other the Cleddau Bridge at Milford Haven in Wales, the Secretary of State for the Environment, in December 1970, appointed a technical committee to look into the basis of design and method of construction of such bridges. The committee, which was under the chairmanship of

Whitehaughs Arch

Dr (later Sir Alec) Merrison, found that there was no reason to doubt the soundness of the design provided it conformed to stricter rules which they recommended. The Department of Environment made these rules available to all engineers engaged in the design of this type of bridge.

Varley,[141] from his position as Superintending Engineer (Bridges) at the RCU Headquarters at the time, gives a graphic account of the steel box girder travails. His letter to the writer together with his account is an archive paper of some moment written as it were from 'within the Ministry'. Extracts, only as they relate to the bridges in question, are recorded here which give an insight into how matters were dealt with by the Department in London. A full copy of the letter has been deposited in the Archive.

> ... I recall Leslie Greenaway phoning me one morning in February 1971, calling me down to St Christopher House. The Merrison Committee Secretary had given him an outline of the recommendations contained in its first, and interim, report* which he would have that afternoon. It was likely that NERCU would be immediately and seriously affected because of the stage of construction of Hylton Bridge to carry the A19 Trunk Road [the bridge is not covered in this historical account] ... When I met Leslie the following morning (and I seem to recollect Jim Ford, Phil Lee, Sriskandan, with him, all bearing expressions which conveyed that this was pretty serious matter) BE [Bridges Engineering Division] had made its first reading of the Report. The Merrison Committee considered that design of their steel box girders, as currently practised, was not sound, and that the design of all steel box girders built, or in course of building, must be re-appraised and proved in accordance with new criteria which it was preparing ... I asked for a copy of the Report to take back with me; although the M62 Kirklees Viaduct with its integral concrete top flange was not a complete steel box girder except over the piers it appeared to fall within the class of box girder as defined by the Committee. The Kirklees steel was under fabrication in the yards ... and so there may be time to apply the new design criteria and add any necessary strengthening without significant delay to the M62 opening. Leslie refused. BE had not yet had time to assess the full implications of the Report, and until the CHE had advised the Minister of its contents and what they meant, which would have to be done pretty quickly, he could not release it ...

The effect of the new design rules meant that the steel beams being manufactured for the Kirklees Viaduct and Blakelaw Bridge by Cleveland Bridge & Engineering had to be delayed whilst they were checked for conformity with the new rules and strengthened if necessary. In the meantime, the support columns had been constructed, and it was hoped that erection could still commence early in November, which would allow the bridges to be completed within the contract period.

---

* The Merrison Committee issued Interim Rules in May 1971.

It was with great credit to both designer and constructor that the strengthening requirements were completed well ahead of the many bridges involved at the time, without a suspension of the works. There were, of course, additional costs to pay amounting to some £700,000 and involving an additional 175 tons of steel. Although an extension of 40 weeks was granted, this section of motorway was opened, in part, in December 1972 on time and completed in July 1973 – an overall delay of some 28 weeks.

The Contract Manager was Stephens and the Agent John Young. The Resident Engineer (Roads) for this contract was Andrews with Brian Gillard the Resident Engineer (Bridges).

Hartshead to Gildersome

The contract for this 5¼-mile section was awarded to Dowsett Engineering Construction Ltd and cost £7.6 million of which £1.2 million was for structures. The contract, which included the construction of ¾ mile of the M606 motorway and a similar length of the M621, was started in June 1970, opened in part in October 1972 and completed in July 1973.

Leaving Hartshead, the motorway passes through the 60-feet-deep Cleckheaton cut to the three-level Chain Bar Interchange. This connects with the A58 Halifax–Leeds road, the A638 Bradford–Dewsbury road, as well as having south-facing slip roads connecting the M62 with the M606 Bradford South Radial motorway.

On the latter 1¼ miles of motorway between the Chain Bar and Gildersome interchanges the motorway crosses two class A and three unclassified side roads and this length includes some of the largest cuttings and fill areas on the scheme. The total amount of excavation was approximately five million cubic yards of which about three million cubic yards was rock.

This length of motorway runs through the Yorkshire coalfields and special precautions had to be taken to minimise the effect of old workings on the motorway. Eleven abandoned mine shafts were located on the line of the works all of which had to be specially backfilled and capped.

There are 17 bridges and a major retaining wall. Six of the bridges which carry the motorway are of standard construction, having pre-cast pre-stressed I-beams, from the Fairclough Factory.

Four of the three- or four-span bridges over the motorway are of cantilever and suspended span construction. The decks consisting of pre-cast reinforced concrete beams with an *in situ* concrete deck slab. The decks are supported on reinforced concrete piers and bankseats.

The Chain Bar interchange comprises five bridges, four of which are of standard construction. The bridge carrying the M606 over the interchange was built to a plan radius of 749 feet and consists of four simply supported spans of 40, 86, 105 and 43 feet.

Agreement had been reached between the Ministry of Transport, British Rail and the writer for certain of the railway underline bridges to be designed by the West Riding Engineers – another 'feather in their cap'.

Chain Bar Rail Viaduct carries the Bradford to Cleckheaton single track railway over the motorway, having five simply supported skew (23º) spans. **Whitehall Road Rail Bridge** carries the same line over the diverted line of the A58 Trunk Road. Unfortunately, soon after the opening of the motorway, this line was closed. However, both of these bridges now serve as part of the Spen Valley Greenway cycle route.

Hunsworth Lane Bridge has three continuous spans, two side spans of 62 feet 6 inches and a centre span over the motorway of 159 feet. The construction is of twin steel box girders with a pre-cast composite reinforced concrete deck slab, the slabs making up the deck having a full highway width of 43 feet. The deck construction was something of a first. The girders were jacked up before laying and jointing the pre-cast deck sections, and after obtaining the required strength in the concrete jointing, the deck was lowered onto its bearings at the piers providing a pre-stress in the deck slab. Although falling under the new Merrison rules during construction, additional stiffening was carried out without delay to the main contract.

It was intended that the two retaining walls should be built to support the westbound motorway slip road embankment adjacent to the works of Hunsworth Dyers Ltd. The walls, over 400 feet long, varied in height up to 25 feet and were of reinforced concrete on bored pile foundations.

Dalton and Hoban[142] record: 'Above the wall the embankment was to have a sideslope of 1 in 2. However due to the difficult ground conditions found locally during piling, the retaining wall was omitted and the sideslope increased to 1 in 1.4.

In February-March 1977, some five years after the motorway was opened to traffic, shallow slips occurred. Failure was almost certainly induced by the inflow of water into the embankment through holes excavated as part of a later tree-planting programme. The holes were dug in autumn 1976 and remained open through the winter acting as traps for surface water. With wetting of the embankment fill material, the factor of safety against rotation reduced to 0.97.

Chain Bar Interchange M62/M606

A box-girder bridge with precast slab deck a new innovation

As the progressive nature of the slips would ultimately threaten the motorway, it was considered necessary to obtain a permanent solution. Regrading the side slope to 1 in 2 would ensure the long-term stability of the embankment. However, the proximity of the dyeworks at the base of the embankment prevented the gradient of the sideslope being reduced without the construction of a retaining wall. Because of the difficult ground conditions a gabion wall appeared to be a reasonable solution.'

Tyre Wall

A proposal from West Yorkshire's Engineering Developments Section for a tyre wall was found to be £10,000 less than the gabion solution and was submitted to the Department of Transport and approved. The West Yorkshire engineers with their new responsibilities for waste disposal had found another solution to overcome the difficult problem of disposing of worn tyres!

Returning to the main contract, Dowsetts' Contracts Manager was Simpson, and Project Manager Jeffs. The Resident Engineer was Carruthers, Assistant Resident Engineer (Bridges) Peter Shalcross and Measurement Engineer Graham Dawson, who succeeded Carruthers in March 1972. The Sub-Contract for earthmoving was Budge with Sub-Agent Richard Budge.

The formal opening of the Ainley Top to Chain Bar section of motorway was in July 1972 by Mr Keith Speed, Parliamentary Under-Secretary at the Department of the Environment. The remaining Chain Bar to Gildersome section opened in May 1973.

Thus the last gap in the Leeds–Manchester stretch of the M62 was closed. It was to be a further three years before the sections east of the A1, and between Liverpool and Manchester, provided the country with its first coast-to-coast motorway.

Gildersome to Lofthouse

This 5¾-mile contract, which was awarded to Dowsett Engineering Construction Ltd, started in October 1968 and was completed in February 1971 at a cost of £5.8 million.

It commenced at, and included the construction of, the Gildersome Interchange and terminated at the M62/M1 intersection at Lofthouse. It also included the construction of the Tingley Interchange. The Gildersome

Tingley Interchange M62/M621

Interchange forms a junction between the M62 and the existing Leeds–Huddersfield road A62 and also provides a link for the M621 Gildersome to Leeds Motorway. Tingley Interchange links the motorway to the Leeds–Dewsbury road A653. The section between the Interchange and Leeds City Boundary was reconstructed under a separate contract with the West Riding County Council. Both interchanges provide a connection with the Bradford–Wakefield road A650.

The line of the motorway on this section had been chosen to avoid, as far as possible, good agricultural and building land, and in so doing had incorporated along its length an opencast coal site, a disused stone quarry and a colliery shale tip.

During earthwork operations at Gildersome in the areas of the southern roundabout on the Interchange, domestic refuse which had been deposited since ancient times had to be removed from the old Howden Clough Valley and the adjoining Hell Hole Valley and replaced with suitable material before the construction of the motorway embankments could proceed.

Again, an interesting feature of this contract was the geotechnical work, which required special consideration during the first ten weeks of the Contract to locate faults and old mine workings along the line of the motorway, and over 60,000 feet of drilling was carried out to locate areas that were required to be stabilised before the construction of the embankments or bridges could commence.

During the winter 1968/69, some 52,000 tons of clay, which was unsuitable for embankment construction, was transported to Sir Alfred

McAlpine's contract at Scammonden and used in the construction of the dam.

Another feature of the contract was that a section of the disused Gildersome Railway tunnel, which was 1¾ miles long and 90 feet below the embankment, had to be backfilled with some 30,000 cubic yards of colliery waste.

The material used in the upper layers of the embankments consisted of the harder sandstone excavated from the cuttings or imported blast furnace slag or well burnt colliery shale, depending on availability. A total of 312,000 tons of crushed limestone imported from E. Butler's quarry at Maltby was used as the sub-base.

Fifteen structures were constructed but the Tingley Common Bridge, which carries the A650 Trunk Road over the motorway, was built as advanced works to provide continuity for the large volume of traffic using the trunk road. East Ardsley Railway Bridge was subcontracted to Holst Ltd.

The contracts manager for Dowsetts was Hatter, the Project Manager Jeffs. The Resident Engineer was Clay and Assistant Resident Engineers Dave Foreman (Roads) and John Millband (Bridges).

Lofthouse to Hopetown

This £6.5 million contract, started in March 1972, was also awarded to Dowsett Engineering Construction Ltd, and included the completion of the interchange between the M1 and the M62 at Lofthouse together with the construction of two other interchanges at Newmarket with the junction of the A642 Wakefield–Aberford County Road and at Normanton at the junction A655 Normanton–Castleford Road. This length of 6.1 miles of motorway also traverses the Yorkshire coalfields and special precautions were taken to minimise any effect that shallow workings may have had on the pavement and structures. The operations included the excavation of colliery waste from adjacent shale tips and the selection of suitable material for incorporation in the works. Alternative tenders were invited for this contract on the basis of the contractor:

- finding his own borrow pits for some 1,000,000 cubic yards of common fill and
- removing some 1,000,000 cubic yards of colliery waste from West Riding No 3 tip near Altofts.

The use of colliery waste was specified in the contract and was successfully compacted in the embankments, and contributed to the removal of yet another tip with resultant benefits to the environment when final treatment of the tip area was completed.

Erecting steelwork
Altofts River Bridge

There are 12 structures including a river crossing. **Altofts River Bridge** carries the motorway over the River Calder near to the village of Altofts and also provides access along both flood banks of the river and for floodwater to pass between the two areas of marshy wash land behind the eastern flood bank.

Each carriageway of the motorway is supported on two box girders which are continuous across three spans, the main river span being 183 feet and the approach spans 100 feet.

The bedrock at the site is at a depth of about 30 feet below the river level and very soft alluvial materials overlie it. The foundations are therefore supported on piles and hence the lightweight superstructure resulting from the box girder arrangement gave considerable savings in the cost of the foundation. A further advantage was that, during erection, the minimum falsework was necessary and no special foundations had to be provided other than a hard standing for mobile cranes.

This bridge was one of the first in the country to incorporate the requirements of the Merrison Report at the design stage. Although the design was complete before the Report became available, there was time for the appraisal calculation and the independent check to be carried out before any fabrication was started. Where extra strength was found to be required it was possible to increase the thickness of plates. This avoided the necessity for elaborate and expensive systems of stiffeners, which have bedevilled some structures caught during and after fabrication.

Provision was made in the Contract for payment for the preparation of calculations by the Contractors to demonstrate that the method of erection proposed complied with the *Criteria for the Assessment of Steel*

Box Girder Bridges. Also, an item was included for additional steel, which may have been added to the structure to ensure compliance during erection, but this was not required.

The box girders were detailed to be fabricated in 30-feet-long units and connected on site with friction grip bolted joints. These units were of a size and weight that made transport from the fabricators works to site and the erection very straightforward. The bolted joints were quick and easy to make and eliminated all the problems associated with site welding.

Dowsett Engineering Construction Ltd, as Main Contractors, carried out all the foundation and sub-structure work but the fabrication and erection of the steelwork was sub-contracted to Fairfield-Mabey Ltd of Chepstow.

Fairfields elected to joint the first two pairs of units at the works so that the approach spans consisted of 60-feet-long units, which were erected onto a temporary tower at the joint. The heaviest of these units, which included the section over the pier, was about 33 tons in weight. These were lifted into position by a mobile crane standing on a levelled area between the piers and the bank seat. The remainder of the river span was fabricated in five of the 30 feet units and cantilevered from each side to meet at mid-span. The centre three units were lifted by a 40-ton crawler crane mounted on a 'Uniflote' pontoon floating on the river.

Fairfield-Mabey fabricated all the steelwork at their works in Chepstow. Messrs Solus Schall, acting as Specialist Steelwork Inspectorate for the Engineer, carried out inspection and testing of the steelwork. Each box was assembled from its constituent plates, complete with stiffeners and the corners and diaphragms welded. Adjacent boxes were assembled with joints bolted up to ensure a perfect fit when they were lifted into position on the bridge. After completion each unit was checked for distortion against tolerances calculated as laid down by the Merrison document but no difficulty was experienced in meeting these tolerances. Those panels, which include site joints, were checked after erection and again no serious problems emerged.

The protective paint system was applied in the works as far as possible, that on the inside being complete except for the joint areas and the outside having two complete coats to be applied after erection. The system adopted was expected to need no maintenance for five years and major repainting only after eight years or more. Runway beams for a maintenance gantry were incorporated in the design of the bridge to facilitate re-painting over the river.

An extension of 21 weeks was granted on the contract because of a national steel shortage of pre-stressing strand associated with the construction of some of the other bridges; with completion in August 1974.

The Contract Manager for Dowsetts was Simpson and Agent Jeffs. The Resident Engineer was Clay and Assistant Resident Engineer (Bridges) was David Pontin.

Hopetown to Ferrybridge

This contract, which was awarded to Dowsett Engineering Construction Ltd in the tender sum of £5.211 million, started in March 1972 and was completed in March 1974.

This section took the M62 Motorway to its junction with the London–Edinburgh Trunk Road A1 at Ferrybridge and included the construction of a three-level interchange together with a length of embankment and bridge in the middle of the roundabout to carry the future M62 extension over the A1. This interchange was replaced in early 2006 by a substantial free-flow junction associated with the conversion of the A1 to motorway north of Ferrybridge.

A second interchange was also included in this contract at Pontefract at the junction of the A639 Pontefract–Castleford County Road. There are 17 bridges on this 8.4 km length of motorway. Again special precautions to minimise the effect of old mine workings were taken throughout these works.

The Contracts Manager for Dowsetts was Hatter and Project Manager Jeffs. The Resident Engineer was Carruthers, succeeded by Clay. Roger Pickup was the Assistant Resident Engineer (Bridges).

It should be recorded that the engineers in the West Yorkshire RCU Sub-Unit in charge of road design teams for the M62 Ferrybridge to Rawcliffe sections, the M18 from the A1(M) eastwards and the M180 motorways included Group Engineers Booth, Hawes, Saltmarsh and Walsh, and their Senior Section Engineers were Andrews, Brannan, Clark, Dawson and Brian Smith. Howitz headed the Contract Section assisted by Carlton.

Ferrybridge to Pollington

This contract was for the construction of 14.5 km of motorway from the Ferrybridge Interchange on the A1 through to Pollington, west of Snaith, where traffic was temporarily discharged onto the A645 pending completion of the adjacent Pollington to Rawcliffe contract.

The contract was awarded to Sir Alfred McAlpine & Sons Ltd in the tender sum of £5.708 million and commenced in October 1972 and was completed in October 1974. The Contracts Manager for McAlpine was Abbott, and the Agent Brian Melling. The Resident Engineer was David Saltmarsh, Dave Langley was Assistant Resident Engineer (Bridges).

The route passes through the magnesian limestone escarpment, east of Ferrybridge, in cutting before running out onto the flat agricultural lands to the east. There is one interchange with the A19 Doncaster–Selby Road at Whitley.

Of the 22 structures on the contract the most interesting are the Flyboat Canal Bridge which carries the motorway over the Knottingley and Goole Canal on a cantilever and suspended span 25-degree skew bridge, and a reinforced earth retaining wall adjacent to the south subway of the Whitley Interchange.

The **Flyboat Canal Bridge** has abutments and piers supported on steel bearing piles that in turn support anchor (13m) and cantilever (11m) spans. The suspended span beams, 30m long weighing 75 tonnes were placed over the navigable channel.

The **Whitley Bridge experimental reinforced earth retaining wall** embodied a new concept of lightweight hexagonal glass reinforced cement panels acting as permanent shutters to the retained earth which is stabilised by the inclusion of horizontal strips of galvanised steel or fibreglass tied to the front face and running directly back from it.

Although simply described, the development of this wall became the subject of a major patent dispute between the UK and the French – a historic event, worthy of more detailed examination.

The Reinforced Soil / Vidal Saga

Around 1971 a French Engineer, Henri Vidal, sought to introduce into the United Kingdom an engineering process for stabilising embankments by means of burying reinforcement, which is connected to 'facing panels', within the soil of the earth fill. The process was called 'reinforced earth', an alternative to the conventional retaining wall. Vidal formed a company to exploit the patent and the process.[143]

The Department of Environment was keen to explore the potential of reinforced soil and sought expressions of interest from within its Sub-Units. It was from the West Yorkshire Sub-Unit, known for its innovativeness, that the process aroused an immediate interest. One of its staff, Dr Colin Jones, was asked to examine thoroughly the potential for 'reinforced earth'.

Jones[144] takes up the story: 'The Department had provided no information with regard to the physical characteristics of a reinforced soil, as a result we started the investigation of the concept with a clean sheet of paper.'

Because the technical description and commercial release was deficient in explaining the theoretical principles which governed the workings of the components, Jones and his assistants set to work it out for themselves and developed a design theory from first principles of soil-mechanics. In order

Whitley Bridge experimental reinforced earth retaining wall

to do so it was decided to design and construct a trial structure, as stated by the Department of Environment 'to monitor structural performance and to study the economics compared with conventional methods of construction'. Such an approach required a design, the development of facing elements, a study and selection of possible reinforcing elements and a study of the analysis of the structure.

The analysis, using design methods developed by Bannerjee in the Department of Environment and finite element analysis developed at Cardiff University, became known as the York Method. This alternative analytical approach to the design of reinforced soil was considered very significant by the patent agents (and Patent Office) in establishing the independent 'York' patent referred to later.

The Sub-Unit evolved a practicable method of designing a reinforced soil retaining wall which eschewed the conventional forms and relied upon 'dry' wall facing units, not bonded to each other but reliant for their collective efficiency upon being linked loosely to tensors buried within the compacted fill of the embankment.[145]

An initial decision was to make all facing elements of the structure small enough so as to be portable (i.e. maximum weight approximately 20 kg). Sixteen different facing elements were eventually used in the trial structure, some proving unacceptable, others being completely satisfactory.

The field trial chosen was at the Whitley Bridge Site on the M62. The work was innovative and experimental, so it necessarily involved participation by the Ministry Bridges Engineering Standards Division and the Transport & Road Research Laboratory. The project was approved and the Contractor commenced work, materials brought in, the Sub-Unit and TRRL engineers agreeing the principles of design and the number, positions and functions of the buried instrumentation that would measure the soil-structure reactions.

The cost of the facing elements used at Whitley Bridge, which measured 600 mm across the flats, was £2.73 (1973 prices). In the next two years the cost of these units was escalated approximately 10 times and the use of small facing units was abandoned in favour of full height units. These were first used on the A1 at Darrington in 1978 already referred to, and in 1979 featured in the BBC programme *Tomorrow's World*.

The involvement of Pilkington in the manufacture of the facing units introduced the use of fibre glass reinforcement (FRP) based upon conventional 'E' glass embedded in polymeric resin and manufactured using the 'pull trussion' technique. This reinforcement proved to be completely satisfactory and arguably the most durable material so far used in a number of structures. However, the lack of a proper marketing system eventually resulted in the material not being recognised by the potential users.

Following their initial involvement with the Whitley Bridge project, Pilkington conducted a patent search and came to the conclusion that the concept being developed by the County Engineers was innovative.

Initially, both the DOE, through the RCU and the West Riding County Council, displayed no interest in the potential intellectual property and refused to consider a patent application. The onus then fell on Jones to act alone and the initial patent application for the York method was funded by Dr Jones and dealt with by Patent Agents in Leeds.[146]

The publicity of the Whitley Trial Wall alerted Vidal to the activities that were going on and the patent application also came to his notice. Vidal began action against the DOE for infringement of his reinforced soil patent. 'The commercial attaché at the French Embassy complained to the Minister of Transport, and the spaghetti hit the fan.'[147]

At this stage the presence of the York patent application became important to the DOE who requested the transfer of the benefits of the patent to them. Dr Jones agreed to assign the rights of the patent to the Crown in exchange for repayment of his costs.

Consolidation of the patent application, now that it had been assigned to the Crown, was a function of the Ministry of Defence which processed all Crown technical patents. The experienced staff, veterans of many patents infringement actions, who now dealt with the patent, soon reached an opinion that Jones had provided, by assignment, a sound patentable process to the Department of Environment. The approach from first principles had led the Sub-Unit engineers to a solution that incorporated allowance for movement, which was not present in the Vidal application.

In the circumstances, a worldwide patent was not possible, but protection in the UK was. In due course engineers, lawyers, patent advisers, and counsel all assembled at Whitley Bridge to conduct a thorough detailed, extensive photographic and agreed written description of the wall that was being built on that site in accordance with the 'York' method.

A few weeks after this formal inspection there was pressure from 'on high' that it would be expedient to settle matters quickly. Sure enough, it was not long before staff at TRRL dealing with the West Yorkshire application were told to stick closely to the soil mechanics aspects and not to discuss with us anything appertaining to the patents position. Soon it was being put about that 'the West Yorkshire patent was really not all that good!'…'The Crown would not have a leg to stand on if it contested Vidal's claim' and even if the patent originators insisted 'the Department had really no moral ground for giving support', 'it would be in the Department's best interests to make an amicable arrangement!'[148]

Very soon Bridle, the Chief Highways Engineer, issued a press release saying that he had reached a favourable settlement. The designers working for the Department on the central government projects would be able to use reinforced earth without restriction, but otherwise the field was left clear for the existing licensee, Vidal.[149]

The validity of the 'York' patent, which covered a construction process, notably the use of a sliding connection with any form of facing and reinforcement, remains and this technique is acknowledged as one of the three established construction methods for Reinforced Soil in modern textbooks and education media.

A full account of the design, construction and monitoring of this experimental wall is given in a paper by Barton, Dalton, Jones and Mumujee[150] entitled *Reinforced Earth Wall on M62 at Whitley Bridge* and is an Archive paper.

The Whitley Bridge trial structure was deconstructed in 1995 after more than 20 years' use – no discernible reduction in strength or durability of the FRP reinforcement or the vertical connection poles was found.

Jones says: 'The majority of the bridge abutments and retaining walls constructed as part of the A1/M1 link were built using reinforced soil with hexagonal units. The savings in costs identified in the M62 Whitley Bridge trial were finally acknowledged – 25 years late!'

WYCET

The entrepreneurial activities of West Yorkshire Engineers was such that at the writer's instigation a company was set up much later in 1984 called WYCET (West Yorkshire Civil Engineering Technology Ltd) to enable active participation in joint ventures with private sector companies and to exploit engineering developments and patents.

Notable activities included development of Traffic Control Systems, demountable gritter bodies, ice alert systems, tyre walls, reinforced earth (mentioned above) and the 'Beany' block drainage channel developed by Neil Beanland,[151] for which royalties have been paid to the successor authorities by Marshalls. In addition, opportunities were taken to bid with Consultants for consultancy support work including some overseas. Directors of the company were Gaffney, Hunter and the writer. The company was short lived and was disbanded on abolition of the Metropolitan Counties in 1986.

Pollington to Rawcliffe

This contract was awarded to W. & C. French in the tender sum of £5.773 million and work started in April 1973. The contract covered approximately 6½ km of the M62 motorway extending from Pollington to Rawcliffe together with approximately 6½ km of single carriageway and half a mile of M18 motorway to provide the Rawcliffe Interchange between M62 and M18.

The motorway is formed on embankment throughout, apart from one very small cutting, with the height maintained at two metres minimum above ground level. A total of 1,500,000 cubic metres of fill, generally bunter sandstone, was imported, including the granular drainage blanket to the base of the embankments.

Immediately to the east and west of Goole–Thorne Road (A614) the route crosses the course of the old River Don and here recent alluvial deposits in the form of peat and soft organic clay of up to seven metres thick were present. These included up to four metres of soft silty clay (warp) at the top. Because consolidation settlement of about a metre could be anticipated it was decided to surcharge this area under an advanced earthworks contract in order to obtain the majority of the settlement prior to constructing the motorway and diversion of the A614. This was successfully carried out using colliery waste from Moorends Tip, near Thorne, in a contract awarded to French which cost £354,509 and commenced in November 1972 with completion in May 1973.

Of the eight bridges on the contract, all of which were founded on piles driven to the underlying sandstone, the most interesting were the Interchange bridges at Rawcliffe and the Viaduct over the Goole Canal and the Dutch River. There was also a railway bridge carrying the motorway over the Pontefract–Goole line.

Langham West, East and South Interchange Bridges. These three bridges are identical and carry connecting roads over the motorway. They are curved in plan and have four continuous spans of 35 metres, 40 metres, 40 metres and 35 metres, and are 14 metres wide. Each deck is a single box spine beam with cantilevers and consists of concrete segmental units supported on reinforced concrete piers and skeleton abutments.

The method of construction was novel in that the units for each bridge, prior to stressing, were supported on a temporary embankment as 'falsework'. This method was adopted as the most economic means of overcoming the poor ground conditions and the then predicted settlement in the area. Each embankment was constructed well in advance of placing the units and was monitored regularly for settlement. The units were supported on reinforced concrete plinths with provision for jacking each unit to its correct position prior to making up the *in situ* joints between the units. Following post-tensioning the embankment 'falsework' was removed. Faircloughs manufactured the units.

Langham Viaduct carries the M18 motorway and a connecting road over the Goole Canal and the Dutch River on an eight-span simply supported structure. The spans are 18 metres, 30 metres, five at 25 metres and 18 metres and the deck varies in width from 42 metres to 52 metres. The structure is supported at its ends on reinforced concrete skeleton abutments and in the intermediate positions on piers formed of reinforced concrete portal frames, two of the piers were founded in permanent cofferdams within the tidal river.

French's Contracts Manager was Peter Stephens, and the Agent was Reg Varney. The Resident Engineer was Hunt, succeeded by Gillard. Ken Corrie was the Resident Engineer on the adjacent Thorne East Cowick M18 Contract but eventually the two contracts was combined under

Langham Interchange Bridges M62/M18

Langham Viaduct

Gillard. Towards the end of the M62 contract Gillard was succeeded by John Holroyd.

The opening of the Lofthouse to Whitley Bridge section of the M62 motorway was by County Councillor Fred Pennington the Chairman of the West Yorkshire Metropolitan County Council's Public Works Committee.[152]

Rawcliffe to Balkholme including the Ouse Bridge

The following account has been taken from the opening brochure[153] and other documents.[154,155]

Scott Wilson Kirkpatrick & Partners on behalf of the Department of the Environment undertook a transportation study into road communication between the Great North Road and Kingston-upon-Hull in 1964. The route of the Rawcliffe to Balkholme Section on the M62, including the crossing of the River Ouse, resulted from that study. This section relieved the A614 between Rawcliffe and Howden and the A63 between Howden and Balkholme.

These roads carried a large volume of traffic with a high proportion of heavy commercial vehicles proceeding to and from the City of Hull. Traffic flow on the A614 was restricted at the Boothferry Bridge over the River Ouse. It was a swing bridge and frequently closed to road traffic to allow passage of shipping, which in the past resulted in long queues of waiting vehicles.

The dominant feature of this section of the M62 is the Ouse Bridge, a structure nearly 1.6 km long and rising to a height of about 30 metres above the surrounding countryside. The motorway was designed to be built on a small embankment on both sides of the Ouse Bridge because of the low flat nature of the surrounding countryside, much of which is liable to become waterlogged in winter and is below the high-tide level of the river.

At the preliminary design stage a comparison was made between the costs of a bridge and an immersed tube tunnel, but a tunnel would have been much more expensive.

Scott Wilson Kirkpatrick & Partners were appointed the consulting engineers to the North Eastern Road Construction Unit of the Department of the Environment for the design and supervision of construction of the Ouse Bridge and of the lengths of motorway on the two adjacent contracts let in April 1973.

The West Roads Contract

This contract comprised five kilometres of motorway beginning near Dobeller Lane just south of Rawcliffe and extending to an interchange on the A614 to the West of Goole.

The Works included three side road re-alignments, one interchange and three overbridges together with drainage works including both pipe and box culverts. The earthworks are embankments of imported fill material.

The locality is below the high-tide level of the River Ouse and ground water and surface water levels are influenced by tidal conditions within the flood bunds of that river. The land is drained by a system of Farmers' Drains connected with Main Drains leading to outfalls at the bunds. In some cases these consist of a simple outfall with flap gates, which close on the rising tide, twice daily. In other cases pumping stations were provided, which work intermittently depending on the water level in the Main Drain. Sometimes a combination of the two methods was used. The Internal Drainage Boards for the area carried out improvement works to cater for increased rainfall run-off from the motorway concurrently with this contract.

The Contract was awarded to Sir Alfred McAlpine & Son Ltd of Hooton, Cheshire, at a Tender figure of £3,058,465. It was completed in March 1975.

The contracts manager was Abbott, the Agent Mike Graham. The Resident Engineer was Ken Barrett succeeded by Mike Hillcoat.

The A614 Interchange at Airmyn

The Ouse Bridge

The £6.75 million contract for the Ouse Bridge was awarded to a consortium of Redpath Dorman Long (Contracting) Limited and Costain Civil Engineering Limited, and commenced in January 1973.

In common with several other medium span bridges, which were tendered for in 1972, the contract was awarded for the construction of a plate girder alternative submitted by the contractor. The cost of constructing steel box girders to comply with the latest requirements had made the box girder uneconomical for these spans, at least at that time.

Redpath Dorman Long designed the superstructure of the bridge and G. Maunsell & Partners designed the substructure on behalf of Costain. Scott Wilson Kirkpatrick & Partners checked the design on behalf of the Road Construction Unit.

In former times the River Ouse meandered over a wide area and extensive deposits of peat and soft clays required a total length of 1,310 metres to be bridged, although the river is now constrained by flood banks to a width of 290 metres at the bridge site.

A self-elevating platform barge equipped with steam hammer was used for pile driving. Piling for the river section and abutment foundations consisted of 120 large steel cylinder piles 1.5 metres diameter and 20 metres long with reinforced concrete plugs to below the corrosion level.

The river section has three main spans of 89 metres and 62.5 metres side spans, approached by multiples spans of 39 metres on each side. Both approach and river spans consist of eight steel plate girders with a reinforced concrete deck. Fabrication of steelwork was undertaken at RDL's Teeside works, and Raymond International (UK) Ltd carried out the piling works as sub-contractors.

David Hayward records in *New Civil Engineer*, 14 August 1975:

> Steel supply problems have been a chronic headache to engineers toiling to finish the 29-span Ouse crossing and the major reason for the eight-month delay in the bridge's construction timetable.
>
> But, three weeks ago, the project suffered another setback: bolts joining the top of an inclined trestle tower to a braced cross-beam unit sheared, causing a partial collapse of the falsework. The mishap, which has added about another month's delay to the job, occurred when the trestle tower shifted outwards causing the beam to slip. The beam, which was supporting the ends of eight 36-ton haunched girders, was prevented from collapse by the bracing of the standard military trestling.
>
> Results of an internal inquiry by steelwork contractors Redpath Dorman Long point strongly to negligence during erection as the main cause of the near disaster. Evidence suggests that four of the 16 bolts required for the fixing were never positioned, and the remaining bolts sheared in very quick succession. Extensive safety and stabilising measures are now being carried out, and consultant Scott Wilson Kirkpatrick is satisfied that the falsework design was never at fault.
>
> The 60-metre-long girder units for the river spans were erected in three sections using a 35-ton Henderson floating derrick. Each end of the 22-metres-long central haunched section is supported on a temporary cross beam unit. It was during a repeat operation over the second main river pier that the falsework slipped ... Shipping was immediately stopped while timber cribbage and tie supports stabilised the girders ...

Ouse Bridge

The recent falsework failure, which could so easily have ended in disaster, suggests more haste, less speed and let the Country wait just a bit longer for that final link in the Trans-Pennine motorway.

On either side of the approach viaducts earth embankments extend about 40 metres at a gradient of 1 in 33 and rise to 13 metres above ground level at the bridge abutments. This gradient was the steepest permissible on motorways. The embankments were constructed mostly from materials imported from existing pits and quarries, but industrial waste material from an old tip in Goole was also used. The volume of fill in the embankments was 320,000 cubic metres. Surfacing works were sub-contracted to Val de Travers Asphalte Ltd. Pre-earthworks site investigation was undertaken by Foundation Engineering Ltd.

The main contractor's Construction Manager was Brian Egan. The Chief Resident Engineer for the Consultants was Nick Greyling who was succeeded on his death during the contract by Geoff Graycroft.

The bridge was officially open to traffic in May 1976 by John Gilbert, the Minister of Transport.

Self-elevating platform barge

The East Roads Contract

This contract comprised eight kilometres of motorway commencing east of the River Ouse just south of Howden and extending to the A63 near Balkholme and was awarded to Clugston Construction Ltd.

The Works included one interchange, the construction of the 0.7 km dual carriageway Howden Spur (a connection to A614), two side road alignments and three overbridges together with drainage works including pipe and box culverts. The earthworks in the embankment was imported fill material.

The construction of a surcharged embankment in the Hail Farm peat area was completed in advance under the adjacent Ouse Bridge Contract and these works were monitored by instrumentation installed under that contract. Possession of that part of the Site was not granted until after the commencement of the Works.

Alternative designs for flexible and rigid carriageway construction were prepared for part of the motorway. All side roads, interchanges, slip roads, Howden Spur and the motorway main carriageway in Hail Farm peat area and west of that area were of flexible construction.

The adjoining contracts, the M62 Ouse Bridge Contract to the west and the M62 Balkholme to Caves Section to the east, were in progress concurrently with this contract.

Mike Hillcoat the Resident Engineer recalls:[156]

> The contract period was 24 months and the works should have been completed within this period with ease. In the event it was almost three years before the works were finished in March 1976.
>
> The contract did not include the alternative item for use of imported colliery shale because it had been decided that it was not viable. Unfortunately at a meeting in Beverly between the East and West Riding Planners they agreed that borrow pits should not be allowed in the East Riding whilst the supplies of Colliery shale were available in West Riding. This led to a very long delay before Planning Permission was granted by the East Riding County Council, and the Contractor rather unwisely did not progress the works until the Planning Permission was agreed.

The combined value of the East and West Road Contracts was about £6 million. Clugston's Contracts Manager was David Grounds, the Site Agent Mike Aspinal.

The Resident Engineer was Mike Hillcoat, the Assistant Resident Engineer for Roads and Bridges being Ian White and Richard Curry. The Partners in charge for Scott Wilson & Kirkpatrick were Mac McDermott and James.

Balkholme to Caves

This scheme was designed and supervised by the Durham sub-unit of the NERCU. The following is abstracted from notes provided by the Resident Engineer, Roger Elphick.[157]

Balkholme to Caves, 10.3 km in length, is the easternmost section of the M62 Trans-Pennine motorway linking Liverpool and Hull and by-passes the villages of Gilberdyke and Newport, rejoining the existing A63 Trunk Road to Hull at a grade-separated interchange near North Cave. There are ten major structures including crossings of the main Selby to Hull railway and the Market Weighton Canal and 7.6 km of associated single carriageway side road works to various standards. Over much of the eastern half of the contract, the motorway follows the line of the abandoned Hull and Barnsley railway line.

The contract was let to Sir Alfred McAlpine (Northern) in April 1974 for £6.1 million, and incorporated Britain's first lengths of continuously reinforced concrete pavement (CRCP), to carry the motorway over unfavourable ground at the eastern end of the contract. Prior to the commencement of the main contract, advance drainage works were completed over some sections of the scheme to drain the ground and improve its bearing capacity. In addition, advanced earthworks were carried out where the motorway partially overlaid a disused railway embankment and an area of variable depth compressible material including peat, which would create both general and differential settlement problems within each carriageway. A surcharged embankment, 4.5 metres in height, was constructed with sand drains installed from ground level enabling a large proportion of the anticipated settlement to occur prior to the construction of the motorway pavement. Soils instrumentation in the form of inclinometers, hydraulic piezometers and horizontal settlement gauges were incorporated to monitor the behaviour of the embankment. It was in this area where the continuously reinforced construction was adopted.

As the motorway was constructed entirely on embankment, the earthworks mainly involved the import of almost a million cubic metres of bulk fill materials, including a hard rock chalk, which formed a 0.5 metre-

The finished pavement

thick pervious drainage blanket at ground level. The shallow embankments, which form the major part of the contract, were constructed generally of Bunter Sandstone and rock chalk whereas the higher embankments, which carry the motorway over the Selby to Hull railway, consisted of clay, extracted from a borrow pit adjacent to the site, capped with 0.5 metre of chalk at formation level and in addition pulverised fuel ash was incorporated within the high sections to minimise settlement.

Drainage was by means of *in situ* concrete channels, laid virtually level in many areas, designed to drain hydraulically. Over 12 km of large open ditches, constructed on either side of the motorway, provide drainage outfalls and 1,000 metres of culverts form 20 interconnections under both the motorway and side roads.

In advanced earthworks area, where the surcharge had been removed, by correlating the continuing output of the soils instrumentation and laboratory consolidation test data it was possible to predict the rate and magnitude of the long-term settlements. As it was anticipated that further limited settlement of the embankment would continue for a considerable time, the CRCP (described on pp.198-200) was adopted. The continuously reinforced slab, 230 mm thick, was constructed in two sections, 540 and 840 metres in length, and was heavily reinforced with a total of 200 tonnes of reinforcement. A 60 mm-thick layer of bituminous roadbase was laid under the concrete, providing a uniformly rough base upon which to set up the bar reinforcement mat on purpose-made stools in advance of the paving operation and also act as a waterproof membrane, protecting the sub-base from water which might subsequently percolate through the slab. The absence of joints has elsewhere been found to improve the riding quality and reduce maintenance costs.

On the remainder of the scheme, an unreinforced concrete pavement, 280 mm thick, was used for the 11.2-metre-wide three-lane carriageways, including the marginal strips. The adjacent hard shoulders were of flexible construction. Both concrete and flexible pavements were laid on a crushed limestone sub-base which provided a firm running surface for the heavy paving machinery. The concrete slab, which has contraction joints at six-metre centres, was constructed in a single pass using McAlpine's Guntert and Zimmerman slip-form paver with SGME ancillary equipment. The transverse joint dowel bars were supported on fabric cradle assemblies, which were set up in advance of the paving together with the bottom crack inducer and the longitudinal joint tie bars; these were fixed into the sub-base on top of the polythene sheeting.

At the eastern end of the contract, the machine was also used to form two short lengths of two-lane carriageway with an integral hard strip. Short lengths of flexible construction incorporating transfer slabs were used for the motorway pavement adjacent to over-bridges, which cross the Market Weighton canal and Selby to Hull railway.

The Project Manager for McAlpines was Abbott, agent Brian Melling. The Resident Engineer was Roger Elphick.

The Ouse Bridge, opened in May 1976, completed the M62 Lancashire-Yorkshire motorway in the North East Region, and although the M62 terminates at North Cave, the A63 Trunk Road provides direct access from this point to Hull and the East Coast. Later that year the final M62 link, in Merseyside, came into operation and completed the direct motorway link between the ports of Liverpool and Hull, which has become the country's 'biggest trade route' (p.126).

10 Urban Motorways in the North East Conurbations

Land-use transportation studies

We again go back in time. In 1958 the Ministry of Transport invited local authorities in the conurbations, several of which were highway authorities, to form area review committees so as to co-ordinate road plans. These committees undertook some traffic studies, but by the early 1960s it was clear that more extensive studies were needed. With encouragement from the Ministry local authorities then took a more comprehensive approach to road and transport policies through the use of land-use/transportation studies. The Department contributed half the cost and participated in the technical direction of these studies.

Studies set up in the North East of England included the West Yorkshire Transportation Study (WYTS) and the Tyne and Wear Plan (TWP), which were completed by 1970. There was debate as to the value of the studies because of 'inadequacies in techniques', such as mathematical modelling.

The consensus of opinion was that the studies were an essential tool in planning urban roads, motorways and public transport systems, but needed to be developed to include social and environmental factors.

In the 1980s, with the development of more sophisticated computer tools for modelling studies, more data could be handled and alternative road and transport plans tested. Long term forecasting of traffic with any accuracy still remained a matter of considerable uncertainty.

Urban motorways

In 1958 the principal Highway Authorities set up a Review Area Committee to report on the long-term highway needs of the West Riding Special Review Area, which included Leeds and Bradford.

The committee did not report until 1964 but proposed that urban motorways should be built in Leeds and Bradford to link the trunk road motorways in the County.

In 1965 a further study by the combined Ministries of Transport and Housing and Local Government together with the Leeds City Council recommended similar proposals in respect of Leeds City.

A start was made on the first stage of the Leeds Inner Ring Road Motorway A58(M) in 1964 under Thirwell until suceeded by Naylor in

178 / Building the Network: The North East of England

1970. An ebullient character and highly respected engineer, Naylor[158] in his writing for the Archive gives the following account of the work of the City Engineers Department and West Yorkshire Metropolitan County Council (after 1974) in bringing these schemes to fruition.

A58(M). The Leeds Inner Ring Motorway, the First Urban Motorway.

The former Leeds County Borough was foremost in transportation thinking. The focus was on the city centre, to create a pleasant and attractive place for shopping, business and recreation enjoyed by pedestrians. This formed the basis of the internationally acclaimed policy 'The Leeds Approach'.

The crux of the problem was the north–south road, Briggate, around which the City had developed, and the east–west road, The Headrow, that crossed it in the centre. Through-traffic was in excess of 40 per cent and the answer proposed in 1955 was an inner ring road. By 1963 this had been raised to the status of a motorway, the first City Centre motorway in the UK. As it was to be constructed in the heart of the City, land was at a premium, environmental intrusion on housing, business and

The motorway in cutting retained by vertical walls

hospital had to be minimised and the many existing main access roads kept functioning.

The solution was a dual 24-feet carriageway road in a cutting approximately 20 feet below ground level retained by vertical walls. The result is a road generally hidden from view except at bridge crossing points. The design differed from rural motorways in that kerbs were provided as a safety measure and the narrow five feet verges and 10-feet central reserve were paved with concrete slabs to reduce maintenance. A 40mph speed limit was imposed.

The line passed through large areas of condemned housing and obsolescent industrial premises. The opportunity was taken to clear them and re-house the people in a rational and phased manner, keeping them together as far as possible. Such were the times that work started in 1964 but the Public Inquiry by the then Ministry of Transport was not held until 1966 when Leeds pioneered the Urban Motorway Procedure and Stages I and II were confirmed as a Special Roads Scheme.

The first two stages formed a ring of 1,860 feet and the slip roads were 'braided' to minimise land take and in one case the exit slip was from the right, hand lane. At the western end the University lay a little distant to the north and the Infirmary to the south. It was agreed to form a University/Hospital precinct by roofing the road for a distance of 1,200 feet, thereby creating useable space of one hectare. The University provided the design and the two bodies paid the extra cost of £300,000. In the event the financial climate prevented the building of a teaching hospital but the City funded a temporary lightweight construction for a contemporary theatre, The Leeds Playhouse.

Ground conditions at foundation levels were highly variable and included the line of a major fault. Situated in a former coal mining area, many small bell holes were encountered. A large pocket of coal was found near Woodhouse Lane crossing and some 2,000 tons were extracted under licence from the National Coal Board.

Particular research was carried out regarding the possible effect of diesel and oil spillage by heavy lorries in the tunnels. To avoid the problem of cleaning the build up of oil deposits on asphalt the main carriageways were constructed of reinforced concrete. Similarly, to alleviate the cleaning problems caused by pollution in the tunnels, the walls were faced with one-inch-square mosaic tiles.

Considerable use was made of rock anchors and rock bolts as special underpinning and permanent support works to various factories etc, which were to remain virtually on the edge of the cutting.

A novel feature, not included in the original scheme, was the construction of an elegant footbridge over the section to the Quarry Hill Flats complex. Thousands of people lived there and complained that they were cut off from the social area of the church, school and clubs. One empty flat was cleared and the footbridge sprang from this across the road and access was from the inner part of the complex. The flats, demolished in the 1990s, have been replaced by the Leeds Playhouse and a much-criticised DHSS Headquarters building.

A forerunner of today's contracts was one negotiated for the second stage works. This was with the successful contractor for the first section, Lehane, McKenzie and Shand, entailing some design, programming and agreeing all rates in the agreed Bill of Quantities, which meant breaking down confidential information on costs, profit and overheads.

The Woodhouse Lane Multi-Storey car park for 1,320 cars is constructed over the motorway, thus reducing land take, and is easily accessible from the motorway for quick access to the centre by foot or park and ride.

In addition to the main tunnel there are another four under-intersections averaging 70–100 metres in length. The end sections of the ring connecting it to the main road network are on viaducts. Two are multi-span design. The third at the eastern end, as it runs into York Road, is a two-level viaduct 560 metres long, carrying the motorway at the top level and the general traffic at the lower. There are eight bridges carrying roads over the motorway and it bridges over the River Aire and the Leeds Liverpool Canal. Four footbridges and two subway complexes cater for pedestrian movement.

The motorway, of length two miles, was constructed in four sections commencing in 1964 and completed in 1975. The contractors were for Stages I and II, Lehane, McKenzie & Shand, for Stage IIa, W. & C. French & Sons and for Stage III, C. Bryant. The total cost including side road alterations was £12.5 million at 1970 prices.

Viaduct sections at eastern end

Stourton Link and M1 Interchange

In 1967 the M1 had been completed to the south of Leeds at Stourton and linked to the local road network. In March 1970 a contract was let to A.F. Budge (Contractors) Ltd at a cost of £1.26 million for the final scheme to link the M1 with the Leeds South Eastern Urban Motorway.

The scheme, completed in October 1971, was designed by the West Riding Sub-Unit and provided a link road with the motorway from the Pontefract–Castleford road A639, improvement of the Wakefield to Leeds A61 and an interchange with two underbridges to carry the M1. It also provided access for the development of a Road/Rail Freight line Terminal with a storage depot at the end of the M1.

M1. Leeds South Eastern Urban Motorway[159]

The route of two miles length commences at the Stourton interchange, officially the end of the national M1. It follows the line of the disused Hunslet East–Beeston Junction railway in cutting. It then rises on embankment to cross over Belle Isle and Old Run Roads providing panoramic views of the city centre on the skyline. The motorway then swings to the north and sweeps across Hunslet Moor in cutting until it

The Urban Motorway joins M1

reaches the South Leeds Interchange which distributes the traffic onto the existing network.

It was intended that the final motorway network would be based on three interconnected motorways running tangentially to the city centre linking the Inner Ring Road to the M1 and M62. The final link was to be a North-East Motorway running from the South Leeds Interchange to the eastern end of the Inner Relief Road at York Road. This was never built because a wider city by-pass, the A1–M1 link, later constructed to the east of the city, diverted a considerable part of the likely traffic. However, with the advent of Urban Traffic Control (UTC) the considerable volumes of traffic using the South Eastern Urban Motorway were managed and controlled on widened all-purpose surface links across the proposed route.

Sensible land acquisition was made possible by a clause in The Leeds Corporation Act which enabled the Council compulsorily to acquire land and property beyond the limits of the highway boundary for amenity purposes. This allowed substantial landscaping and earth mounding to be provided to reduce intrusion and noise by using all of the surplus materials. At that time legislation limited such purpose to the boundary and resulted in disasters such as Westway. Subsequently, the Leeds clause was incorporated into the Highways Act.

Hunslet and Beeston were redevelopment areas and the scene of considerable dereliction. Although the use of the former railway line saved many good properties, 400 houses and 600 industrial and commercial premises were demolished.

From nearby, 250,000 tons of colliery waste from a tip, partly surrounded by houses, in Old Run Road were used to form embankments and residents were delighted that at last they had a pleasant view instead of a shale tip at the front door. Adjacent to the tip the motorway, on a 30-feet-high embankment, crosses the line of the Middleton Colliery Railway. The route of this historic railway line, which was still in use, into the former colliery has been preserved by building a corrugated steel 'Armco' tunnel under the motorway, which at 260 feet long and 19 feet in diameter was the largest structure of its type in Britain. In 1758 this line was the first railway system to be authorised by Act of Parliament. For the first 50 years the carriages were horse-drawn, the change to steam being made in 1812 using a rack rail system and a maximum speed of 10 miles per hour.

The idea of using standard lighting columns creating a 'wall' across South Leeds was unacceptable. The Ministry, however, refused to consider the relatively new high mast lighting – it not being in the book! However, after much discussion a grant based on the cost of normal lighting was given and the City was allowed to provide anything more expensive at its own cost. Hence, 100-feet-high lighting columns with High Pressure

High mast lighting

Sodium lights spaced at wide intervals were provided, illuminating the road and landscape areas.

Generally the motorway, which has a design speed of 50 mph, is 110 feet wide with dual three-lane carriageways. The motorway structures include 11 road bridges, three of which span the Leeds–Derby main line, four footbridges, 13 retaining walls, four subways and a railway tunnel. In addition, there is a dual 24-feet-wide carriageway, half-a-mile long, known as the Hunslet Distributor leading to Hunslet Road.

The total cost of the scheme was £7.67 million of which £2.87 million was land purchase and £0.85 million service diversions. Tarmac Construction Ltd completed the works three months ahead of schedule.[160]

This was thought to be Tarmac's first urban motorway. Brian Georgel records:[161]

> It was soon realised that urban motorways had their own particular problems, which were not generally encountered on rural motorways. In particular, the services in Leeds, both existing and new, were a nightmare.

Earthworks were sub-let to E.W. Ambrose, a local company. Both red and black shale was imported from local sources and used in embankments in large quantities, necessitating the use of sulphate resisting concrete for all drainage works. Large quantities of machine laid extruded concrete kerb were used on this contract.

The contract commenced in early 1971 at the same time as the '3 day week' was affecting the whole country. The first few weeks were spent without power, trying to keep warm and working by Tilley lamps in the evenings.

The contract also experienced the 'builders strike' of 1972. The strikers eventually descended upon the contract and the Project Manager was faced with a baying mob demanding that he shut the job down. He managed to persuade them first to let him have all the plant and equipment brought into the compound, which was successfully carried out – an ugly situation involving some physical violence. The site was closed for about three months.[162]

The Contracts Manager was Bill Redston, the Project Manager Georgel, the Road Agent Ian Isley and the Bridge Agent was Harry Mehra. The Resident Engineer was John Carter.

The road was opened by The Rt Hon. Geoffrey Rippon QC MP, Secretary of State, the Department of the Environment, in December 1972.

M621. Leeds South West Urban Motorway[163]

This motorway forms the continuation of the M621 which was constructed by the West Riding County Council as the Leeds Motorway from the M62 to the Beeston Ring Road. The M621 comes boldly down a long steep hill for over a mile and affords a view of almost all of the city. The motorway continues from the Beeston interchange, passing Elland Road (Leeds United) Football Ground and links with the South East interchange. Its length is 1.66 miles and is constructed mainly on embankment. The connection to the Inner Ring Road is provided by the Ingram Road Distributor (0.77 miles), which starts at the Elland Road Interchange. The distributor has dual two-lane carriageways but no footways.

Of the three motorways this was the only one to have serious objections at the CPO Inquiry stage in 1972, a remarkable achievement considering the complexity of the land requirements. The line of the road had been revealed in development plan submissions in 1963 with no objections. The majority concerned individual properties but one was a considered alternative route and one was from the staff of the Mathew Murray Secondary School built in 1961 and adjacent to the distributor. Concern was rightly expressed at the proposal to cross playing fields adjacent to the school in open cut with the resultant disturbance. The Council had proposed to the Ministry that a cut and cover solution at an extra cost of approximately £200,000 would be preferable, relying on the knowledge gained on the Inner Relief Road. However, they required the cheapest solution. The lady 'civics' teacher brought her pupils to the City Hall to take note and photographs (early tuition for the protest groups!) and appeared at the Public Inquiry. She was known as 'The Barefoot Contessa', no shoes, and she accompanied the Inspector on his site visit across old tips in this manner. The Inspector quietly asked the Engineer what his views were regarding the school and he had no hesitation in replying 'cover the road – the Council would be delighted'. His recommendation was to do that and, to be fair, the Ministry readily gave grant for the work. The cross examination of the Engineer seemingly collapsed when the Counsel thundered, '… and do you know how much this school cost?', to which he replied '£530,016 14s. 5d.!'

The motorway is 90 feet wide comprising dual two-lane carriageways and is subject to a 50-mph limit from the city to Beeston Ring Road. There are six road bridges, two rail bridges, two footbridges and 360 feet of tunnel. In addition, British Rail were responsible for another bridge carrying the main London line over the motorway. Typical of the Leeds area, bad ground conditions were met and preliminary work to locate and fill old mine workings was undertaken. Large quantities of toxic material also had to be removed.

The contractor was A.F. Budge Ltd and the work, which commenced in December 1974, took 20 months to complete against the contract period of 27 months. The total cost of the scheme was £10.5 million of which land purchases accounted for £1.86 million. The Project Manager was Ian Green, the Agent (Roads) John Smith, and the Agent (Structures) Peter Gothard.

When the latter two sections of the motorway were completed the municipal bus undertaking ran a 'fastaway' bus service on them providing a fast, non-stop service from the outlying estates to the city.[164]

These schemes were designed and supervised by the City of Leeds Engineer's Department with the exception of the contract supervision of the South West Urban Motorway by the West Yorkshire Metropolitan County Council which completed the scheme. The Resident Engineer was David Camm. George Kidd was Assistant City Engineer (Roads) and 'Derry' Davies held a similar position and headed the Bridges Section.

M621. Gildersome Street to Leeds Motorway

For something of an account of the motorway the writer has used the submission for Associate Membership of the Institution of Civil Engineers by John Land,[165] a graduate engineer in his Bridge Department at the time.

The M621 Motorway is basically a two-lane dual carriageway of approximately three miles in length forming the link between the M62 Lancashire–Yorkshire Motorway and the Leeds South East Urban

186 / Building the Network: The North East of England

Armco multiplate arch

Motorway. For most of its length, however, an additional crawler lane is provided on the steep gradient of the northbound carriageway. There are 12 structures on this length of motorway.

The contract was won by Messrs. W. & C. French (Construction) Ltd at a tender price of £2.9 million. Work started in September 1971.

Acres of rhubarb were cleared when the M621 earthmoving programme began in September 1971. In addition to the tipping of night soil over centuries the secret ingredient, say the local farmers, is the sooty atmosphere characteristic of the region, in the heart of the industrial north.

The scheme included approximately 1.5 miles of slip roads from the M62 Gildersome Interchange to their conjunction as M621 dual carriageway. Crossing the route of the slip roads is the A650 Trunk Road, and this is carried on two individual over-bridges. Both bridges span approximately 60 feet at slightly different skews, due to the horizontal curvature of the A650. The parapets being curved both in plan and elevation, and extending over 300 feet, required much effort and co-operation between the engineer and the contractor in order to achieve a satisfactory line.

At the other extremity of the site two similar bridges were being constructed as part of the Beeston Interchange. Between the two Beeston Interchange Bridges, an 'Armco' multiple arch spans 26 feet over the existing road with the YEB and CEGB electricity services beneath. This solution was considerably cheaper than diverting the services around the roundabout, but still provides access to them for maintenance. Settlement of the footings and deflections of the crown of the arch, both vertically and horizontally, required careful supervision during backfilling operations and were monitored in order that the final profile should be as near circular as possible.

In addition to the erection of lighting columns it was necessary to erect a double-sided tensioned safety barrier throughout the length of the motorway and single sided on the slip roads. Despite this additional work, the building strike of 1972 and the steel shortage, the motorway was opened in November 1973, only two months behind schedule.

The Agent for W. & C. French was Jack Hollis. The resident Engineer was Hunt, and John Evans was his deputy who eventually succeeded him.

M606. Chain Bar–Bradford Motorway

The M606 was designed by the Highways Department of the Bradford Corporation headed by Reg Atkinson who was fiercely protective of the status of the Borough Engineer. He would not have taken kindly to County engineers designing anything on his 'patch'.

The realignment of the M62 nearer to Bradford and Leeds presented an opportunity to provide a direct connection from the city to the motorway. Alternatives were examined, but the logical connection was thought to be a new road following a 100 feet improvement line included in the City's Development Plan. This extended southwards, through the green belt, from the City's Ring Road (now A6177) towards Chain Bar, intersection of the A 58 and the A638 to Dewsbury.

The Bradford South Radial Motorway, between the Ring Road and the City Boundary, was designed and approved by the City Council in 1964. The outline scheme also extended from the Ring Road, through the City Centre and northwards as the 'Bradford North Radial Motorway', on the same reserved improvement line but, unfortunately, the reserved width was insufficient to allow the provision of service roads, and a full motorway scheme would have involved substantial property demolition and was never built.[166]

During the design process there was close liaison with the West Riding County Council which proved fruitful, and they were able to design an interchange at Chain Bar which provided free-flow facilities for traffic heading towards Bradford from the south.

The M606 motorway contract was awarded to A. Monk & Co. Ltd. Work started in June 1971 and was completed in May 1973, at a cost of just over £2 million. Largely constructed on embankment, the features of the scheme were the interchange with the Bradford Ring Road and the provision of slip roads to provide access to the development of the Euroway Industrial Trading Estate.

The ¾-mile-long section of the M606, to link with the M62, was designed by the West Riding RCU Sub-Unit and was constructed by Dowsett Engineering Construction as part of the Hartshead to Gildersome Section of the M62. The work started in 1970 and was completed in 1972 (see pp.155-7).

In 1974 the maintenance of the M606 came under the Directorate of Engineering of the West Yorkshire MCC. Several 'holes' opened up on this section of motorway in its early life due to the collapse of old mining shafts. Extensive drilling was carried out to investigate the extent of these old shafts and a contract let for the filling and capping of identified shafts.

Newcastle Urban Motorways

Newcastle Central Motorway East, a trial Urban Motorway, is referred to on p.64 together with the Newcastle Western By-pass.

11 Rotherham to Goole Motorway M18 – East of A1(M)

The construction of the M18 Motorway provided a motorway link between the M1 near Rotherham and the M62 near Goole and closed the motorway box around the towns of Pontefract, Wakefield, Barnsley, Rotherham and Doncaster. The motorway is also linked to the A1(M) at Doncaster (Wadworth) and the M180 south of Thorne. The M18 from Rotherham to the A1(M) Doncaster By-pass has already been described. This account covers the motorway to the east of A1(M) to Goole.

This length of the M18 was divided into the following contracts and takes us from Thorne back to the Doncaster By-pass.

- Thorne to East Cowick
- Hatfield to Thorne (Thorne By-pass)
- Armthorpe to Hatfield
- Wadworth to Armthorpe
- Wadworth Viaduct

The North Eastern Road Construction Unit and the West Riding and West Yorkshire Sub-Units carried out the contracts over a period of six years from 1970 to 1978.

Thorne to East Cowick

This contract connected the M62 Pollington–Rawcliffe Interchange (junction 35) to the Hatfield–Thorne (M18) section, which had already been completed and opened.

The contract, which included the completion of the two-level interchange at Waterside (Junction 6), was awarded to W. & C. French in the sum of £2.46 million. Having also won the Pollington–Rawcliffe contract on the M62, French combined both the jobs under the same site team.

Work on the two contracts started in May 1973, this contract being completed in June 1975, some three months ahead of that on the M62.

This contract was initially under the supervision of Corrie as Resident Engineer and then it was later combined with the Pollington-Rawcliffe Resident Engineers' Office under Gillard.

Hatfield to Thorne (Thorne By-pass)

This contract was awarded to Sir Alfred McAlpine & Sons in the tender sum of £4.798 million and work started in September 1970.

189

This 3.6-mile section of M18 was opened to traffic in June 1972 and runs from a point on the Hatfield–Thorne Road A1146 to join the A614 at Waterside to the north west of Thorne. The Tudworth link (originally numbered A18(M)) is approximately one mile in length, stretching east from the two-level motorway interchange at North Ings to a point near Tudworth Hall Corner.

Some two million cubic yards of fill material was imported and included unburnt colliery shale from Hatfield tip near Thorne and bunter sandstone.

Of the 14 structures on the contract the major one is the **East Ings Canal Bridge**, which carries the motorway over the Stainforth–Keadby Canal. The bridge has three spans, an overall length of 242 feet with two piers founded on piles and the bank seats on embankment filling. 175,000 cubic yards of peat (with bog oak), located on each side of the canal, had to be excavated up to a depth of 20 feet prior to commencing filling.

Moglia recalls that 54RB Draglines were used standing on timber mats to spread the load. Material was passed from machine to machine until firm ground was reached. The work involved the prior protection of the canal banks with sheet piling, in order to avoid the possibility of draining several miles of canal. Unfortunately, the piling did not toe into the underlying Bunter Sandstone, and so led to the removal of all the peat from under the south bridge abutment and to the need to jack up the bridge deck later in the contract.

In 1966 the West Riding County Council acting with the Ministry of Transport initiated some tests into the earth pressures acting on the retaining walls (Sims *et al*.[167] 1970). In 1970 further field research was conducted at the North Ings Interchange and is reported by Jones and the writer in *Geotechnique*.[168]

The Contracts Manager was Sutherland, and the Agent Abbott. The Resident Engineer was Moglia, and the Assistant Resident Engineer Ralley.

East Ings Canal Bridge

Armthorpe to Hatfield

This contract comprised the construction of about six km of motorway between a point 1.5 km to the east of Armthorpe and the southern end of the existing section of M18, Thorne By-pass, one km to the north east of Hatfield. In addition, a link road for traffic from the east side of Doncaster was constructed from the railway bridge at Edenthorpe to an interchange at the southern end of the new section of motorway. Diversions to six existing roads, the construction of six structures and the excavation for a new service area at Hatfield completed the works. The Contractor for the scheme was A. Monk & Co. Ltd and the value of the tender was £4.72 million. It commenced in December 1975 and was completed in July 1977.

A 2.5-km length of the motorway in the middle of the contract was constructed over poor ground consisting of about one metre of soft clay containing lenses of silt and decomposed vegetation overlying sand. To overcome the problem of instability resulting from this clay, a half-metre thickness of rock was placed directly on existing topsoil, prior to the construction of the remainder of the embankment.

The fill requirement for the scheme amounted to 550,000 cubic metres, almost all of which came from the excavation for Hatfield Service Area, which, for environmental reasons, was constructed about three metres below existing ground level and further screened by two-metre bunds around its perimeter.

Drainage through the low-lying area was a particular problem. Run-off from the carriageway is collected in specially designed concrete drainage channels, set at the back of the hardshoulder, which discharge at regular intervals into large drainage ditches excavated alongside the motorway embankment. The gradients of these stretches are very flat and flow depends entirely on the hydraulic gradient of the water in the ditches.

Water drained from the motorway, with the exception of a small quantity outfalling into a stream at Edenthorpe, passes into the man-made drainage system of the area at West Moor Drain and Woodhouse Sewer, both of these large ditches passing under the motorway in two-metre culverts. To cater for the more rapid run-off from paved surfaces, Woodhouse Sewer was deepened and widened and a new pumping station constructed at Waterton Farm.

Three thousand three hundred and thirty metres of side road diversions were constructed. These included the re-alignment of Holme Wood Lane, the diversion of Waterton Lane over the motorway, the re-alignment of Moss Croft Lane C252 over both the motorway and the A18 Trunk Road and the construction of 1,100 metres of a new unclassified County Road – Carr Side Lane. Thorne New Road A1146 was realigned to form a temporary connection with the existing Hatfield to Thorne Section of M18.

Bridgeworks included West Moor North and South overbridge carrying the West Moor North Link to interchange with the M18. Moss Cross lane overbridge has a skew of 27°. Waterton Lane overbridge has four simply supported spans. All the above bridges were expected to be subject to mining movements in the future.

Epworth Road overbridge has two spans and is curved in plan. Epworth Road Services culvert carries a foul sewer, water and GPO services beneath the M18 on the line of the existing A18. The culvert is of reinforced concrete box-construction. Mere Lane Pedestrian Subway crosses the West

Moor Link and, as it could be liable to flooding, two automatic self-starting electric pumps are provided in a sump at one end. Hatfield Service Area Subway under the M18 provides access to the Service Centre.

The Contracts Manager was Shields, and the Agent Dave Clarkin. The Resident Engineer was Alan Short who, sadly, died in harness, Neville Criddle succeeding him. The Assistant Resident Engineer was Richard Whitely.

Wadworth to Armthorpe

This contract for the construction of 12 km of two-lane motorway connected the M18/A1 Interchange with West Moor Interchange, Armthorpe, which was then under construction. Five diversions of side roads and several diversions of farm access roads were constructed as part of the scheme, together with ten bridges, two underpasses and a number of other structures, mainly for drainage. Dowsett Engineering Construction Ltd won the contract for the scheme, with a tender of £9.54 million. The contract commenced in December 1976 and was completed in February 1979.

The southern end of the Works included two 15-metre rock cuttings and three areas of fill, one being 15 metres high on the approach to the A1 / M18 Interchange, and the other two approximately 10 to 12 metres high over the East Coast London Edinburgh Main Line and a Mineral Railway Line. The northern 4.5 km is in shallow cut or fill in generally flat terrain.

The earthworks were considerable with approximately 1.6 million cubic metres of cut and a similar amount of fill. However, nearly 300,000 cubic metres of excavation was unsuitable material, about 35 per cent coming from the Loversall Carr area. The deficit of suitable material was made up with colliery shale from Rossington Colliery. About 1.5 km from the M18/A1 Interchange is Loversall Cutting in limestone, the material from which was used below embankment for the rock blanket, specified over a 3.5 km length of the contract. High approach embankments and the Loversall Carr Railway Bridge carry the motorway over the East Coast Railway Line. Underlaying peat, alluvial and laminated clays were excavated and the remainder of the rock from the Loversall Cutting used as replacement. The East Coast Main Line created a major barrier for the earthworks operation – a problem resolved by the use of a 100-metre four-span Bailey bridge over the railway. Approximately one km north of this area is the other major cutting in Bunter Sandstone. Whilst excavated as rock, the material was only suitable as a general fill. This source of material was used to complete all areas of fill north of the cutting and in addition provided fill for much of the southern end moved via the Bailey bridge. Completion of the embankments of the southern five km was made with colliery shale. Because of anticipated settlements, the Loversall Carr approach embankments were instrumented and staged construction employed at both railway crossings.

There are four standard two-span bridges and a further three standard four-span bridges carrying side roads and farm access tracks over the motorway. In addition there is a single-span piled bridge carrying the motorway over the Mineral Railway, a four-span structure carrying the A638 over the motorway, and the Loversall Carr Railway Bridge. The latter structure, costing approximately £1.25 million, is of interest because of the need to produce negligible settlement of the East Coast Main Line. The 40-metre depth of the peat and soft clays in the area rendered it impractical to found the structures on piles. The two central piers were designed with hollow polystyrene filled bases so that the resultant loading was equal to the weight of the material being excavated. Consequently, in the immediate vicinity of the railway tracks the loading should be no greater than prior to construction. The ends of the structure rest on bankseats on the approach embankments. The archive contains a paper by Ken Hunt on the *use of compensated foundations* for the Loversall Carr Bridge.[169]

The A638 was a particular problem in that a perfectly straight road crosses over a 15-metre cutting on the alignment of the original road. The number of services in the A638 verges further aggravated the situation. As it was desirable to build the bridge on the line of the A638, a temporary diversion on a 15-metres-high bund had to be constructed to allow excavation of the bridge site. Consequently, all the services had to be temporarily diverted and on completion of the bridge diverted back into the bridge. Not more than 300 metres from this area is Hatchell Wood Railway Bridge. As the motorway is in a 15-metre cutting it passes beneath a local railway line already in the cutting. The contract for this was let and supervised by British Rail. Prior to excavation beneath the line, a bridge deck with lines *in situ* was placed upon cast *in situ* bored piles, involving closure of the line for 24 hours. Upon excavation the piles were faced with concrete to give a final appearance as conventional bridge piers and abutments.

Some 47 kilometres of piped drainage along with 10 km of open ditch was employed in draining the motorway and intercepted existing land drainage. In addition, two pumping station contracts were let by the local Drainage Boards to facilitate outfalls.

Statutory undertakers' works involved the diversion of nine medium and high voltage overhead YEB supplies and several underground diversions, four high-pressure gas main diversions, one being a twin 600mm diameter national gas grid main, protection measures to existing sleeved mains and several low pressure diversions, one major and three minor Post Office Telephone diversions, two major and three minor Water Supply diversions and minor diversions of foul and surface water sewers.

The Contracts Manager was Jeffs and Project Manager Peter Heslop. Peter Brannan was the Resident Engineer.

Wadworth Viaduct

The contract covered road and bridgeworks and extended the existing Barlborough to Wadworth section of the M18 across the A1(M) Doncaster By-pass to link with the Wadworth to Armthorpe section of the M18.

Wadworth Viaduct carries the M18 over the A1(M) interchange roundabout, White Cross Lane and the A1(M). The viaduct has seven 39.25-metre spans and there is a longitudinal joint between the carriageways.

The deck for each carriageway is constructed of six longitudinal steel plate girders. The girders were fabricated in approximately 20-metre sections and welded on site to form a continuous construction. Generally two beam sections were welded together on the ground to give a lifting length of 39.25 metres, which were lifted into place in pairs for stability during erection.

Each deck is supported on reinforced concrete abutments and six pairs of reinforced concrete piers, each pier is tapered and widens out at the top to form a crosshead. All piers and abutments are supported on steel H-piles, with an average length of 12 metres. Steel H-piles were selected because of the aggressive ground conditions, with sulphate concentrations up to Class 5. This rendered the use of concrete piles impracticable, and necessitated the waterproofing of the pier and abutment bases, in addition to the use of sulphate-resisting cement.

Roadworks entailed the construction of approximately 250 metres of motorway connecting the completed section of the M18 from the west with the viaduct together with its surfacing. The Main Contractor was Dowsett Engineering Construction Ltd, and the subcontractor for the steelwork was Fairfield-Mabey Ltd. The contract commenced in November 1976, and was completed in January 1979. The Contracts Manager was Jeffs and the Agent Carl Morehouse. The Resident Engineer was John Bowerman and the Assistant Resident Engineer Alan Phillips.

The Wadworth Viaduct

12   Motorways in Humberside (formerly Lindsey County)

History

The South Humberside Feasibility Study recommended a new east–west route replacing the existing A18 to link Scunthorpe, Grimsby and Immingham with the national motorway network. The *Yorkshire and Humberside – Regional Strategy* report[170] prepared by the Yorkshire and Humberside Economic Council and Board in 1970 concluded:

> The future development of the region will demand better communications, in which roads will have special importance. The impetus which road construction has developed must be sustained both between and within our urban areas.

The major industrialised developments in the area included:

- The British Steel Corporation Anchor Works to the east of Scunthorpe
- The docks at Immingham with associated development – the growth of these was probably more rapid than in other parts of the country.
- The development of the docks and industry at Grimsby.

The planning, design and supervision of construction of the M180 was undertaken by North Eastern Road construction Unit – its West Riding (later West Yorkshire) and Durham County Sub-Units – and Scott Wilson Kirkpatrick & Partners.

South Humberside Motorway M180

The M180 South Humberside Motorway connects from the Tudworth Hall Link Road (A18(M)), which was built under the Hatfield-Thorne Contract, to the A18 South of Scunthorpe at Bottesford Moor.

From this point the motorway runs south of Scunthorpe, north of Brigg and thence to Grimsby, Immingham and the East Coast. The M180 connects to the Humber Bridge via an improved Trunk Road, A15. The motorway, which forms part of the complex of new roads linking both North and South Humberside with the rest of the country, has special significance for trade with Europe.

The completion of the M18 provided a link between the M1 near Rotherham and the M62 near Goole with connection to the M180. This completed the motorway 'box' between the industrialised centres of West and South Yorkshire and Lancashire, the East Coast 'Euroports' and the nation's motorway system. The M180 was divided into eight contracts, which are described below.

Tudworth to Sandtoft Advanced Earthworks

A contract for advanced earthworks was let to Sir Alfred McAlpine in the sum of £331,596. Work started in November 1975 and involved the placement of embankment fill for this section of the motorway crossing the alluvial plain of the River Don. This contract was let at the same time as the Advanced Earthworks Contract for the Trent Approaches and involved the same contractor and supervisory teams. The works were completed in July 1976.

Thorne to Sandtoft

The 24-month contract was awarded to A. Monk & Co. Ltd in the sum of £4.8 million in May 1976. The works consisted of the construction of approximately seven km of dual three-lane motorway together with the addition of a third lane to the existing A18(M) for approximately one km. An advanced earthworks contract was completed near to the county boundary, overlying the alluvial plain of the Old River Don. Surcharge was removed from this embankment at a later stage in the contract.

There is one partial west-facing interchange at Tudworth. Two side roads, A18 Doncaster to Scunthorpe Trunk Road and Crow Tree Bank, together with two accommodation tracks, were diverted on embankment and bridges over the motorway.

Tudworth Road Bridge over the M180, a two-span structure, carries the A18 at a 25° skew. Crow Tree Bank Bridge, a four-span structure carries an unclassified road at a 5° skew. Dale Mount and Plains Lane Bridges are three-span square accommodation bridges. Three 2.9-metre diameter Armco multiplate culverts were constructed to maintain the flow of the existing main drainage together with numerous smaller culverts.

The site of the Works generally overlies Bunter Sandstone covered by a mixture of alluvium, peat, wind-blown sand, clay, silts, sands and gravels, some of which are glacial deposits. Extensive treatment was necessary in certain locations to minimise the effect of the underlying alluvium and peat particularly in the disused watercourses. Generally the land is flat and has been substantially improved by man-made watercourses leaving many disused channels. Substantial drainage ditches were excavated on each side of the motorway and major improvements involving the construction of new channels, flood banks and pump houses were provided by the Severn Trent Water Authority to accommodate the drainage from both the M180 and M18.

The motorway is generally on shallow embankment approximately two metres high. There is one small cut section adjacent to the A18 where the motorway passes through Tudworth Hill. Excavated material from the cutting and the ditches was, where possible, used in the embankments. Unsuitable material was deposited in landscape areas and on a noise attenuation bund at Tudworth. Additional filling material for the embankment was obtained from workings adjacent to the route. The amount of excavation was 400,000 cubic metres and the filling required was 760,000 cubic metres.

The contract was completed in May 1978. The Contract Manager was Shields and the Agent Mike Clark, later Brian Venn. The Resident Engineer was Dawson, the Assistant Resident Engineer Roger Haith.

Sandtoft to Trent

This contract, awarded to Sir Alfred McAlpine & Son (Northern) Ltd in the sum of £6,783,300, started in November 1976.

It involved the construction of dual three-lane motorway between Sandtoft and the River Trent together with a 'diamond' interchange at Woodhouse. The carriageways of the motorway are of rigid construction, the majority being experimental Continuously Reinforced Concrete Pavement (see description below, pp.198-200), of varying depths and reinforcement position, with the remainder as comparative lengths of unreinforced and reinforced pavement with variations to joints and underlay. The design and construction of the experimental pavement on the M180 is covered in a paper by Don Hunt,[171] the *Journal of the Institution of Highway Engineers* April 1981 and in the *C & CA News Release* of August 1978.[172]

The hard shoulder is also unreinforced concrete pavement. The Transport and Road Research Laboratory monitored the experiment. Only 340 metres of the motorway is of flexible construction, at either side of the two underbridges and at the tie-in to the adjacent Thorne-Sandtoft section. The slip roads and side road diversions are also of flexible construction. The three main side road diversions are North Idle Lane (unclassified), the A161 and Mutton Lane (C108).

This length of motorway crosses flat agricultural land which is generally only one to two metres above OD and consists of wind-blown sand at the western end and alluvial clays peats at the eastern end with the underlying Keuper Marl of the Permo-Triassic Series surfacing in the central area which forms part of the old Isle of Axholme. The marl is divided into two by a deposit of alluvial sands.

The motorway is basically formed on shallow embankment throughout, apart from the central Interchange area where superior ground conditions permit construction at or near ground level or in very shallow cutting.

In the past, in order to drain the land, a close and complex network of artificial channels and pumping stations had been constructed. The slow moving water in these channels is below the level of the water in the floodbank-enclosed river except at low tide, and pumping stations were used to discharge into the River Trent. Because of the increased run-off resulting from the paved motorway it was necessary for the local Internal Drainage Boards and River Authority to improve the whole drainage of the area. Side ditches dug along both sides of the motorway and intersected by culverts carry carriageway and embankment drainage.

All bridges to the west of the Woodhouse Interchange are founded on piles driven to the underlying marl and associated gravels with the remainder on spread footings. North Idle Lane and Mutton Lane Bridges have four spans and carry unclassified roads. Hatfield West Drain Bridge carries the motorway and has a span of 11 metres. Woodcarr Farm and Belwood Farm Bridges carry farm accommodation roads. River Torne and South Engine Drain bridges of two spans carry the motorway over the river and the drain. Woodhouse Bridge of two spans takes the A161 road over the motorway. A 6.3-metres span Armco pipe arch with concrete headwalls carries the motorway over Folly Drain and a 2.1-metres diameter Armco pipe provides pedestrian access.

The contract was completed in October 1978. The Contracts Manager was Abbott succeeded by Howard Stephens. Brian Melling was the Agent. The Resident Engineer was Hunt, and Barry Griffiths the Assistant Resident Engineer.

Continuously Reinforced Concrete Pavement (CRCP)

The first uses of Continuously Reinforced Concrete Pavement in the United Kingdom were on two short lengths of the M62, Balkholme to Caves contract (see pp.173-6).

This form of construction operates on the principle of promoting hairline cracking at frequent intervals of 1.5 to 2.0 metres with a relatively heavy longitudinal reinforcement (0.6 per cent by area) restricting the cracks to a width which maintains aggregate interlock load transfer and do not require sealing. This results in increased flexibility of the slab which will cope with any settlement of sub-soil that may occur. The basic design was developed by the Transport and Road Research Laboratory and was based on Belgian practice where it had been extensively used. It was refined by the West Yorkshire and Durham Sub-Units at the design stage of the two contracts.

The overall carriageway construction depth is 460 mm, the CRCP being 210 mm, 230 mm and 250 mm thick, the remainder is made up in sub-base, for which the Contractor used the cement-bound granular alternative. There are two lengths of identical thickness, one containing

CRCP reinforcement

the reinforcement at mid-depth and the other at one-third depth. There is an additional section containing fabric reinforcement 7.6 km long. The unreinforced concrete hard shoulder was paved, after the 11.2-metre-wide slab, by a mini-paver, which constructed the trapezoidal drainage channel at the same time. Elsewhere, the overall rigid construction depth is still 360 mm, but is made up of 180 mm unreinforced or reinforced pavement and 180 mm sub-base. The unreinforced concrete pavement has narrow, unsealed, contraction joints 3 mm wide and no polythene underlay.

Concrete was mixed on site using an automatic batching plant and transported to the paver using purpose-built four-axle non-tipping ejector trunks with a 7.5-cubic metre capacity, which matched the batch size. The trucks were fitted with hydraulically actuated sliding ejector bulkheads and tailgates which enabled a rapid but controlled discharge to be made onto the belt conveyors feeding the paving machine.

The principal element in the paving unit was a wire guided Guntert and Zimmerman slip form paver incorporating a two-metre-long conforming plate, capable of laying the full carriageway width slab. The machine ran on a pair of crawler tracks and was adjusted for line and level by wires that were positioned outside the machine. The unit was also capable of forming the longitudinal joints. The other units in the train were a transverse joint groove former, transverse joint finisher and a combined brush-texturing and curing spray machine, all of which were carried on rubber tyres and made to McAlpines' specification by SGME. They were also wire-guided, preformed rigid cellular filler strips were inserted by a vertical vibrating blade,

The slip form paver

a removable upper portion was subsequently pulled from the hardened concrete and the resultant groove filled with a neoprene compression seal. The joint finisher incorporated a wide surface float and two vibrating plates adjacent to the filler strip, which traversed the slab across each joint. A two metres-wide wire brush applied the texture transversely and an aluminised curing agent was subsequently sprayed onto the slab.

Trent Approaches Advanced Earthworks

The contract was awarded to Sir Alfred McAlpine (Northern) Ltd in the sum of £1.85 million in November 1975. The contract period was 14 months and the Works consisted of the construction of the approach embankments for the proposed bridge carrying the motorway over the River Trent.

The site of the works overlies alluvial deposits and was, at one time, a plant-covered marsh, which has been reclaimed by controlled warping, resulting in highly fertile Grade I agricultural land. It has, however, a very low bearing capacity and controlled rates of filling were specified to prevent failure. In addition, extensive drainage was carried out to reduce the time for pore water dissipation and more than five hundred instruments were installed within the ground and the embankment to monitor movement and pressure changes. Up to two metres of settlement were anticipated. A drainage layer consisting of rockfill sandwiched between two layers of a permeable membrane formed the base of the embankment. The main core of the embankment consists of lightweight fuel ash surrounded by a bund of heavier material. The works were divided into three stages and included a cessation of filling between stages one and two. Stage I was generally six metres high and eight metres in the future bank seat area. Stages II and III were only executed when the analysis of the instrument readings indicated that it was safe to proceed.

The adjacent West Butterwick Road was raised, in the vicinity of the bridge, to provide additional weight and stability at the end of the embankment. Also included in the contract was approximately one km of shallow embankment, overlaying a peat area where high settlement was anticipated and also a 1½ km-access track from Burringham Road.

Considerable strengthening and widening was carried out by Humberside County Council, on behalf of the Department of Environment, on certain local roads, to cope with the import of material required for this and other M180 contracts, and special measures were included to reduce the nuisance caused by the works.

It is of note that, throughout the duration of the pre-construction soil survey, the existing water table was monitored at ground level, and the design of the embankment and instrumentation scheme was based upon this information. However, the water table when construction commenced was monitored at three metres below ground level, a result of the dry summer and mild winter of 1975/76. This drop in the water table had the effect of reducing the anticipated ground movements, and considerably improved the overall stability of the works when construction commenced.

The Contracts Manager was Abbott and the Agent Mike Graham. The Resident Engineer was Graham Dawson, Assistant Resident Engineer Stephen Kaye.

Glued Segmental Bridge Construction in Yorkshire

The first bridge in the United Kingdom to use glued segmental construction techniques was the Dutch River Bridge in the West Riding, constructed in 1967. The method of construction was proposed to the writer by Tony Dunster of Shepherd Hill & Co. Ltd and the design undertaken by Stewart Woodhead's team was modified.[173, 174]

Tests were carried out during the early stages of the contract to compare the behaviour and suitability of different types of resin and involved the Universities of Leeds, Bradford and Sheffield.

Dutch River Bridge. The first glued segmental bridge in the UK.

Although at this time not far behind the French engineers, who had pioneered the technique, it was to take a further 10 years before Yorkshire Engineers were to get their next opportunity to use glued segmental construction for a major bridge.

In looking at the bridges required for Yorkshire's road programme at least three, including the Trent crossing, were considered for glued segmental construction. This led to the need to look at continental practice and in particular at the launching girders being used. Economy of construction depended on re-use of the launching girder. A visit in 1973 to Enterprises Campenon Bernard in Paris by Gaffney and the writer, followed by a tour of bridges and the casting yards making the segments, confirmed the view that at the first opportunity glued segmental construction should be adopted based on a launching girder similar to that of the French. Approval was given for the West Riding Sub-Unit to proceed with the design of Trent Bridge.

Trent Bridge

The design and construction of the Trent Bridge is well-documented.[175,176] An internal paper by Chaffé[177] deals with the claims issues during construction.

The M180 crosses the River Trent about three kilometres upstream of the existing Keadby Bridge west of Scunthorpe. The design of the Trent Bridge was commenced in 1969 by the West Riding Sub-Unit to carry the dual three-lane motorway over the River Trent and over two side roads, one either side of the river. The river is approximately 150 metres wide and navigable as far as Gainsborough, the main river traffic being barges and coasters. At the bridge site there is a tidal range of about five metres with current flows of up to five knots.

It was necessary for the bridge to be in service and during its construction to provide sufficient headroom and waterway for shipping. However, the soil conditions either side of the river consisted of soft silty river deposits which restricted the height of the approach embankments to about nine metres. The depth available for the deck construction was therefore limited.

Two designs for the bridge were prepared to meet these constraints, one with a deck consisting of steel plate girders with a reinforced concrete deck and the other of continuous pre-cast concrete box construction to be erected using an overhead launching girder, a technique new to this country but used widely on the Continent.

Each design was of four spans with a pier in the centre of the river. E.W.H. Gifford & Partners and Durham Sub-Unit were appointed to undertake the independent design checks of the concrete and the steel solutions respectively under the Department's technical approval procedures.

At the Public Inquiry in December 1973, the Port of Gainsborough Development Association, representing the shipping interests, objected to the proposals on the grounds that shipping would be inhibited by the restriction on headroom and that the centre pier would upset the regime of the river, cause scouring of the river bed and the formation of shoals in the navigation channel.

Prior to the Public Inquiry, the Hydraulics Research Station (HRS) had carried out a float-tracking survey of the river on behalf of the Department. After they had carried out further work, including a hydraulic model test on various shapes of pier to minimise the effects on the regime of the river, and after the design headroom over the river had been increased by one metre, the proposals were confirmed following a second Public Inquiry in October 1974.

The HRS acted as the Department's expert eye-witness at both inquiries. On their advice regular surveys of the river bed by the British Transport Docks Board were instigated, which were to continue throughout the construction period.

In August 1976 tenders were invited for construction of the Trent Bridge. Tenderers were required to price two alternative designs, namely the steel plate girder design and the pre-cast pre-stressed concrete glued segmental design. The Instructions for Tenderers drew attention to the mobile nature of the river-bed material and the likelihood of erosion around any temporary works placed in the riverbed. It was stated that allowance should be made for measures to detect and control erosion which the tenderer deemed necessary to enable him to fulfil his general obligations relating to the temporary works. An HRS Report – *Effect of Pier Shape on Erosion around the Pier* – was included with the tender documents. At the request of one of the tenderers, the results of the float-tracking surveys in the river were sent to all tenderers.

Tenders were returned in November 1976, the lowest being from Cementation Construction Ltd for the concrete design for the sum of £3.34 million. The lowest tender for the steel design was £3.48 million. The two-year contract was awarded to Cementation. Work started in January 1977 and the due date for completion was January 1979.

The local geology consisted of a layer of soft silty river deposits, with peat inclusions of varying thickness, overlying marl at a depth of 15 to 20 metres. In order to allow time for settlement the approach embankments, which have a core of lightweight fill, were built as part of the advanced earthworks contract already referred to.

Instrumentation of the ground below the embankments was undertaken in order to monitor their stability during construction and the rates of filling were adjusted as necessary. Information was also obtained on ground movements both vertically and horizontally, particularly in the area of the west bank seat.

Balanced cantilever construction

Pier construction

The design provided for a symmetrical bridge of four spans of 48.5, 85, 85 and 48.5 metres. Each carriageway was supported by an independent superstructure of twin concrete box girders varying in depth, from approximately 4.9 metres at the piers to 2.1 metres at mid-centre spans and 1.7 metres at the bank seats. Each box girder was made up of 91 pre-cast concrete units three metres long and four metres wide with two metre deck slab cantilevers. The units varied in weight from 35 to 75 tonnes.

The units were constructed by counter-casting one unit against another to form the faces to be joined. The joint faces had a corrugated profile to carry the shear force at the joints before the adhesive cured.

The box girders were designed to be built by the 'balanced' cantilever method of construction using a launching girder to position the units. The unit over a pier is first erected and then units are added to each side in turn to complete the balanced cantilevers. The ends of these cantilevers are then joined at mid-centre spans and extended at the bank seats onto the bearings to form a continuous box girder.

The units were joined using epoxy resin adhesive and stressed together first by a temporary pre-stress and then by permanent pre-stress following some two units beyond the advancing ends of the balanced cantilevers. The temporary pre-stress is removed in stages.

The epoxy adhesive is spread on both faces of the joints to a thickness of one to two mm. Whilst initially performing the function of a lubricant to assist in the mating of the units, it eventually cures to provide a water and grout tight gasket at the joints and to develop sufficient strength to transmit shear and comprehensive forces across the joint in conjunction with the permanent pre-stressing.

The centre river pier has a specially shaped base and sheet pile skirt to minimise the effects of scour and is designed for vessel impact. The shape was determined on the basis of tests carried out at the Hydraulics Research Station.

The drainage was by continuous entry hollow cast iron kerb units. Navigation lights were fixed to the centre and west piers and over the navigation channel.

Cementation sub-contracted the supply of the launching girder and the manufacture of the pre-cast concrete units to PSC Ltd and Dowmac Concrete Ltd respectively. Instead of a launching girder of the type shown on the Contract Drawings and used on the Continent by Campernon-Bernard, who together with PSC Ltd were associated with Freyssinet International, the Contractor engaged A.R. Gee & Partners Consulting Engineers to design a form of girder operating on different principles.

A number of problems occurred during the contract, and the following is a very brief summary:

  a) Exceptionally bad weather occurred whilst constructing the cofferdams for the east and west piers, which led to an extension of contract
  b) Serious problems were encountered with the centre cofferdam. Dewatering was not initially successful and a diving survey revealed there was a lack of structural integrity of the cofferdam. It was some time before successful dewatering was achieved.
  c) Scour problems were experienced under the jetty and the box piles supporting it were strengthened.
  d) There were teething problems with the manufacture of the 364 deck units. By mid-March only 105 units, instead of 223 units programmed, had been cast.
  e) The Contractor experienced considerable difficulties in commissioning the launching girder and it was not until February 1978 that the first concrete deck unit was erected, some 19 weeks behind programme.
  f) The slow progress on deck erection and its effects on reducing the earnings of the site workforce led to industrial action in the form of working to rule, overtime bans and then to strikes intermittently for the remainder of the year.
  h) In January 1979, the delivery of units to site was prevented by the national transport strike and work was suspended for a period.
  i) Throughout the winter there were delays owing to the abnormally bad weather.

The four cantilevers on the east pier were completed in mid-September 1978 approximately 29 weeks behind programme. By mid-November 1978, five out of 12 deck cantilevers had been erected and the launching girder moved forward to erect units on the west pier. Deck erection was however by this time 35 weeks behind programme and progress was bedevilled by mechanical failures and strikes.

By the end of June 1979 all 364 units had been erected. Completion of the finishing works allowed the westbound carriageway to be opened to traffic in July 1979 by Kenneth Clarke MP, Parliamentary Secretary for Transport. The eastbound carriageway was completed in October 1979 and opened to traffic later that month.

The Contracts Manager for Cementation was Tom Moss, the Agent Colin Scargill who was to succeed Marshall. Alan Moreton was the Resident Engineer and Keith Jones the Assistant Resident Engineer. Trent Bridge was the first motorway bridge in the UK to be built by the cantilever method using 'glued' segmental construction.

Despite the trials and tribulations of both Contractor and Engineer, this splendid bridge enables a quick crossing of the River Trent and the tedium to motorists of the bottleneck at the old Keadby Bridge is long forgotten.

Trent to Scunthorpe including M181

The contract was awarded to A.F. Budge Contractors Ltd in the tender sum of £4.44 million and commenced in July 1976.

The Works consisted of the construction of approximately 2.1 km of dual two and three lane motorway from the River Trent eastwards, the 4.1 km M181 Scunthorpe Link motorway northwards from the Midmoor Interchange, and approximately 1.7 km of connecting roads and slip roads. The main earthworks and pre-earthworks drainage from the River Trent eastwards for approximately one km were constructed as part of the Advance Earthworks Contract already described.

The motorway was formed on embankment throughout with a height maintained at a minimum of two metres above original ground level. On completion a total of 600,000 cubic metres of fill was imported, made up of slag waste rock fill as a granular drainage blanket at the base of the embankments, PFA and sand fill from borrow pits adjacent to the motorway. Throughout the Contract length the motorway crossed over flat agricultural land, which was generally one to three metres above OD. The Advanced Earthworks embankment on the eastern approach to the River Trent was constructed early in order to obtain the majority of settlement prior to carriageway construction. Additionally the higher fills in Midmoor Interchange stood for 40 weeks prior to commencement of carriageway construction.

Because of the increased run-off which resulted from the paved motorway it was necessary to improve sections of the local drainage system and this was carried out by the appropriate Internal Drainage Board. The Contractor elected to provide a flexible pavement with *in situ* concrete drainage channel.

All bridges are founded on piles driven to the underlying Keuper Marl. Midmoor Bridge carries the M181 over the M180 motorway on a two-span bridge. The M181 Burringham Road Bridge carries the B1450, Brumy Common Lane Bridge carries an unclassified road on a four-span bridge and White House Farm and Grange Farm Bridges carry farm accommodation roads on three-span identical bridges.

The contract was completed in December 1978. The Contracts Manager was Gordon Muir, and the Agent David Threadkell. The design and supervision of construction of the M180 contracts so far described were undertaken by the West Riding (later West Yorkshire) Sub-Unit. The Resident Engineer was John Holroyd, the Assistant Resident Engineer Dave Coldwell.

Bill Rogers MP, Minister of Transport, who became one of the 'gang of four' in the Social Democratic Party (SDP), performed the opening ceremony.

The Scunthorpe Southern By-pass

There had been continuous pressure by local interests to speed up the programme for completion of the whole of the M180 from Thorne to Immingham/Grimsby. The section from Thorne to the Woodhouse Interchange on the A161 was then open to traffic, as was the M180 Brigg By-pass from the A18/A15 junction at Castlethorpe west of Brigg to the Elsham Interchange.

The Scunthorpe Southern By-pass, which followed, commenced to the east of Midmoor Interchange and connected with the Brigg By-pass at Castlethorpe. Links into Scunthorpe were formed by Midmoor Interchange and the M181 from the west, and Ermine Street Interchange and the A18 from the east.

The 13.9 km by-pass is carried in an easterly direction on a shallow fill over the River Trent Flood Plain. The motorway on low embankment joined the Brigg By-pass to the west of the River Ancholme.

Two balancing reservoirs have been constructed to take the surface water run-off from the carriageways and discharge it slowly into the existing land drainage systems.

From west of Scotter Road to Ermine Street Interchange the motorway has dual two-lane carriageways and from Ermine Street to Castlethorpe dual three-lane carriageways. 6.4 km of side roads were constructed. The £13.5 million contract for the M180 Scunthorpe By-pass was awarded to the Balfour Beatty/Clugston Joint Venture.

The Works, which started in November 1976 and were completed in November 1978, involved 1.5 million cubic metres of earthworks, 167,000

Scunthorpe By-pass

cubic metres of sub-base, and 420,000 square metres of surfacing. The spans of the bridges vary between 16 and 30 m.

Mike Hillcoat[178] the Resident Engineer recalls an amusing episode. 'The Contract Manager on one of his routine trips stopped at Twigmoor Lane Bridge site where considerable activity was in progress for a concrete pour. One man at the top of the cutting was eating sandwiches and the General Foreman was told to go and tell the man he was sacked. He came back and told Rush that he was a local man who had just come to watch!'

The A18 Springfield Bridge, with a span of 45 metres, has a 48-sided central column support. The Bottesford Beck and Scotter road culverts are 80 metres and 45 metres long respectively. Drainage involved 50 piped culverts.

Scott Wilson Kirkpatrick and Partners undertook the design and supervision on behalf of the North Eastern Road Construction Unit. Their supervising Partners were 'Mac' McDermott and James. The project engineers for design were Dave Flint (Roads) and Dudley Ings (Bridges). The Chief Resident Engineer was Hillcoat. The Resident Engineers were Mike Smith, Don Lee and John Richardson.

The Contracts Manager for Balfour Beatty was Tony Rush with Mike Welton Project Manager, and Rod Storr Construction Manager.

Brigg By-pass

The following has been taken from an archive paper prepared by Ted Purver.[179]

> Brigg is a small market town (population 5,300) in North Lincolnshire. Its full name Glanford Brigg derives from the location of the town at the crossing of the Ancholme. Prior to the construction of the New River Ancholme and major drainage works in the 1630s the Ancholme valley or level was a marshy swamp and would have reverted to such condition had it not been for the drainage improvement works carried out under John Rennie and his son between 1800 and 1844. The construction of dykes and a system of low level catchwater drainage channels with sluices and locks at Ferriby on the south bank of the Humber greatly improved the drainage and reduce flooding in times of heavy rainfall. Following the Land Drainage Act 1930 further improvements were carried out including the provision of pumped drainage of the low-level system administered under the Ancholme Internal Drainage Board.
>
> The Doncaster–Immingham–Grimsby Trunk road A18 carrying very heavy traffic passed through the centre of the town's Market Place and shopping streets. The narrow Wrawby and Bigby Streets had been

made one-way. Traffic included a high proportion of heavy goods vehicles with oil and chemical industry tankers from the oil refinery at South Killingholme.

Plans for a trunk road by-pass of Brigg dated back to the early 1930s but it took the massive explosion at the chemical plant at Flixborough near Scunthorpe in 1974 to prompt urgency for the town to be by-passed. Political pressure resulted in an earlier start to the South Humberside Motorway.

Tender documents were hurriedly prepared to achieve a contract commencement as soon as possible in the spring of 1975. Further site geotechnical investigations were carried out and these revealed the need for design reconsiderations. The original design preparation by Lindsey County Council had by then been passed on to the newly formed Humberside County Council, whose Director of Technical Services was Len Crossley. At the beginning of 1975 Scott Wilson Kirkpatrick and Partners, who were already appointed Consultants for the design of the South Humberside Motorway to the east and west of the Brigg By-pass section, and had carried out a Transportation Study for Humberside, were invited to take over the design responsibility and supervise the construction of the Brigg By-pass.

Design changes were made to several of the eight bridge structures and slope stability changes were necessary to both Elsham and Wrawby cuttings. The approach embankments to the New River Ancholme Bridge were also changed to use lightweight fill material (PFA and Cement Works flue ash), constructed in stages at controlled rates of fill. These embankments were surcharged in order to increase the rate of settlement.

These late changes necessitated the negotiation for the acquisition of some additional land not included in the original compulsory purchase orders. These negotiations were completed in four weeks preceding the commencement of the 27-month contract in May 1975.

Typical overbridge

The £9.25 million contract for the 7.37-km by-pass was awarded to Sir Alfred McAlpine & Co. The Contracts Manager was Abbott and Paul McMillan was Agent. Scott Wilson's partner James was the Engineer with Purver the Chief Resident Engineer and Richard Curry his Deputy.

It was originally intended that a two-level roundabout interchange would be constructed at Scawby Brook with a link southwards to the A15 Lincoln road and that this would form the Western end of Brigg By-pass. However, a decision to re-route the A15 along the line of Ermine Street, by-passing Redbourne and Hibaldstow, was pending, so Brigg By-pass western end was made 500 metres west of New River Ancholme Bridge and a temporary link road to the A18 was provided. This reduced the length of the dual three-lane motorway to 7.2 km with the two-level roundabout junction, A15 North link road to the Humber Bridge, at the Eastern end of the by-pass.

A confirmatory geotechnical investigation was carried out at the beginning of the contract and instrumentation was installed in the settlement areas east and west of the New River Ancholme. These were monitored throughout the construction of the staged controlled rate embankment construction. Embankments were constructed on a

450-mm-thick drainage layer of crushed rock to assist relief of pore water pressures. It was found that the very hard chalk material from Elsham quarry was suitable for drainage and capping layers under the pavement construction, generating a substantial cost saving to the contract.

The Oxford Clays in Wrawby cutting required one in six slopes for stability and where this slope could not be achieved because of existing housing development countefort drains were provided. The cutting slopes at Elsham cutting and the A15 Interchange slip roads were stabilised by chalk fill material.

Eight bridges were constructed, the new River Ancholme Bridge, a three-span structure, being the largest with its centre span crossing the navigable river channel. Piled foundations were provided at the river bridge, three road overbridges and the railway underbridge at Elsham. It is noteworthy that one of the country's first 'badger' tunnels under a motorway was provided beneath the embankment at Elsham woods. A 'badger' bridge was also provided at a diverted watercourse.[180]

John Horan, Parliamentary Under Secretary of State for Transport, officially opened the Brigg By-pass in September 1977.

The Humber Bridge

Although not a motorway bridge, no story of the strategic motorway system in the North East would be complete without some record of the Humber Bridge. When constructed in 1981 with a main span of 1,410 metres it held the record for the longest span suspension bridge in the world until overtaken by the Japanese.

The bridge which links the M180 with the M62 via the A15 and A63 Trunk roads resulted from studies by Freeman Fox & Partners the first in 1935, the second in 1955 and the promotion of a Parliamentary Bill in 1958 by the Kingston upon Hull Corporation. The Humber Bridge Acts of 1959 to 1973 gave powers to the Humber Bridge Board to construct, operate and maintain the bridge and acquire the necessary land and finance for its building and to take tolls for its use.

In 1969 the Government produced a report entitled *Humberside – A Feasibility Study*, which recommended that the bridge should be built to enable the Humberside region to develop in the 1980s and induce commercial and industrial expansion.

In 1971 the government decided to lend the finance for the project to the Humber Bridge Board following which Freeman Fox & Partners were instructed to proceed with the design work.

The bridge has many innovatory features and the superstructure follows closely the concept first used for the Severn Bridge completed in 1966. An unusual feature, which resulted from topographical and geological considerations, is the inequality in length of the side spans; 280 metres at the north end and 530 metres at the south.

A record span

Wind tunnel tests were carried out at the National Maritime Institute, Feltham on models of the deck and towers to establish their aerodynamic stability. The foundation for the Hessle tower was designed as a massive reinforced concrete slab founded in chalk some eight metres below ground level. On the Barton side the ground conditions were much more difficult due to erosion of the sound chalk. The alluvial and glacial materials overlaying the Kimmeridge clay were too variable to support the heavy foundations. Because the clay stratum was also susceptible to exposure it was decided to sink two 24-metre diameter concrete caissons of two concentric cylinders joined by six cross walls, eight metres into the clay where the bottom slab was founded.

The main towers consist of two hollow reinforced concrete legs 155.5 metres high braced by four horizontal beams, the lowest of which supports the deck. The box-section of the deck is 22 metres wide and 4.5 metres deep with three metres cantilevered panels on each side carrying the walkways. Prior to assembly the deck steelwork was given a thorough protective treatment and after erection two further coats of chlorinated rubber paint.

Each main cable carries a load of about 19,000 tonnes and consists of 14,948 galvanised drawn wires of five mm diameter; the wires are grouped into 37 strands for ease of erection and anchoring. For each cable on the Hessle side an additional 800 wires were provided for the increased tension due to their steeper inclination.

The contract for construction was awarded to British Bridge Builders, a consortium of companies comprising Sir William Arrol, Cleveland Bridge and Engineering, Redpath Dorman Long and John Howard and Company. Work started on the southern approach road in July 1972. In March 1973 John Howard commenced the 26-month contract for the sub-structure construction. Construction was not without its difficulties in dealing with the wrath of the Humber, the elements, and problems with steelworkers endemic in the industry at the time. The bridge has an advanced toll system.

Her Majesty the Queen opened the Humber Bridge in July 1981.

13 The Demise of the Road Construction Units

Following a review of expenditure on motorways and trunk roads and the announced cuts of £60 million in the White Paper on *Transport Policy* of June 1977, consideration was given to the future organisation for road construction.

In 1978 a further paper from the Department set out the staffing needs to complete the trunk road programme into at least the late 1980s. Discussions took place with the Local Authority associations and the unions.

In March 1980, following the study by Sir Derek Raynor, the Minister announced to the House of Commons the results of the study and his policy on the future of the Sub-Units. Alarm bells rang for the Counties. On the phasing out of the Sub-Units the Minister reported, 'I intend in particular to make increased use of Consultants who have a large part to play; and also of agency arrangements where the case made for them by the County Councils concerned clearly makes sense'.

Government policy was now directed toward privatisation and the transfer of work to the private sector. Consultants were short-listed and those offering the 'best deal' for staff to transfer with their schemes were recommended.

In the North East Region in 1981, Bullen and Partners were to take the Durham Sub-Unit Schemes and Pell Frischmann, Babtie Shaw and Morton, and John Burrows, the West Yorkshire Sub-Unit schemes, which included Airedale and Settle, Kirkhamgate to Dishforth and the Lincoln relief road. Certain schemes did fall to be undertaken by the County Councils.

Many of the local authority sub-unit staff took early retirement and a wealth of older experience was lost. Others saw joining the private sector as an opportunity and a number went on to become Partners or achieved prominence in their new firms as Divisional Directors, Technical Directors and Associates.

With the reorganisation of local government in 1986, when Margaret Thatcher 'saw off' Ken Livingstone and the Metropolitan County Councils, the major conurbations lost their strategic planning, highway and transportation authorities.

This was another major drain of local authority expertise and more work was transferred to consultants.

It was then that the writer 'retired' from local government and joined Pell Frischmann as Chief Executive to set up a new company within the Group, Pell Frischmann Consultants Ltd. The Company had early success in tendering and winning a large portfolio of motorway and trunk road schemes from the Ministry. Both Babties and Bullens achieved similar success with later Motorway and Trunk Road Contracts in the North East.

14 A1 Improvement Schemes Carried Out in the Mid-1980s to Early 1990s

In the mid-1980s traffic measurements and forecasts suggested that traffic on the A1 had been growing at a higher rate than the national average. The proposed A1 scheme standard of dual three-lane all-purpose was therefore appropriate for design year flows of 40,000 vehicles per day and above.

The Secretary of State for Transport indicated a commitment to the upgrading of the trunk road link between the motorway system in Yorkshire and the road network in the North East of England, and the Department had embarked on a comprehensive programme of improvements. The following schemes were completed on the Trunk Road A1 in the 1980s and 1990s.

Bramham to Wetherby

In the 1990s traffic flows on this section of the A1 exceeded the recommended capacity for a large part of the year. Average traffic flows were 43,000 vehicles per day and were expected to increase to between 57,000 and 70,000 vehicles per day by the year 2007. Other factors, including a very high content of heavy commercial vehicles (40 per cent during the normal working day), unsatisfactory features such as the numerous central reserve gaps and direct private access, the use of A1 by slow moving agricultural vehicles and cyclists, pedestrians crossing at grade, and the need to reduce traffic to a single lane in each direction during maintenance works, all led to a high accident potential and unacceptable traffic delays.

Pell Frischmann Consultants Ltd was responsible for feasibility and design studies, detailed design and contract documentation on behalf of the Department of Transport. They were employed as Engineer for the Works, which were constructed by Monk Construction Ltd at a value of £15 million. Work started in June 1990 and was completed in March 1993. Under the scheme the A1 was widened to dual three-lane plus hard shoulders, enabling at least two lanes to be maintained in each direction, even during major maintenance works.

All central reserve gaps and direct private accesses onto A1 were closed, and the several junctions in the Bramham area were rationalised to provide single points of entry and exit linked by local distributor roads. The use of the A1 by agricultural vehicles has been minimised by the provision of an extensive network of new access roads and the construction of a farm accommodation bridge.

A separate cycleway has been provided between Boston Spa and Wetherby and appropriate signing to use local roads between Bramham and Boston Spa has facilitated cycling. The need to cross the A1 on foot has been removed by linking footpaths to overbridges at Bowcliffe Hall, Tenter Hill and Clifford Moor.

The existing A1 lay immediately to the west of Bramham village on a high embankment 18 metres above the village square. Even though traffic had been screened visually by mature planting, noise levels were very high.

The A1 has been realigned away from the village into a nine-metre cutting and is completely hidden from the village by the existing A1 embankment. One carriageway of the existing A1 has been retained as a local distributor road and carries only local traffic. Noise levels in the village have been reduced by more than half and the local distributor road acts as a by-pass of Bramham for local traffic accessing the A1.

The work involved the improvement by a combination of widening and realignment of some 6.5 km of the A1 from dual two-lane to dual three-lane carriageway. Full width hard shoulders were provided throughout except for the section between the existing Bowcliffe Hall retaining walls where insufficient width was available.

Six new slip roads were constructed, two at each of the Tenter Hill and Grange Moor interchanges on the northbound carriageway, and one at each end of the Wetherby Road and Aberford Road junctions on the southbound carriageway. Some 3.7 km of side roads and 6 km of private accommodation accesses were diverted or reconstructed.

Four overbridges were constructed over the A1: Paradise Farm Accommodation Bridge (four-spans); Bowcliffe Hall Bridge a single-span replacement deck; Tenter Hill Bridge (four-spans); and Clifford Moor Footbridge (two-spans). The two existing bridges at the Grange Moor interchange were demolished and replaced by four three-span bridges. Other structures included a pre-cast reinforced concrete sign gantry spanning the northbound carriageway, and crib walls supporting the A1 embankment.

For Pell Frischmann Consultants Ltd the Director in Charge and Engineer was John Gallagher, the Resident Engineer was John Land, toward the end of the contract succeeded by Barry Drewett who was Assistant Resident Engineer together with Saltmarsh.

For the Contractor, Monk/Trafalgar House Construction, the Project Manager (Agent) was Geoff Wolfenden. The Agent Roadworks was Rod Barrett, with Agent Structures Gordon Grey.

The second Wetherby
By-pass
Swan Photography

Wetherby By-pass and Wetherby to Walshford Junction Improvements

Pell Frischmann Consultants Ltd was appointed by the Department of Transport in 1981 to undertake feasibility and design studies for the schemes. Following preparation of detailed designs, drawings and contract documentation, the consultants were employed as the Engineer to supervise the construction of the Works.

The 2.5 km by-pass runs between Sweep Farm and the B1244, York Road and was constructed to dual two-lane all-purpose trunk road standards. The contract was let at the end of July 1986 to John Laing Construction Ltd in a tender sum of £9.93 million. The Works commenced in August 1986 with a contract period of 24 months in the case of the by-pass and 21 months for the Junction Improvements.

A turf-cutting ceremony was held in Wetherby Grange Park in September. Councillor David Hudson, the Mayor of Wetherby, cut a sod from the cricket pitch, using the spade which had been used by his father at the inauguration of the construction of the original Wetherby By-pass in 1957. Chilton, the Resident Engineer, said, 'I did advise him to keep it for possible future use for the next Wetherby By-pass in another 30 years time!'

Tony Homer, the Director of Transport for Yorkshire and Humberside, did reveal after the ceremony that the dual carriageway would eventually be made three-lane to the north and south of Wetherby.

The scheme removed two major accident blackspots and sources of delay to A1 users; namely Walton Road central reserve crossing and the

218 / Building the Network: The North East of England

River Wharfe New Bridge

Wetherby Roundabout. Substandard horizontal and vertical alignments, particularly in the vicinity of the disused railway, were improved and a central reserve safety barrier was installed.

It was a challenging project involving a major bridge across the River Wharfe and five other bridges, three of which were advanced works to minimise traffic delays during the next phase of A1 improvements to the north of Wetherby.

The DTp were most concerned at the effect of the scheme on local residents and landscaped earth bunds and noise barriers were incorporated to minimise noise and visual intrusion. The scheme was also designed to minimise the impact on Wetherby Racecourse, Wetherby Grange Park and other farming interests.

A feature of the scheme was a 450-metre dual-carriageway temporary diversion designed to facilitate the demolition of the disused railway bridge located to the south of Wetherby racecourse. Traffic was diverted away from what was basically an on-line improvement to permit the permanent works to proceed without interference to road users.

Extracts from Laing's in-house magazine *Team Spirit* for April 1988[181] give an insight into construction problems.

> When your shortest haul for muck shifting is the same as your longest haul; when a most important route north in the country is your site access, as well as your haul road; and when no contraflow system you

set up lasts longer than two weeks – then as a civil engineer building a road – you face a few problems.

Because the A1 had to be used as a haul road, this necessitated the use of licensed vehicles, which were not allowed to make any right-hand turn, even at crossovers. This meant that whichever of the structures the excavated fill from the by-pass was destined for, vehicles had to go on a 17-mile round trip to the junction of the A59 before they could turn south again. Bearing in mind the normal volume of traffic on the A1, the build up caused by the necessary roadworks and occasionally the addition of traffic from the racecourse, the planning and programming of hauls was one of the major aspects of the contract. Additionally, it was an expensive and time consuming, although absolutely necessary operation, to ensure mud was not spilt on the A1.

Specialists within both the West and North Yorkshire Police forces worked closely with Pell Frischmann and the Contractor during the construction of the scheme. The side road works included the construction of 250 metres of single carriageway road to connect north- and south-bound slip roads and modification of the Wetherby Roundabout to provide an access to Wetherby Grange Park.

The existing A1 carriageway was modified to form a Class 1 County road, linking the Wetherby and the new Walton Road roundabouts. The C78 was carried over the by-pass.

The bridge to Wetherby Grange is a three-span concrete, and the deck was constructed in one continuous pour, which involved placing 800 cubic metres of concrete in a day.

The **River Wharfe New Bridge** is worthy of mention and comprises a two-span curved plate girder deck. A demountable suspended cradle has been provided for maintenance and inspection of the bridge. Walton Road Bridge has three-spans, and the piers and abutments are on piled foundations because of poor ground conditions.

The Project Director for Laings was John Vyse. The Agent for the contract was Martin Corrigan who was succeeded by Dermot Kelly. The Engineer for the contract was Gallagher of Pell Frischmann, the Resident Engineer, Chilton, who also project-managed the design.

The new Wetherby By-pass was opened in August 1988. Although nothing officially was planned an 'unofficial opening' did occur. This took the form of a tape cutting, performed by 'Wilf', the tractor brush driver, 'in a suit!', as Chilton's diary records; this was his retirement present from Laing – he was also allowed to keep the engraved garden shears used for the purpose!

Although the consulting engineers had pressed the Department of Transport to construct the by-pass to dual three-lane motorway standards, this was not acceded to. The wisdom of this decision comes into question when in December 1991, some three years after completion, a further by-pass was added to the Department of Transport's Programme.

220 / Building the Network: The North East of England

Ox Close Lane diversion

Wetherby to Walshford Junction Improvements

Three diversions including three bridges were constructed under the Wetherby By-pass contract by Laing as advanced works for the next A1 up-grading scheme between Wetherby and Walshford.

Mark Lane Diversion takes the unclassified road over the existing A1 trunk road, and provides a connection to Loshpot Lane and a junction with the A1 southbound carriageway.

The C273 Ox Close Lane Diversion over the trunk road has connecting links to both carriageways of the A1, and Moor Lane Diversion provides similarly for the C278. Pell Frischmann developed a standard bridge for these diversions of four and five spans.

Although these advanced works were completed in 1988, construction of the Wetherby–Walshford Improvement had not received the Ministers approval to proceed.

Dishforth Interchange

The following information is taken from the opening brochure[182] prepared on behalf of the Department of Transport and involved Bullens as Consulting

Engineers. The last remaining roundabout on the A1 in Yorkshire was situated in the rural area of Dishforth, at the junction of the A1 and A168 Trunk Roads and the C233 County road.

Both the A1 and A168 are designated national high and heavy load routes providing links to the industrial areas of Tyneside and Teesside. An unusually high proportion of commercial vehicles, over 30 per cent, contributed to two-way traffic flows which then exceeded 43,000 vehicles per day on the A1 and 17,000 vehicles per day on the A168. Heavy congestion and substantial delays to traffic became commonplace and it had a poor accident record. The situation was deteriorating as traffic volumes increased.

The Dishforth Interchange contract was awarded to Henry Boot Northern Limited in April 1988 and was completed in October 1989. The works consisted of 1.8 km of new main carriageway, 3.3 km of side roads and include three reinforced concrete bridges. It was designed to provide free movement both for A1 through-traffic and for traffic between the A168 and A1 south of the interchange.

Two underbridges carried the A1 over the eastbound link road between the A1 and A168 and over the link road between the C233 and A168. It was not possible to take these roads over the A1 because of restrictions imposed by the flight path for Dishforth Airfield. A new side road network providing links between the A1, A168 and C233, incorporated an overbridge that enabled closure of the Dishforth–Rainton A168 crossroad.

In order to soften the impact of the works several areas are designated for landscape treatment. Some 50,000 cubic metres of surplus material excavated was used to contour the grassed areas within the interchange. In due course these areas were planted with shrubs and trees. In the vicinity of the A168 overbridge it was possible to retain some existing hedgerows and trees to gain immediate landscape benefit.

Extensive traffic management measures were necessary during the contract including the construction of a high standard temporary dual carriageway diversion of the A1 itself. Connection to the A168 and C233 were provided at a temporary roundabout some 250 metres south of the old roundabout. The diversion, which operated successfully for 12 months, enabled the construction of the two A1 bridges. Although the cost of these temporary works was substantial, the delays to traffic during construction were greatly reduced.

Throughout construction, efforts were made to reduce disruption to traffic. Lane closures and contraflow systems were kept to a minimum. No A1 lane closures were permitted during the six weeks' summer peak holiday periods or during bank holiday weekends. Some lane restrictions were unavoidable and these resulted in long traffic queues, but the durations were minimised by working up to 24 hours per day, seven days per week.

Tingley Interchange
M62/M621

For the Highways Agency the Project Manager was Mick Malton and Norman Kemp the Project Engineer. Barry Stone was the Project Director for Henry Boot, Jim Allan was the Contracts Manager and Andy Butler the Agent. Ken Rutter was the Project Director for Bullens, the Resident Engineer Keith Young, and the Assistant Resident Engineer Saltmarsh.

Robert Atkins MP, Minister, opened the new Dishforth interchange, completed at a cost of £9 million, in October 1989.

Baldersby Junction Improvements

Pell Frischmann Consultants Ltd was appointed by the Department of Transport to undertake the feasibility study, design and site supervision of the improvement of the A1 Trunk Road at its junction with the A61 near Baldersby St James.

The Project Manager and Engineer for the Works was Brian Dean, Peter Boulton carried out the roads design and Ian Harkness the bridge design.

The works comprised the construction of a full diamond grade-separated interchange replacing the existing roundabout. This involved the construction of four sliproads, reconstruction and overlay works of one km of dual carriageway on the trunk road and a 1.25 km diversion of the single carriageway A61 over a new bridge spanning the A1. The maintenance of the heavy traffic flow through the site was of paramount concern and strict limitations were imposed on traffic management phasing.

The £2.4 million contract was awarded to Henry Boot Ltd with start of works in April 1986 and completion in June 1987. The Contracts Manager was Jim Allen and Mick Moseley was the Agent. John Tirrill was the Resident Engineer and Jon Buxton was the Assistant Resident Engineer.

There was no official opening. Tirrill recalls walking the A1 with Mick Moseley while he hand-swept the loose chippings off the carriageway before the cones were moved away and the police were signalled to let traffic through, which they had been holding up.

Sadly, the improvements came too late and Tirrill says he attended a number of inquests on drivers who didn't make it through the site during construction.

Gatenby Lane Junction Improvement

The redevelopment of RAF Leeming in the late 1980s had resulted in increased traffic flow at the base with its access from the trunk road. The A1 then carried over 38,000 vehicles per day at Gatenby of which 30 per cent were heavy goods vehicles. These traffic figures were steadily increasing on this national highway and heavy load route. The Department of Transport appointed Pell Frischmann Consultants in 1986 to undertake feasibility and design studies for a new access to RAF Leeming via Gatenby Lane.

The £2.7 million Gatenby Lane Junction Contract was awarded to Mowlem Northern in March 1991 and the scheme was opened to traffic three months ahead of schedule.

The Works consisted of construction of a new two-level junction to the north of the old junction, closure of the existing southbound slip roads at Londonderry, improvements to the RAF access via Gatenby Lane, together with resurfacing 2 km of the A1. An unusual feature was the provision of gates on the southbound slip roads at Londonderry, which were only to be used by abnormally high loads.

The new junction was designed to provide free movement of traffic between the A1 and Gatenby Lane in all directions, with on and off slip roads. The new overbridge carries Gatenby Lane over the A1 and the bridge has been designed to accommodate abnormally high vehicles on the trunk road. A new retaining wall was built at Theakston Grange Farm.

The overbridge is a two-span, reinforced concrete structure. Theakston Grange Retaining Wall is a reinforced concrete structure 110 metres long and incorporates a section above road level to provide additional safety and traffic noise attenuation for the farmhouse.

Junction construction

Traffic management measures on the A1 were necessary during the Contract mainly for surfacing work and placement of the bridge beams. Both of these operations were carried out during a contraflow but for as short a period as possible in order to keep disruption to a minimum. Other necessary operations were carried out under night-time lane closures. Lane closures and contraflow working were not allowed during the six-week summer peak holiday period and Bank holidays.

The new bridge was designed to accommodate the Department of Transport's proposals for the future upgrading of the A1 between Dishforth and Scotch Corner to a dual three-lane motorway with hardshoulders, which is dealt with later.

Those involved with the project were Project Manager Mick Malton and Project Engineer Mick Barbier. For Pell Frischmann Gallagher was the Project Director, Coldwell was Project Manager for the design, the Resident Engineer Drewett; Assistant Resident Engineers Buxton and Sam Addison. For Mowlem the agent was Peter Samuel.

The Earl of Arran, Parliamentary Under Secretary of State for the Armed Forces, opened the A1 Gatenby Lane Junction in December 1991.

15 The Up-Grading of Trunk Road A1 to Motorway Status in the North East Region after 1990

On a typical day increased traffic, of up to 50,000 vehicles, was using the Trunk Road A1 with every third vehicle a lorry travelling at relatively high speeds, resulting in a dangerous mix of users; cars and lorries, low speed agricultural vehicles, cyclists and pedestrians.

With such heavy traffic flows, maintenance of the two-lane highway had also become a problem with long queues forming and traffic diverting onto local roads causing congestion and disturbance reminiscent of the '50s and '60s. There were many at-grade unclassified roads, isolated properties, petrol stations and cafes and as a result many gaps in the central reservation.

The significance of the A1 to the economy of the Country was unquestioned. Although those engineers involved in early improvements of the Great North Road had pressed for increased standards to be applied, it was not until the 1990s that the Department of Transport turned its attention to its upgrading to motorway status.

The Department of Transport at this time had reorganised itself in the North East into two regional offices – namely Yorkshire and Humberside, and Northern – each having a Construction Programme Division (CPD) and a Network Management Division.

It was estimated that the nine proposed A1 schemes in Yorkshire and Humberside would cost £500 million. Selected consulting engineers, who had performed well on other schemes were invited to tender for the new schemes. On the basis of the tender offers the following firms were selected: W.S. Atkins, Bullen and Partners, Carl Bro Kirkpatrick, Pell Frischmann Consultants and Sir Owen Williams and Partners.

The problems of up-grading the A1 were to be more difficult than those encountered on the original dualling due to the requirement to up-grade the road mainly along its existing heavily used corridor, maintain

Heavy traffic flows on Trunk Road A1

two lanes of traffic in each direction during construction, and provide alternative routes for non-motorway and local traffic.

On some sections, notably north of Dishforth, the alignment of the old Roman road permits on-line widening. Off-line sections are needed where the bends on the existing road are too tight to be followed by the new motorway and, in the vicinity of Ferrybridge, where extensive roadside development makes on-line improvement impracticable.[183]

The aim of the Regional Office, subject to completion of the statutory procedures and availability of funds, was to complete the upgrade of the Yorkshire section of the A1 by the turn of the century.

For each scheme alternative routes had to be investigated, public consultations held, the preferred route announced, the route investigated further, Statutory Orders published and objections invited and a Public Inquiry held if necessary. Following the Inspector's decision, the Minister would announce his decision following which land could be acquired, by compulsory powers if necessary, and, having completed the contract documents, tenders invited and construction started.

Due to changes in Government Policy and the availability of public finance for roads, the awarded schemes, although having progressed to varying stages, became caught up in the Private Finance Initiative launched by the Highways Agency in 1994.

Many of the schemes were 'to fall to the axe' and consultancy agreements terminated. The schemes were to be subsumed and 're-engineered' into a major Design, Build, Finance and Operate (DBFO) project which was to take in the whole of the A1 from Doncaster to north of Scotch Corner. The Hook Moor to Bramham section was the exception and became part of the M1–A1 Link Road DBFO.

The Department's brochure[184] dated June 1993 and introduced by John MacGregor OBE MP, Secretary of State for Transport, provides details of the proposed schemes. The following is an account of the stages reached and of the schemes that 'got away'.

Redhouse to Ferrybridge

This section was being designed by Sir Owen Williams and Partners, assisted on environmental matters by Anthony Walker and Partners and on traffic matters by the MVA Consultancy.

Detailed studies concluded that there was only one viable route option. This was presented to the public at a modified Public Consultation procedure in January 1992. In December 1992 the Secretary of State confirmed this as the Preferred Route.

The scheme was to start at the northern end of the Doncaster By-pass with an off-line section running to the west of the existing A1 past Skellow. On-line widening to the east of the A1 was to be adopted up to the crossing of the River Went. North of the river the A1 bends too sharply to be followed by a motorway. The new route was therefore to diverge eastwards and rejoin the existing A1 at Darrington. North of Darrington the route moved off-line to the west to tie into the Ferrybridge to Hook Moor Section.

Full motorway junctions were to be provided at Redhouse (A638) and at Barnsdale Bar (A639). A partial interchange catering for limited traffic movements was proposed just to the north of Darrington.

Redundant sections of the A1 were to be converted into a local access road. The most significant feature along the route is the River Went Valley. A new motorway bridge, 250 metres long and 30 metres above the valley floor, was to be located on the eastern side of the existing Wentbridge Viaduct, which had listed status and was to be retained to carry local traffic.

Work proceeded in preparation for the publication of draft orders and Environmental Statement. In December 1995 the consultancy agreement was terminated and the length of the A1 was included in the DBFO scheme for operation and maintenance.

Ferrybridge to Hook Moor

On 14 February 2003, AMEC announced that Road Management Services (a consortium which is jointly owned by AMEC, Alfred McAlpine, Dragados, and Kellogg Brown & Root) had finalised contracts with the Highways Agency to upgrade and operate a 53km-section of the A1 in Yorkshire to motorway standard. The three-year project had an investment value of around £245 million.

Total funding for the DBFO contract, which covers the A1 between Darrington and Dishforth, was secured through a £114 million index-linked bond and a £110 million facility from the European Investment Bank. The remainder was equity investment from the consortium shareholders.

Payment to the consortium on this new contract was through a pioneering new system developed by the Highways Agency – based on the consortium's ability to deliver a high quality road operating service, minimise congestion and reduce road accidents. Revenue for the consortium was based on a sliding scale dependent upon the volume and speed of traffic using the road. This acted as an incentive to conduct essential activities, such as maintenance works, at off peak times and to attend incidents on the network quickly, thereby benefiting road users.

The A1 Darrington to Dishforth DBFO project consisted of the operation and maintenance of 53 km of the A1(M)/A1(T) between Darrington, on the A1 just to the south of the existing A1/M62 Interchange, and the existing A1/A168 Interchange at Dishforth, east of Ripon. It also included the design and construction of two Targeted Programme of Improvement (TPI) schemes, which would provide 24 km of new dual three-lane motorway. The two TPI schemes were: A1(M) **Ferrybridge to**

Hook Moor (estimated cost £183 million) which formally opened in early 2006, and A1(M) **Wetherby to Walshford** (see pp.229-30).

The Ferrybridge to Hook Moor section was substantially defined by physical constraints, environmental considerations and the need to achieve a safe alignment. The southern section of the route deviated substantially from the existing A1 corridor, as improvement 'on-line' would cause extensive demolition of property in Ferrybridge.

The new motorway followed the line of the A1 before veering off to avoid the Neolithic Ferrybridge Henge, which is a Scheduled Ancient Monument. Further north the route passed through the eastern side of Fryston Park, a former deer park, with the loss of part of the woodland designated as a Site of Special Scientific Interest. Substantial landscaping was necessary in this area to mitigate the effects of the new road.

After crossing the navigable River Aire, the route crossed the Brotherton Ings Ash Lagoons, which contain a depth of almost 20 metres of ash waste from the Ferrybridge Power Stations and required substantial engineering works to stabilise the ash to support the motorway.

Routing the alignment over the ash lagoons and by-passing Fairburn to the east avoided the RSPB Nature Reserve at Fairburn Ings. This reserve is the most important ecological resource in the area and has been designated a Site of Special Scientific Interest.

From Fairburn to Selby Fork the route passes through open agricultural land but in cutting to reduce the impact on the landscape.

North of Selby Fork the route rejoins the existing A1, remaining mainly in cutting as far as the Boot and Shoe Junction. Thereafter the route re-crosses the A1 to pass Micklefield to the east of the existing A1.

A junction links the new motorway to the A63 Trunk Road, and a substantial 'free-flow' interchange west of Ferrybridge Power station links the new motorway to the M62.

In addition to benefits to the road user, this scheme benefits the communities of Ferrybridge, Brotherton and Fairburn by taking traffic away from their centres. At Micklefield the road is some 50 metres further away from the village.

Hook Moor to Bramham

This section was designed by Pell Frischmann Consultants Ltd. The Hook Moor–Bramham Section formed part of the proposals for the new motorway link between the M1 and the A1, described later (pp.237-43).

Bramham to Wetherby Conversion

This section was awarded to Carl Bro Kirkpatrick and Partners. The Bramham to Wetherby section was added to the road programme in

December 1991. Its purpose was to convert the recently completed road to motorway.

Under an agency agreement with Pell Frischmann Consultants Ltd the newly improved carriageway had already been built to dual three-lane standards with hardshoulders as described. However, it could not become a motorway until the local access road had been built and the junction strategy considered. The scheme was to start just to the north of the A64 junction. Public Consultation was to be held towards the end of 1994.

The consultancy agreement was subsequently terminated and this length of A1 was incorporated into the DBFO scheme for operation and maintenance only.

On 25 June 2002 the Minister for Transport announced a package of improvements on the A1 which included a scheme to upgrade 10 km of the A1 between the A64 Bramham Crossroads and Wetherby to a dual three-lane motorway at an estimated scheme cost of £51 million.

The Public Inquiry into the objections to the Orders was held in early 2006 at the *Bridge Inn*, Walshford. The Inspector's recommendations were not available at the time of writing.

Wetherby By-pass Upgrading

This section was also to be designed by Carl Bro Kirkpatrick and Partners. The Wetherby By-pass scheme was added to the programme in December 1991.

The A1 passed through Wetherby until 1962 when a dual carriageway by-pass was opened. This by-pass was improved in 1988 when the Mickelthwaite roundabout was removed and is referred to earlier (pp.217-19).

Upgrading this three-mile section to motorway was to use as much of the existing road as possible. The crossing of the River Wharfe valley and the nearness of Wetherby Racecourse were major considerations in the upgrading scheme.

Public consultation was to be held towards the end of 1994. The Consultancy Agreement for the scheme was subsequently terminated. The by-pass was included within the DBFO scheme for operation and maintenance.

Wetherby to Walshford

This section was awarded to Pell Frischmann Consultants Ltd and the improvement was in the course of design.

The alignment of the existing road could not be followed by the new high standard motorway, which was to be routed to the east, starting from just south of the existing York Road Bridge and rejoin the A1 north of the Moor Lane Bridge at Walshford.

At York Road the existing bridge was to be replaced by a new structure offering higher headroom clearance to enable high loads to stay on the A1 rather than travelling through Wetherby as at present. One carriageway of the existing A1 was to be converted to a two-way single-carriageway local access road between Wetherby and Walshford. The other carriageway was to be broken out and either returned to agriculture by agreement or landscaped using mounding and/or planting.

Under the DBFO arrangement described in 'Ferrybridge to Hook Moor' above, construction work started in April 2003, and the scheme opened in April 2005 at an estimated cost of £46 million.

Walshford to Dishforth

Details of this scheme have been taken from the Highways Agency's opening brochure.[185]

> Whilst predominantly used by long distance traffic this part of the A1 also served as a connection between local villages and towns such as Boroughbridge and Marton-le-Moor and gave access to adjoining properties and fields. Sections of the alignment of the existing road were substandard. Minor accidents were common during busy periods resulting in long traffic queues ...
>
> Following the Secretary of State's announcement to upgrade to motorway standard it was decided following entry of this section into the road programme in July 1990 to fast track the programme to ensure that early benefits were delivered.

The planning, design and site supervision of the scheme was awarded to Bullen and Partners. The partner in charge was Desmond Scott with Associates Ken Rutter and Fred Shepherd heading the project teams. A Public Inquiry was held in March 1992, with the scheme orders made in the following July. By November of that year CPOs were made and tenders could be invited for construction of the works.

The contract was awarded to the Joint Venture of Alfred McAlpine/Amec and work commenced in May 1993. The Agent (Roads) was Mike Parke and Agent (Structures) Tommy Smith. For Bullens Ken Slater was the Resident Engineer and Wyne Rhodes his Deputy.

The 13-mile-long section of dual three-lane carriageway runs along the west side of the existing A1 from just north of Walshford to the A168 junction at Dishforth. Grade separated interchanges have been provided on the A59 at Allerton and at Aldborough Gate to the south of Boroughbridge.

Having completed the provision of the new A1(M) motorway, the joint venture then modified the existing A1 trunk road to a single carriageway local access road, with part of the southbound carriageway retained and realigned where necessary to improve visibility. A number of new road junctions and bridges have been provided to meet modern loading

The Up-Grading of Trunk Road A1 to Motorway Status in the North East Region after 1990 / 231

Arrows Bridge

standards. The northbound carriageway was broken up, covered with earth mounds, grassed and tree planted to provide a landscaped screen between the two roads.

A total of 35 structures was involved in the motorway works including nine overbridges. A further four bridges were constructed for local access roads and 12 existing bridges demolished on the existing A1. By virtue of the rural nature of the motorway corridor only three dwellings and three commercial properties required demolition.

The biggest structure is the **Arrows Bridge** carrying the motorway over the River Ure at Boroughbridge. This is a three-span bridge with a total length of 125 metres.

The contractors opened borrow pits adjacent to the motorway from which most of the road pavement materials were produced. The pits were subsequently backfilled to the original ground levels with surplus excavated material from the motorway and the areas restored to agricultural use.

The ecology of the area has benefited from the provision of 40 hectares of new tree and shrub planting. The drainage system for the new motorway was designed to minimise the effects on the existing watercourses by the construction of balancing ponds, which regulate the discharge, and oil interceptors to provide pollution control.

Before construction work started archaeological surveys were carried out initially by geophysical techniques to identify areas of interest and then by excavation in areas where positive signs of historical activity had been identified. Excavations revealed both Neolithic and Roman remains the most significant of which was a large Roman Fort clear of the line of the motorway, which remained undisturbed.

The Walshford to Dishforth Section was opened in November 1995, by John Watts MP, Minister for Railways and Roads, only five years after the Secretary's announcement of the project. It was the first of the Yorkshire upgrade schemes to be completed. This length was to be included in the DBFO scheme for operation and maintenance.

Dishforth to Leeming

This section, having been awarded by the Highways Agency, was being designed by Pell Frischmann Consultants Ltd.

North of Dishforth the A1 follows the alignment of the Roman road, Dere Street, and is inevitably fairly straight. This lent itself to on-line upgrading.

The Preferred Route was announced in 1991; since then design had continued taking account of the many comments received from local people and public bodies. The Highways Agency and the Consultants were particularly conscious of the need to minimise the impact of the scheme on houses bordering the A1 and to improve conditions if at all possible.

Providing bridges across the motorway was to offer the opportunity to re-establish the east-west footpath, bridleway and cycle routes that had effectively been severed by the increase in A1 traffic.

The detailed design was well on the way and there had been public consultation when in 1995 the Consultancy agreement was terminated. The scheme was to be incorporated within the Highways Agency's DBFO scheme for operation and maintenance.

Leeming to Scotch Corner

This section had been awarded to W.S. Atkins–Northern. Parallel widening techniques were to be adopted to maintain existing traffic flow on two lanes in each direction during construction.

On-line improvement had been selected after careful consideration of all the alternatives. This had been made possible because this section of existing road was almost straight. Improving and widening the existing road – rather than a totally new 'green-field' alignment – generally required less land, caused less disruption to communities and reduced the need for demolition of existing properties.

The existing junctions at Catterick North and Catterick South were to be replaced with a single, central junction. This would have taken traffic out of Catterick Village and Catterick Bridge whilst providing for all the local traffic movements.

The Roman history of the A1 has been mentioned previously. This particular section is one of the most sensitive along the whole route. The existing road generally follows the line of Dere Street both to the south and to the north of the Catterick area. The Catterick By-pass, which was built in the 1950s, unfortunately passed through the buried remains of the former Roman town of Cataractonium, now a Scheduled Ancient Monument (SAM). At this point the existing road is in a coutting up to eight metres deep and 61 metres wide.

The consultancy agreement was terminated in 1995. This length of the A1 was then to be incorporated into the DBFO scheme for operation and maintenance only.

This concludes the story of the Trunk Road A1 to date. Although a great deal of work had been done, the Government's aim to upgrade the Great North Road in the North East to full motorway status by the millennium was not to be realised.

The Future – a Brief Note

Since this book was first drafted, an additional 24 km of the A1 has been converted to motorway, as described above. A further 10 km, from Bramham crossroads to Wetherby, is in the advanced planning stage, the public inquiry having been held in early February 2006.

There do not appear to be any further motorway proposals in the pipeline, but the future of communications on the whole of the East Coast was the subject of an 'East Coast Motorway Feasibility Study' which investigated a route which started in the South of England and passed close to Kingston upon Hull and York before terminating near Newcastle upon Tyne. This study, which was commissioned in 1990 by a total of 38 public and private sponsors, investigated the need for improved road communications in Eastern England and is covered more fully in Volume 2, in this series, *Building the Network: Southern and Eastern England*.

16　The Role of the Department of State with Responsibility for Transport

Great credit falls to the County Surveyors, Consulting Engineers, the contractors and their staffs in the planning, design and construction of the motorways and improvement of Trunk Road A1 in the North East. The role of, and contribution made by, the Ministers and Government officers is covered in other 'Motorway Achievement' volumes, but some attempt has been made in this account to identify the people who headed the 'government side' in bringing to fruition the motorway network in the North-East Region.

Harry Pashley[186] who was at Ministry of Transport HQ, St Christopher House, Southwark in 1964 and later a Superintending Engineer of the North Eastern Road Construction Unit gives a view, summarised here, of some of the workings of the Department of Transport.

Headed by a Director of Highways (formerly Chief Highways Engineer) the Department was made up of various divisions and branches and Regional Offices headed by Divisional Road Engineers. Included in this departmental structure were Engineering Intelligence, a Bridges Engineers Division and a Motorways Division in which Motorways 'B' covered the North Eastern Region. Contracts Branch dealt with contracts in the region and Lands Branch dealt with all Compulsory Purchase Order Publications and Land Acquisition. A Standards Division was responsible for the standards for planning and design of motorways and their construction. The Engineering Intelligence Division worked closely with the Road Research Laboratory to this end.

Government policy decided how much of the national funds were to be allocated for motorway construction. Every year a proposal was put forward by the Motorways Division (later a white paper draft). Funding fluctuated considerably, so there was a need regularly to revise the programme accordingly. Underspend was avoided since that could influence future spending.

Either Agency Agreements were drawn up with County Councils or Consultants were invited to bid for preparation work. The Government wanted Consultants to have experience to bid for work overseas. Headquarters staff dealt directly at that time with the Agents, and included liaison on route location for preparation of line, road orders and then side road orders and land acquisition plans. All proposals had to be agreed by the Department for acceptance by the Minister.

When orders were published, all objections to them were sent to the Ministry who replied and resolved matters where possible (in consultation with the Agency). The aim was to avoid a Public Inquiry if possible, as these caused considerable delays to the project. Land acquisition was particularly difficult since if any objection to Compulsory Purchase Orders (CPOs) were outstanding there had to be an Inquiry. In the early days the Minister could overrule the need for an Inquiry, if only a few objections were not withdrawn and these objections were minor. Very few major Inquiries were ever held on the M1 and M62.

Once a line and side road order was made the preparation of contract drawings and documents proceeded. Tenders were invited and returned to the Department of Transport. The Agents then made a detailed appraisal of these with recommendations. Following contract award, the cash flow was a very important control for the Department and all claims came to the Department for approval.

At the time of the design and construction of the Doncaster By-pass Motorway and the A1 improvement schemes in the West and North Ridings the Divisional Road Engineer at Leeds was J.G. Taylor. Charles Gair dealt with the Northumberland schemes. The first Director of the North Eastern Road Construction Unit in 1968 was Gilbert Norris followed by Denis Hall, Jim MacKenzie and Ken Westhorpe.

In 1981, following the demise of the RCUs, the NERCU amalgamated with the Yorkshire and Humberside Regional Office in Leeds under its Director Jim Blows. Work for Northumberland, Durham, Tyne and Wear and Cleveland transferred to Newcastle. R. Green was the Director. Blows was succeeded by John Jefferson, who died in harness and has the Departments' offices in Leeds named after him. Tony Homer followed. In 1990 the Yorkshire and Humberside Contract Programme Division was formed under Homer. Bob Bineham was appointed Director in 1995. Under the Highways Agency further reorganisation took place involving Alan Whitfield, David York and Derek Oddy.

Many names go unrecorded in this brief overview of the North Eastern Regional Offices of the Department of Transport in all its forms. More names are mentioned in the Archive. Some future researcher may wish to delve more deeply.

17   The M1–A1 Link

History

In 1973 the Department of Transport commissioned a study known as the *South Yorkshire to North East Traffic and Economic Study (SYNETES)*, the brief being to forecast traffic on the main road network in the region and evaluate alternative proposals.

In 1975 the Department of Environment put forward proposals based on this study for a road to link the M1 motorway south of Leeds at Kirkhamgate with the A1 and A19 Trunk Roads at Dishforth, and invited public views.

Two basic options were proposed; a western corridor passing between Leeds and Bradford and to the north east of Ripon, and an eastern corridor, passing to the east of Leeds and then following the existing A1 north of Wetherby, both corridors joining at Dishforth. Each corridor had two variations.

The West Yorkshire Metropolitan County Council responded to the Department's invitation by preparing a report in October 1975, which supported the Kirkhamgate–Dishforth route but reserved its position pending the results of the West Yorkshire Transportation Studies.

The Studies considered the implications to West Yorkshire of both corridors, and a report[187] on the Route to the North, prepared by the County's Directorate of Planning, Engineering and Transportation dated November 1977, concluded that an 'east of Leeds route is preferable'.

In July 1977, whilst this report was in preparation, the Secretary of State announced his decision that his department's preferred route was the 'Brown' variation of the east of Leeds corridor. This route required a shorter length of new road and made greater use of the existing A1.

The West Riding Sub-Unit of the North Eastern Road Construction Unit initially undertook the planning and design of the new route. The 1981 privatisation of the RCUs saw the scheme transferred to Pell Frischmann Consulting Engineers, together with the relevant Sub-Unit staff.

In May 1982 a Public Inquiry commenced on the Kirkhamgate–Dishforth Scheme before Air Marshal Sir Michael Giddings, KCB OBE DFC as the Inspector. The Minister's decision confirmed the schemes to upgrade the A1 between Bramham and Dishforth, but not the link road between the M1 and A1 because of concerns over its environmental impact.

As a result, a further study was commissioned in 1985. Following detailed investigations, the Secretary of State for Transport announced a recommendation for a new route for the M1–A1 Link Road in November 1987.

Further public consultation was conducted in November 1989 and the preferred scheme published and considered at Public Inquiry in January 1993. The decision to confirm the scheme and proceed towards construction was announced by the Minister for Roads and Traffic in November 1993. Pell Frischmann's scheme had finally got the go ahead.

The Private Finance Initiative

The first consultation paper on private finance for roads was the Secretary of State for Transport's Green Paper *New Roads by New Means*,[188] presented to Parliament in May 1989, which proposed 'new procedures for authorising privately financed roads'.

> The government is looking for genuine private sector ventures with appropriate risks and rewards. There is no place for financial devices, disguised government borrowing or guarantees ... shadow tolls, for example, where the government makes payment to the private sector according to the number of vehicles using the road, are ruled out for this reason.

In November 1992, in parallel with the development of the M1–A1 Scheme, the Department of Transport announced that private sector companies might be invited to tender for Design, Build, Finance, and Operate (DBFO) road contracts. This was discussed in the Green Paper *Paying for a Better Motorway*,[189] published in May 1993.

The Highways Agency formally launched its use of the Private Finance Initiative (PFI) to procure parts of the motorway and trunk road network in August 1994 with payment through 'shadow tolls'. The M1–A1 Link Road was selected as one of eight DBFO projects and was the largest and most complex of the national schemes to be procured by this method.

The decision was something of a blow to Pell Frischmann Consultants Ltd who had developed the scheme almost to tender stage. Although Pell Frischmann had achieved success within the new DBFO initiative, the decision had to be faced, whether to remain the Department's Agent or join with contractors bidding for the concession. In the event they were awarded the Agent's role, which was to become more involved than at first envisaged, to ensure that the contractor operated in accordance with his Quality Plan.

Following the pre-qualification stage, which began in August 1994, four bidders were selected for the next stage in the demanding tendering and negotiation process leading to the selection of 'Preferred Bidder'.

The £218-million contract was originally awarded to a joint venture of Trafalgar House and Wimpey, but, after the contractor withdrew, Yorkshire Link Ltd, a consortium of Kvaerner and BICC, was selected as 'preferred Bidder'. The financing of the £200-million project was a significant aspect of the tendering and negotiation process. They decided to finance the project by means of a combination of equity provided by the two consortium shareholders and by loans from some 32 banks.

In March 1996, the Minister for Railways and Roads awarded Yorkshire Link Ltd a 30-year concession to deliver, operate and maintain the M1–A1 Link Road, and to receive payments based on tariffs for road usage, from the Highways Agency. In the year 2026, the project will be handed back to the Secretary of State, subject to meeting residual life conditions contained within the agreement.

The Construction

For construction Yorkshire Link formed a Joint Venture of Kvaerner Construction and Balfour Beatty, with the Babtie Group acting as their consulting engineers. In addition to the Link Road, 20 miles of side roads and diversions had to be constructed which were to be handed back to Leeds City and North Yorkshire County Councils on completion.

Jim Cohen, Chairman and Peter Dyer, Managing Director of Yorkshire Link said: 'As the country's largest and most complex DBFO road contract to date, it provides a superb example of the advantages which partnership between the public and private sectors can bring to the provision of national infrastructure. The completion of the project ahead of programme and to cost is a fine demonstration of technical competence on the part of all those involved ...'

To manage the construction of the project, a Project Forum was established, which comprised senior management representatives from Yorkshire Link, Balfour Beattie, Pell Frischmann, the Highways Agency and the Babtie Group. Their function was to oversee the design and construction programme of work.

One of the biggest challenges was that for the Babtie Group to produce a design in advance of the construction phase – a task made more difficult because of the demanding timescale. The engineers in seeking innovative and cost effective solutions to the design of the project had to take account of the contrasting requirements of lowest capital cost for construction and of whole life costing for maintenance, and produce a total value engineered solution. The main areas of design where this was achieved were Earthworks, Drainage, Pavement and Structures.

The scale of the work involved over 36 months in the construction of the 30-km M1–A1 Link Road, is impressive: approximately five million cubic metres of excavation, building over 150 structures, widening/re-aligning 12 km of existing carriageway on the M62, M1, A1 and A64, constructing 18 km of new, continuously reinforced concrete road and providing two motorway interchanges and five junctions.

The Works divided three distinct sections:

1. The M1–M62 widening;
2. A new motorway built on a green field site between Stourton and Hook Moor;
3. The parallel reconstruction of A1 between Hook Moor and Bramham.

The road design incorporated a balance between cut and fill resulting in the excavated material largely being re-used within the project. John Jones was a major sub-contractor for earthworks. Several landscaped balancing ponds have been provided for drainage from the motorway to surrounding watercourses and to provide habitat for wild life.

The carriageway pavements have been designed for a 40-year life and should only require resurfacing to maintain skid resistance. Most carriageways have fully flexible pavement construction, with a continuously reinforced concrete pavement used for the central 15 km between Stourton and Hook Moor, where subsidence may be expected over backfilled open cast mining areas.

The structures included one viaduct, two tunnels, 37 bridges, eight underpasses, two footbridges, three culverts, the remainder being signal gantries and CCTV masts. The structures have been designed for low maintenance, throughout their 120-year design life, and balance aesthetic appeal with economy. Fifteen integral bridges have been provided. Two cut and cover tunnels were constructed to take the M1 to M62 free flow link under the two motorways.

Cut and cover tunnel

Aire Valley Viaduct under construction

Traffic management was a major challenge to ensure that the motorway traffic could be maintained throughout their construction. The innovative design of the £3 million tunnels allowed them to be simultaneously constructed whilst 12 lanes of traffic were kept moving on both motorways. Both tunnels cross the motorways at a skew, with the longer of the two, under the M62, measuring 147 metres.

St George's Bridge forms the gateway to Leeds and is a two-span steel/concrete bridge curved both in plan and elevation. The 140-metre-long bridge cost £3.5 million and carries the new M1 northbound carriageway around the south east of Leeds over the re-numbered M621 motorway.

Two of the bridges carry the motorway over busy railway lines, which necessitated much of the construction work being carried out during night and weekend possessions. The largest structure on the scheme is the £9-million **Aire Valley Viaduct**, at 250 metres long, which carries 10 lanes of motorway, including slip-roads over the River Aire and the Aire and Calder Navigation Canal. The viaduct is a five-span steel beam structure – the longest span being 73 metres. The structural steelwork for this and nine other bridges was fabricated by Kvaerner Cleveland Bridge in Darlington and transported to site by road.

The Aire Valley Viaduct contains approximately 4,000 tonnes of structural steelwork, and with beams weighing up to 150 tonnes some of the largest mobile cranes in the country were used to lift them into place across the waterways.

A coating of highly durable glass flake epoxy was painted on all steel structures. However the construction of the Aire Valley Viaduct, and other sections of the scheme, was not without its problems, which could have been disastrous.

The main girders, having arrived on site, were found by a Babtie engineer not to be in accordance with the consultant's design, and modifications had to be made, and exhaustively tested, before being accepted.

There were also the problems of constructing the road through the coal measures and a CRCP carriageway (see pp.198-200) was adopted.

On one section, when the drainage had not been completed before the concrete carriageway had been constructed, water found its way into the fill and caused collapse and dipping of the carriageway. The drainage was completed but this section of pavement had to be reconstructed.

This was not the only problem with water. Water contaminated with chlorides got into the supply to the concrete mixing plant and a bridge pier had to be demolished when this problem was discovered by the contractor's laboratory engineer during routine testing.

Under this new arrangement of procurement a large number of things were discovered as potential non-conformities and the client's Agent had progressively to increase staff numbers to undertake its role fully although that is not to say that construction under the older established forms of contract weren't without problems.

The debate will continue as to whether the PFI route or the traditional ways in which most of the network of motorways was built with government funding, and defined roles for client, engineer and contractor, provides the best technical and economic motorway in the long term.

Whichever way is adopted the public can still influence construction even when built, none more so than on the M1–A1 Link. The section of carriageway between Garforth and Parlington had been constructed with rough textured CRCP and, because of local objection on noise grounds from traffic, a thick black top paving had to be overlaid.

This short account of some of the problems encountered during the construction of this fine section of the motorway is intended to provide a balance with the official account.

The scheme has important safety measures for the travelling public. Extensive signing and signalling has been provided at the numerous junctions and interchanges, in order to provide information to motorists and the monitor and control traffic. In addition to fixed directional signs there are electronically controlled variable message and enhanced message signs. Electronic matrix signals provide the means of controlling traffic speeds in the event of emergencies. PTZ (pan, tilt and zoom) cameras mounted on masts permit monitoring of traffic. The West Yorkshire Police at Wakefield operate these controls, which are also monitored by Yorkshire Link from their Bramham maintenance compound.

Given the scale of the scheme, much emphasis has been placed on the need to safeguard local ecology, and an environmental impact study was carried out. Hook Moor is a Site of Special Scientific Interest and is one of the top two sites for thistle broomrape in Britain.

Along the route of the motorway there are several areas of archaeological interest. These included the discovery of a Bronze-Age cremation cemetery north of Garforth, while evidence of Bronze-Age huts were found at Swillington Common. There were several investigations of Roman field systems, providing an insight into the landscape in Roman times. One group of enclosures at Parlington Junction included a small cemetery with six Roman burials together with substantial amounts of Roman pottery. Two sunken-floored huts here sounds unimpressive, but these were the first Dark-Age buildings discovered in West Yorkshire, and showed that the site has been re-occupied by Anglo-Saxon invaders after the end of Roman rule.

During excavation across the A656 the original embankment and surface of the Roman road from Castleford to Tadcaster was found to have survived intact under the modern road. Surveys and excavations were undertaken by the West Yorkshire Archaeological Services (WYAS) on 35 sites along the route, of which 22 yielded archaeological remains.

A comprehensive landscape scheme has been prepared along the 30-km route with the planting of 550,000 trees and shrubs and wild flower areas which will integrate the road with surrounding landscapes.

The M1–A1 Link was opened in February 1999 by the Rt Hon. John Prescott MP, who recorded it as 'a significant step in the completion of the nation's strategic motorway network'.

St George's Bridge

18   Conclusion

We have come to the end of our journey through the Great North Road, Trunk Road A1 and A1(M) and the motorways in the North East Region. It has taken 50 years to bring this part of the motorway network to its present stage of development and involved well over one hundred construction contracts.

We have seen major changes in local government and County boundaries. The Counties making up the Ridings of Yorkshire are no more. The Metropolitan Counties of West and South Yorkshire were created and then abolished. Road Construction Units were established and lasted almost a decade and a half, before their work was transferred to consulting engineers. All of these changes in organisation and administration had to be coped with during the progression of schemes. A number of the contractors featured here, such as Monk, Dowsett and French, no longer exist, having been subsumed by larger construction companies.

As is the nature of history the 'glory' goes to those who head the many organisations brought together in this achievement. In this effort to record the history of the many schemes that make up the network the writer has attempted to include some names of those whose contribution has been in the detail of the work. For those who read this and feel they should have been included the Archive remains open for their contribution to be added and for future researchers to record.

The engineers initially recruited in the 1950s to the County Highways Departments, Consultants and Contractors regarded themselves as 'pioneers' of the network. The training given to the young people involved produced, in later years, engineers, technicians and administrators of excellence. Thrown in at the deep end they quickly learnt and developed the skills necessary to achieve these major works.

Research and Development provided a stream of developments in highway and bridge construction, too extensive to review here. This, together with the work in planning, specification, design and construction of the motorways in the UK, achieved international recognition.

Although this history is mostly a story of success there were failures. Failure in aspects of planning, in adequacy of design and in construction, all occurred and lessons learned, often painfully, for those involved, occasionally resulting in the ultimate sacrifice of loss of life.

The history of motorways in this respect is no different from that of the canals or railways. Notwithstanding these failures to get things right, the story is mostly of tremendous endeavour, achievement, success and goodwill. There can be no doubt that the motorways in the North East have made an enormous contribution to today's prosperity of the region and the United Kingdom.

This achievement has only been possible with the fullest co-operation between Ministry of Transport officials, planning, design and supervising staff, contractors, research organisations and universities, numerous local authorities, valuers, statutory and nationalised undertakings, financial institutions, landowners, tenants, and the general public affected by these highways.

It remains to be seen what the future holds for the maintenance and further development of the motorway network in the next 30 years under the new methods of procurement, the lessening involvement of the public sector and greater involvement of the private sector under the Private Finance Initiative.

The writer is indebted to all those who have contributed to this piece of work and hastens to add that it is the work of an engineer not a historian!

Notes

1. Bagshawe, R.W., *Roman Roads*, Shire Publications Ltd, 1979.
2. Hutchinson, A.T., 'A Yorkshire Walkabout', Archive Document, Aug. 1994.
3. *Ibid.*
4. *Ibid.*
5. *Ibid.*
6. *Ibid.*
7. *Ibid.*
8. *Ibid.*
9. Varley, W.R., 'Lincoln to the River Tweed', Archive Paper, 1999.
10. Callery, M.F., 'Personal Recollections', Archive Paper, 1999.
11. Race, G., 'Lines, Levels and Earthworks', G.F.S. In-house magazine, 1959.
12. *Ibid.*
13. Hutchinson, A.T., *op. cit.*
14. Buchi, N.H., 'The Design and Construction of Wentbridge Viaduct', *The Surveyor*, Feb. 1962.
15. Markham, R.B., 'The Construction of Wentbridge Viaduct', Jnl. *Reinforced Concrete Assoc.*, Vol. 1, No 12, Nov/Dec 1963.
16. Sims, F.A., 'The Design of Wentbridge Viaduct', Jnl. *Reinforced Concrete Assoc.*, Vol. 1, No 12, Nov/Dec 1963.
17. Base, G.D., 'Tests on Structural Hinges of Reinforced Concrete Hinge No 1 Test Memorandum', Cement and Concrete Association, 23 Dec. 1958
18. Sims, F.A. and Bridle, R.J., *The Design of Concrete Hinges Concrete and Constructional Engineering*, VOL LIX, No 8, Aug 1964.
19. England, T., 'Past Construction Works', Archive Note, July 1999.
20. Jackson, R., *Jacksons Illustrated Guide to Yorkshire*, R. Jackson, Leeds, 1891.
21. Varley, W.R. and Allinson, M.G., 'The River Aire Bridge', *Jnl Inst. Highway Engrs*, Sept. 1966.
22. Green-Armytage, K., '£2 m. by-pass and bridging scheme completed at Ferrybridge Highways and Public Works', Nov. 1967.
23. White, K., 'Completion of Ferrybridge By-pass, England', CN Post, Nov. 1967.
24. Sriskandan, K., 'Recollections', Archive Letter, Jan.1998.
25. Hutchinson, A.T., *op. cit.*
26. England, T., *op. cit.*
27. Jackson, R., *op.cit.*
28. Hutchinson, A.T., *op. cit.*
29. Department of Transport, *The New A1 Motorway in Yorkshire*, White Horse Press, Leeds, June 1993.
30. Couchmann, M., 'Recollections', Archive Note, 1999.
31. Jackson, R., *op.cit.*
32. Scott, F., 'Recollections', Archive Note, July 1999.
33. *Ibid.*
34. Wright, R., 'Hopperton Station Diversion Report on BSP Steel Cased Piling at the Railway Bridge', Site Report, Jan.1962.
35. Hatter, F., 'Recollections', Archive Note, Nov. 1999.
36. Jackson, R., *op.cit.*
37. Woodhead, J.D., 'The Design and Construction of Allerton Park Flyover A1', *The Jnl Inst. Highway Engrs*, Sept 1971.
38. Couchmann, M., *op. cit.*
39. Corby, R.G., 'A1/A638 Redhouse Junction Improvements. Barnsdale Bar

40. *Ibid.*
41. Wilkinson, G.D., 'Notes on A1 – North Riding of Yorkshire', Archive Paper, July 1999.
42. Wilkinson, G.D., *op.cit.*
43. Jackson, R., *op.cit.*
44. *Ibid.*
45. *Ibid.*
46. Supplied by M. Moore, 'Extracts from North Riding County Council Minutes, and Newspaper cuttings', Archive Papers, June 1999.
47. Wilkinson, G.D., *op.cit.*
48. *Ibid.*
49. MacKenzie, J. A. M., 'W. H. B. Cotton' Archive Paper, July 1999.
50. *Ibid.*
51. Durham County Council, *Darlington By-pass Motorway A1(M)*, Durham County Council, 14 May 1965.
52. Durham County Council, *Durham Motorway A1(M)*, Durham County Council, 17 Sep. 1969.
53. Hatter, F., *op. cit.*
54. Durham County Council, *op.cit.*
55. Collins, J., 'Birtley By-pass', Archive Note.
56. Charlesworth, G., *A History of British Motorways*, Thomas Telford Ltd, 1984.
57. Durham County Council, *op.cit.*
58. Best, K., *Best Endeavours*, K. Best, 1992.
59. *Ibid.*
60. *Ibid.*
61. *Ibid.*
62. *Ibid.*
63. *Ibid.*
64. *Ibid.*
65. Harding, R., with notes by Telford, L. and Cockton, J., 'The Great North Road, Newcastle Upon Tyne to Berwick', Archive Papers, Nov.1999, Feb., and April 2000.
66. H.M.S.O., *A1 Felton By-pass*, H.M.S.O. Crown Copyright, 1981.
67. Harding, R., *op. cit.*
68. Cox, J., 'Recollections', Archive Note, July 1999.
69. Shelbourn, J., 'A Professional Career 1962-1965', Archive Paper, May 1999.
70. *Ibid.*
71. Forrester, G.R., 'Soil Surveys Paid Off', *Yorkshire Post*, 18 Oct. 1968.
72. Shelbourn, J., *op. cit.*
73. Senior, G.S., 'Testing Time for Mining Engineers', *Yorkshire Post*, 18 Oct. 1968.
74. Shelbourn, J., *op. cit.*
75. *Ibid.*
76. *Ibid.*
77. Ellis, N.G., 'Roads have changed Britains landscape', *Yorkshire Post*, 18 October 1968.
78. Hutchinson, A.T., 'Functional and pleasing to the eye', *Yorkshire Post*, 18 October 1968.
79. Bradley, D., 'M1–Wakefield–East Ardsley', Archive Paper, Jan. 1998.
80. Hutchinson, A.T., *op. cit.*
81. Sims, F.A., 'Special Problems for bridge designers', *Yorkshire Post*, 18 Oct. 1968.
82. Friston, A.H., 'Tinsley Viaduct – A Personal View', Archive Paper, 1999.
83. Sims, F.A. and Bridle, R.J., 'Design of Bridges in Areas of Mining Subsidence', *Jnl Inst. Highway Engrs*, Nov. 1965.
84. Varley, W.R., 'M1/M62 Lofthouse Interchange 1962-1965', Archive Paper, Feb. 1998.
85. Bowerman, J., 'Smithy Wood Footbridge Hinge Tests', Archive Paper, West

Riding Bridges, Section, 1967.
86. Sims, F.A. and Forrester, G.R. and Jones, C.J.F., 'Lateral Pressures on Retaining Walls', *Jnl. Inst. of Highway Engrs*, June 1970.
87. Sims, F.A., *op. cit.*
88. Varley, W.R., 'Lofthouse Interchange in Yorkshire', *Civil Engineering and Public Works Review*, Vol.62, No 727, Feb 1967.
89. Deuce, T.L.C., 'Lofthouse Interchange Bridges', *Proceedings of Conference on Steel Bridges*, British Constructional Steelwork Association, 1968.
90. Varley, W.R., *op. cit.*
91. *Ibid.*
92. *Ibid.*
93. Bridle, R.J., Recollections, Archive Note, 1999.
94. Sims, F.A., *op. cit.*
95. Friston, A.H., *op. cit.*]
96. *Ibid.*
97. Varley, W.R., 'The Loss of Tinsley Viaduct', Archive Paper, July 1999.
98. Unknown, 'Aston Sheffield Motorway', *The Surveyor and Municipal Engineer*, 22 June 1968.
99. *Ibid.*
100. Walker, M., 'Tinsley Viaduct to meet Merrison soon', *New Civil Engineer*, 26 June 1975.
101. O'Neill, B., 'Two-level Tinsley Viaduct up to date', *New Civil Engineer*, 2 Nov. 1978.
102. *Ibid.*
103. Butler, A.A.W., Wooley, M.V. and Gifford, E.W.H., 'The Calder Bridge Proceedings', *Inst. Civ. Engrs*, Aug.1969.
104. Williams, O.T., *London to Yorkshire Motorway*, Sir Owen Williams & Partners, July 1973.
105. *Ibid.*
106. *Ibid.*
107. Baxter, J.M., 'Barlborough to Thurcroft M1', Archive Note, 1998.
108. *Ibid.*
109. W. & C. French, 'A First Look at the M18 Motorway and Latest on M18 Motorway, Contract Progress No 47', *Friendship Magazine*, W. & C. French, 1967.
110. *Ibid.*
111. *Ibid.*
112. Dawson, T., 'Recollections', Archive Note, Sept. 1999.
113. Millard, R., *op. cit.*
114. *Ibid.*
115. Lovell, S.M., 'The Birth of a Motorway, Part I', *The Surveyor and Municipal Engineer*, 22 Jan. 1966.
116. Lovell, S.M., 'The Birth of a Motorway Part II', *The Surveyor and Municipal Engineer*, 29 Jan. 1966.
117. Ellis, N.G., 'The Planning of the Lancashire Yorkshire Motorway', Lecture Notes, 1964.
118. County Council of West Riding of Yorkshire, Lancashire, Yorkshire Motorway, Chorley and Pickersgill Ltd, Leeds, 1963.
119. Shelbourn, J., *op. cit.*
120. *Ibid.*
121. Department of Environment and Central Office of Information, 'Motorway across the Pennines', HMSO, Jesse Brood & Co, Manchester, 1971.
122. Shelbourn, J., *op. cit.*
123. *Ibid.*
124. West Riding County Council, *An Investigation into the Advisability of letting a Contract for the Bulk Supply of Beams*, West Riding County Council Report, July 1966.

125. Sims, F.A., 'Note of Meeting re Bulk Supply of Beams', West Riding County Council Bridges Section Minute, July 1966.
126. Gray, T., *Road to Success Alfred McAlpine 1935-1985*, Rainbird Publishing Group Ltd, London, 1987.
127. West Riding Bridges Section, 'Pennine, Contract Scammonden Bridge Press Notice', West Riding County Council, 1971.
128. Department of Environment and Central Office of Information, *op. cit.*
129. Mitchell, P.B. and Maguire, F.J., *Scammonden Dam Civil Engineering and Public Works Review*, Nov. 1968.
130. *Ibid.*
131. Department of Environment and Central Office of Information, *op. cit.*
132. Tusler, C., 'M62 Lifeline over the Pennines', *The Surveyor*, 6 March 1970.
133. Department of Environment and Central Office of Information, *op. cit.*
134. *Ibid.*
135. Hunter, G.S.R., 'Recollection of the Pennine Contract', Archive Paper, Dec. 1999.
136. Department of Environment and Central Office of Information, *op. cit.*
137. Institution of Civil Engineers, '20 Years of British Motorways', page 31, discussion F.A. Sims, *Proceedings of Conference*, London, 27/28 February 1980.
138. Gray, T., *op. cit.*
139. Hunter, G.S.R., *op. cit.*
140. Sir Alfred McAlpine, 'Majestic Occasions', Sir Alfred McAlpine Company Article, 1971.
141. Varley, W.R., 'Steel Box Girders', Archive Paper, May 1999.
142. Dalton, D.C. and Hoban, K.M., 'Tyre Walls in Highway Construction', *The Highway Engineer*, Feb.1982.
143. Varley, W.R., 'The origins and surrender of a Reinforced Earth Patent', Archive Paper, Aug.1999.
144. Jones, C.J.F.P., 'Reinforced Soil – A View from the Operational Level', Archive Paper, Oct. 1999.
145. Varley, W.R., *op. cit.*
146. Jones, C.J.F.P., *op. cit.*
147. Varley, W.R., *op. cit.*
148. *Ibid.*
149. Jones, C.J.F.P., *op. cit.*
150. Barlow, S.J., Dalton, D.C., Jones, C.J.F.P. and Mamujee, F., 'Reinforced Earth Wall on M62 at Whitley Bridge', Directorate of Engineering, West Yorkshire Met. C.C., 1975.
151. Sims, F.A. and Beanland, N.S., 'The "Beany Block" Combined Kerb and Drainage System', *DOTHE Design Guide*, West Yorkshire Met. C.C., March 1982.
152. Pennington, F.I., Opening Speech, Archive Paper, 1974.
153. Department of Transport, *The Final Link M62 Motorway-Ouse Bridge Contract*, Department of Transport, May 1976.
154. Scott Wilson Kirkpatrick and Partners, *The West Roads Contract*, Scott Wilson Kirkpatrick and Partners, 1975.
155. Scott Wilson Kirkpatrick and Partners, *The East Roads Contract*, Scott Wilson Kirkpatrick and Partners, 1975.
156. *Ibid.*
157. N.E R.C.U., 'M62 Lancashire to Yorkshire Motorway – Balkholme to Caves Section', N.E.R.C.U. and Durham Sub-Unit, 1975.
158. Naylor, A.E., 'The Leeds Urban Motorways', Archive Paper, 1999.
159. *Ibid.*
160. *Ibid.*
161. Georgel, B., 'M1–Leeds South East Urban Motorway – 1971-1972', Tarmac, Archive Paper, June 1998.
162. *Ibid.*

163. Naylor, A.E., *op. cit*.
164. *Ibid*.
165. Land, J., 'Submission for Associate Membership – Institution of Civil Engineers', Archive Paper, 1999.
166. Hewitt, P., 'M606', Archive Note, 2001.
167. Sims, F.A. and Forrester, G.R. and Jones, C.J.F., 'Lateral Pressures on Retaining Walls', *Jnl. Inst. of Highway Engrs*, June 1970.
168. Jones, C.J.F.P. and Sims, F.A., 'Earth pressures against the abutments and wing walls of standard motorway bridges', *Géotechnique*, Vol XXV No 4, Dec. 1975.
169. Hunt, K., 'Lovesall Carr Bridge, An example of the use of compensated foundations for bridges', West Yorkshire MCC Paper, 1980.
170. Yorkshire and Humberside Economic Council and Board, 'Yorkshire and Humberside Regional Strategy', Yorkshire and Humberside Economic Council and Board, 1970.
171. Hunt, D., 'Experimental Concrete Carriageways on M180', *Jnl Inst. Highway Engrs*, April 1981.
172. News Release, 'UK's First Large Scale Continuously Reinforced Paving on M180', Cement & Concrete Association, August 1978.
173. *Ibid*.
174. Sims, F.A. and Woodhead, S., 'Rawcliffe Bridge in Yorkshire Civil Engineering and Public Works Review', April 1968.
175. Leech, A., 'Glued Segmental Pre-stressed Concrete Construction for New M180 Trent Bridge', News Release, Cement and Concrete Association, July 1978.
176. Cementation Construction, 'Opening of the M180 Trent Bridge, 20 July 1979', *Cementation Construction*, July 1979.
177. Chaffé, J., 'Trent Bridge', NERCU Paper, Sept. 1980.
178. Notes supplied by Hillcoat, M., 'The Scunthorpe Southern By-pass', Archive Paper, July 1999.
179. Purver, T., 'Brigg By-pass', Archive Paper, Oct. 1999.
180. *Ibid*.
181. Laing, 'Wetherby By-pass', Team Spirit, Laing, April 1988.
182. Department of Transport, 'A1 Dishforth To North of Leeming Improvements Gatenby Lane Junction', Department of Transport/Pell Frischmann Consultants, Mowlem, 1991.
183. Hunt, D., *op. cit*.
184. The Department of Transport, *The New A1 Motorway in Yorkshire*, Y.H.P.D.C., Jefferson House, June 1993.
185. Opening Brochure, *Walshford-Dishforth*, Bullens, 1995.
186. Pashley, H., 'Recollections', Archive Paper, Nov.1999.
187. Directorate of Planning, Engineering and Transportation, 'The Route to the North Kirkhamgate-Dishforth', West Yorkshire Met. C.C. Report, Nov. 1977.
188. Secretary of State Green Paper, 'New Road by New Means', HMSO, May 1989.
189. Secretary of State Green Paper, 'Paying for a Better Motorway', HMSO, May 1993.

Index

In this index, the following abbreviations are used: [CD]=County Durham, [N]=Northumberland, [NR]=North Riding of Yorkshire, [WR]=West Riding of Yorkshire, [SY]=South Yorkshire (Metropolitan CC), [WY]=West Yorkshire (Metropolitan CC), [NY]=North Yorkshire.

A1(M)[CD], 62
    Aycliffe to Bradbury, 55, 61
    Birtley By-Pass, 51, 61, 62
    Bowburn to Carrville, 57, 62
    Bradbury to Bowburn, 56
    Carrville to Chester-le Street, 58
    Darlington By-pass, 7, 45, 49, 51, 52
    Durham Motorway, 54, 62, 64

A1(M)[NR], 50

A1(M)[NY]
    Dishforth to Leeming, 232
    Leeming to Scotch Corner, 233
    Walshford to Dishforth, 230
    Wetherby to Walshford, 228, 229

A1(M)[WR]
    Doncaster By-pass, 12, 42, 89, 116, 117, 121, 189, 194, 226

A1(M)[WY]
    Bramham to Wetherby, 234
    Bramham to Wetherby Conversion, 228
    Darrington to Dishforth DBFO, 227
    Ferrybridge to Hook Moor, 34, 227
    Hook Moor to Bramham, 228
    Redhouse to Ferrybridge, 226
    Wetherby By-pass Upgrading, 229

A1[N]
    Alnwick By-pass, 79, 80
    Belford By-pass, 81
    Belford to West Mains, 82
    Berwick on Tweed By-pass, 82, 84

    Brownieside Diversion, 81
    Conundrum to Marshall Meadows, 84
    Felton By-pass, 77
    Haggerston Diversion, 82
    Hitchcroft to Cawledge, 79
    Morpeth By-pass, 75
    Morpeth to Felton, 77
    Newcastle Western By-pass, 64, 74, 188
    Newton on the Moor Diversion, 79
    Pillars to New Mouson, 81
    Seaton Burn to Stannington Bridge, 74
    Stannington Bridge to Clifton Div'n, 75
    Warenford Diversion, 81
    Wide Open to Seaton Burn Div'n, 74

A1[NR]
    Boroughbridge By-pass, 48
    Catterick By-pass, 47
    Catterick N and S junctions, 50
    Leeming By-pass, 47
    Scotch Corner Diversion, 50

A1[NY]
    Baldersby Junction Improvements, 222
    Dishforth Interchange, 220
    Gatenby Lane Junction Impt, 223
    Wetherby to Walshford Junction Improvements, 217, 220

A1[SY]
    Barnsdale Bar Grade Sep. junction, 42
    Redhouse Junction Improvement, 42

A1[WR]
    Aberford By-pass, 35
    Aberford to Wetherby, 36
    Allerton Park flyover, 40, 41
    Allerton to Boroughbridge, 41
    Brotherton By-pass, 31
    Brotherton to Micklefield, 32
    Ferrybridge By-pass and Aire Bridge, 26
    Hopperton Station Diversion, 40
    Micklefield By-pass, 35
    Redhouse to Wentbridge, 20
    Wentbridge to Ferrybridge, 26
    Wentbridge Viaduct and By-pass, 22
    Wetherby By-pass, 217
    Wetherby By-pass/Wharfe Bridge, 37
    Wetherby to Allerton Station, 40

A1[WY]
    Bramham to Wetherby, 215
    Darrington Crossroads, 43
    Wetherby By-pass, 217

A167(M), 64
    Newcastle Central Motorway East, 64, 188

A194(M)
    White Mare Pool to Black Fell, 63

A58(M)
    Leeds Inner Ring Motorway, 178
A6157(M), 64
A66(M), 45, 50, 52, 53
Abbot, Ivan, 98, 150, 162, 170, 198, 210
Aberford, 19, 36
A. Carmichael Ltd., 55, 58, 62, 80
aerial survey, 87, 91, 128
A.F. Budge (Contractors) Ltd, 44, 157, 181, 185, 207; Construction Ltd, 42
Agency Agreements, 235
Aire Bridge, 26, 27, 28, 31
Aire Valley Viaduct, 241
Allerton, 230
    Manleverer, 40
    Park, 40
    Station, 41
Allinson, Maurice, 17, 27
AMEC, 227, 230
Ameys, 58
Andrew, John, 95, 155
archaeological surveys, 232
Armco, 20, 57, 151, 182, 186, 196, 198
Armthorpe, 190, 192
Arrows Bridge, 232
Arthur, Basil, 6, 73
Association of County Councils, 123
Aston, 85, 117
Atkins, Robert MP, 67, 72, 222
Atkinson, Reg, 187
Aycliffe, 55, 62

Babtie Group, 239
Bailey bridge, 14, 24, 192
Baldersby, 50
Baldersby St James, 222
Balfour Beatty Construction Ltd, 66, 77, 79, 81, 84, 208, 239
Bannerjee, 164
Barefoot Contessa, 185

Barnsdale
    Bar, 42, 227
    Bar Railway Bridge, 20
    Forest, 22
Barton, 7, 52, 212
    By-pass, 52
    Motorway Compound, 49
Beany block, 167
Beeston, 182
    Interchange, 186
    Ring Road, 184, 185
Belford, 73, 81
bell-pit mines, 87, 94, 179
Berwick on Tweed, 73
Best, Keith, 64
Birdwell, 85, 95, 102
Birse Construction Ltd, 66
Blackburn, 93
Blackwell Bridge, 45, 52, 53, 54
Blaydon
    Bridge, 64, 65, 66, 68, 72
    Haughs Viaduct, 68, 70
Blyth By-pass, 13, 17
Boot and Shoe, 34, 228
Boroughbridge, 1, 9, 19, 41, 45, 230, 232
    By-pass, 46, 49
Boston Spa, 36, 216
Bowcliffe Hall, 36, 216
    Bridge, 216
box-girders, 147, 153, 154
Bradford, 177
    Institute of Technology, 100
    Ring Road, 187
    University, 201
Bradley, Denis, 96, 98, 150
Bramham, 19, 215
    Cross Roads, 36
    Maintenance Compound, 242
    Moor, 36
    Park, 36
Bridges Engineering Standards Division, 165
Bridle, Ron, 78, 86, 100, 106, 114, 166

Brigg, 195
Brims & Co. Ltd, 50, 54, 63
British Rail, 27, 68, 90, 98, 156, 185, 193
British Railways, 17, 95
British Ropes Ltd, 23
British Steel Corporation, 195
British Waterways, 90
Brodsworth Railway Bridge, 17
Brotherton, 19
    By-pass, 32
    Ings, 228
Buchi, Norman, 9, 10
Building Research Station, 143
Bulk Beam Contract, 134
Bullen and Partners, 64, 82, 213, 220, 225, 230
Burns, Wilfred, 64

Calder Bridge, 10, 92, 96, 107, 114
    collapse, 115
Callery, Michael, 9, 14, 16, 17, 20, 31
Canal
    Aire and Calder Navigation, 241
    Calder and Hebble Navigation, 153
    Goole, 167, 168
    Knottingley and Goole, 163
    Leeds Liverpool, 180
    Market Weighton, 173, 175
    Sheffield-Keadby, 107
Carl Bro Kirkpatrick, 225, 228, 229
Carruthers, Don, 96, 157
Castle, Barbara MP, 123
Cataractonium, 47, 233
Catchwater, 145, 146, 209
Catcliffe, 86, 93
Catterick, 7, 45, 46, 233
    By-pass, 47
    Racecourse, 47
Cementation Co. Ltd, 53
    Construction Ltd, 56, 76, 204
    Projects Ltd, 66, 68

Central Electricity Generating
    Board, 90
Chain Bar
    Interchange, 155, 187
    Rail Viaduct, 156
Chapeltown, 85, 94
Chester-le-Street, 55, 59, 62
    By-pass, 51
Chilton, Rod, 217
Chope, Christopher, MP, 72
Christiani and Nielsen, 28
Clarke, Kenneth, MP, 79, 207
Clay, Bernard, 93, 159, 162
Cleveland Bridge and Engineering
    Co. Ltd, 53, 108, 110, 212
Clifton Interchange, 152
Clugston Construction Ltd, 152,
    172, 173, 208
coal
    seams, 20, 23, 87, 88, 96
    workings, 51, 58, 61
Cofferdam, 69, 206
Compulsory Purchase Order, 90,
    184, 236
continuously reinforced concrete
    pavement, 173, 198, 240
Conundrum, 84
Corby, Gordon, 42, 93
Cornelius joints, 33, 99
Corrie, Ken, 168, 189
Costain Civil Engineering Ltd, 95,
    101, 115, 170
Cotton, Basil, 6, 7, 51, 52, 123, 124
Couchman, Maurice, 37, 95, 106
County Council
    Humberside, 201, 210
    Lindsey, 210
    North Riding, 10, 45, 48
    North Yorkshire, 52
    Northumberland, 73, 77, 79, 81,
        84
    Nottinghamshire, 18
    South Yorkshire Metropolitan, 42
    West Riding, 6, 127, 165

    West Yorkshire, 3, 11, 43, 125,
        237
County Development Plan, 55, 127
County Durham, 3, 7, 10, 45, 49,
    52, 55
County Laboratory, 3, 87
County Mining Engineer, 10, 88,
    129
County Planning Officer, 92
County Surveyors Society, 5, 123
Crigglestone, 85, 89, 95
Crowley Russell & Co. Ltd, 38, 40
Cubitts, Fitzpatrick, Shand, 14
Curry, Richard, 173, 210

Darlington, 45, 52
Darrington, 5, 227
    Crossroads, 44
    Flyover, 44
Darton, 85, 95
Dawson, Graham, 157, 197, 201
Dawson, Tony, 121
DBFO, 226, 238, 239
Deady, Frank, 35, 53
Dean Head, 129, 130, 131, 141
Deanhead Cutting, 146, 148
Department
    of Environment, 110, 163, 165,
        237
    of Transport, 68, 78, 219, 235,
        237
Derwenthaugh, 66, 70
design standards, 40, 86
Deuce, Leslie, 104, 124, 134, 136
Dick Turpin, 22
differential settlement, 18, 34, 101,
    102, 109, 174
direct labour, 6, 7, 8, 10, 53
Dishforth, 50, 221, 226, 230, 232,
    237
Divisional Road Engineer, 6, 47,
    235, 236
Dodworth, 85, 89, 95, 103
Don Valley, 16, 86, 107, 111

Doncaster, 5, 12, 226
    By-pass, 6, 9, 42
    Racecourse, 18
DOPET, 43, 125
Dorman Long, 47, 48, 170
Dowmac's of Tallington, 93, 101,
    206
Dowsett Engineering Construction
    Ltd, 32, 35, 40, 53, 93, 95, 121,
    155, 157, 159, 162, 188, 192, 194
Dragados, 227
Drake, Sir James, 7, 128, 136
Drewett Barry, 216, 224
Dropping Well Footbridge, 103
Durham, 51, 54, 236
    coalfield, 57, 61
    Prison, 63
    Sub-Unit, 62, 63, 82, 123, 134,
        173, 195, 198, 203, 213

E.W.H. Gifford & Partners, 114,
    115, 203
East Ardsley, 85, 96
    Railway Bridge, 159
East Coast Motorway, 234
Edmund Nutall Ltd, 66
Ellis, Norman, 9, 132
Elphick, Roger, 173, 176
England, Tom, 25
explosives, 56, 120

Fairburn, 32, 228
    Footbridge, 33
Fairfield-Mabey, 82, 161, 194
Fairhurst & Partners, 81
Felton, 77, 79
Ferrybridge, 9, 19, 26, 129, 136,
    162, 226
    By-pass, 9
    'C' Power Station, 31, 228
    Henge, 228
    Interchange, 162
    Lock, 29
    Service Area, 127, 138

Fitzpatrick and Son (Contractors) Ltd, 14
Flixborough Explosion, 210
Foote, Colin, 56, 76
Forrester, Ray, 10, 87
Forster, Gordon, 76, 80
Foundation Engineering Ltd, 142, 172
Freeman Fox & Partners, 108, 211

Gaffney, Tony, 41, 43, 124, 151, 167, 202
Gainsborough, 117, 203
Gallagher, John, 216, 219, 224
Gateshead, 64
Gateshead Western By-pass, 65
George Wimpey and Co. Ltd, 20, 239
Gildersome, 141, 143
    Interchange, 155, 157, 186
    Railway tunnel, 159
Gillard, Brian, 155, 168, 189
Girven, Cyril, 6, 73
Glanville, John, 9, 129
Gleeson Civil Engineering, 80, 81
glued segmental, 201, 203
Goldsborough, 41
Goldsborough, Derek, 35
Goole, 189
Graham, Mike, 170, 201
Grange Mill, 94, 103
Great North Road, A1, 2, 12, 64, 73, 77
Green, Ian, 42, 185
Green-Armytage, Keith, 27
Grimsby, 127, 195, 208
Guntert and Zimmerman, 175, 199

Harbour and General Works Ltd, 32
Harding, Ray, 73, 80, 81
Harris, Sir William, 107, 123, 134
Hartshead, 155
Hartshead Moor Service Area, 127, 137, 152

Haslingden Flags, 143
Hatfield, 190
    Service Area, 191
Hatter, Fred, 53, 56, 93, 95, 121, 159, 162
Hatton, Ian, 75, 79, 81, 84
Hawes, Dennis, 90, 125
Henry Boot Northern Limited, 221, 222, 223
Her Majesty the Queen, 64, 71, 138, 150, 212
Higgs and Hill Civil Engineering Ltd, 74
Highways Act 1959, 7, 89, 182
Highways Agency, 11, 226, 227, 238, 239
Hillcoat, Mike, 170, 173, 209
Holland Hannen and Cubitts Ltd, 14
Holroyd, John, 169, 208
Hook Moor, 35, 226, 227, 240, 243
Hopetown, 159
Hore-Belisha, Rt Hon. Leslie, 5
House of Commons, 110, 114, 213
Howden Spur, 172
Howie, Eric, 9, 43
Howieson, Keith Charles, 28, 32, 37
H-piles, 58, 61, 70, 194
Huddersfield, 133, 138
    Corporation, 130, 149, 150
    Water Undertaking, 130
Humber Bridge, 126, 195, 210, 211
    Acts, 211
    Board, 211
Hunslet, 182
Hunslet Distributor, 183
Hunsworth
    Dyers Ltd, 156
    Lane Bridge, 156
Hunt, Don, 150, 168, 187, 197, 198
Hunter, Geoffrey, 35, 36, 128, 143, 150
Hutchinson, A T 'Hutch', 3, 28, 35, 100, 124, 125, 151

Hydes, 'Wes', 51, 53
Hydraulics Research Station (HRS), 203, 206

Immingham, 195, 208
Institution of
    Civil Engineers, 10, 85, 115, 185
    Highway Engineers, 5, 197
instrumentation, 143, 165, 175, 201
Internal Drainage Boards, 137, 170, 198

James, Jimmie, 173, 209
Jeffs, John, 35, 93, 95, 157, 159, 162, 194
John Laing Construction Ltd, 131, 217
John Mowlem Construction, 223, 224
Joint Venture, 208, 230, 239
Jones, Dr Colin, 44, 94, 163, 165

Kellogg Brown & Root, 227
Kinderscout Grit, 131, 132, 142
Kingston upon Hull, 126, 234
    Corporation, 211
Kirkhamgate, 85, 96, 237
Kirkhamgate to Dishforth, 237
Kirklees Viaduct, 153
Kneeton Corner, 52, 54
Knottingley, 27
    Bridge, 28
Kvaerner Construction, 239, 241

Lancashire, 7, 138, 196
    Boundary, 132, 133
    South, 127
Land, John, 185, 216
Langham Viaduct, 168
Lawrence, Howard, 90, 100
Lee, Phil, 134, 154
Leech, 'Gerry', 49
Leeds, 157, 177, 241
    City Council, 3, 177, 178, 239

Corn Exchange, 126
Inner Relief Road, 182, 185
Inner Ring Road Motorway, 177
Motorway, 184
North-East Motorway, 182
Playhouse, 179, 180
University, 201
Leeds/Bradford Airport, 248
Leeming, 45, 47, 232
   RAF, 223
Lehane, McKenzie and Shand, 14, 180
Leonard Fairclough Ltd, 96, 134, 135, 155
Liverpool, 126, 157
Local Government Reorganisation, 50
Lofthouse, 86, 99, 106, 129, 141, 143, 157
   Interchange, 101, 103
Lofthouse Committee, 123
Lovell, Col S. Maynard, 6, 7, 9, 16, 36, 85, 104, 108, 123, 124, 128, 151
Lovell, John, 34, 37, 121
Lowson, David, 9, 14

M1, 48, 62
   Aston-Sheffield-Leeds M'way, 85, 134
   Aston to Tinsley, 93
   Barlborough to Thurcroft, 116
   Blackburn to Tankersley, 94
   Bridgeworks, 100
   completed to Leeds, 116
   Construction Contracts, 92
   Darton to Wakefield, 95
   East Ardsley to Stourton, 98, 105, 134
   First Contract, 98
   Leeds South East Urban Motor way, 181
   London to Yorkshire Motorway, 85, 116
   Meadowhall to Blackburn, 93
   Tankersley to Darton, 95
   Wakefield to East Ardsley, 96
M1-A1 Link Road, 166, 182, 226, 228, 237, 238
M1/M18 Interchange, 86, 93
M1-M62 widening, 240
M18, 89, 167, 189, 191
   Armthorpe to Hatfield, 190
   Barlborough to Wadworth, 118, 194
   Hatfield to Thorne, 189, 191, 195
   Rotherham to Goole Motorway, 189
   Thorne to East Cowick, 189
   Thurcroft to Wadworth, 116
   Wadworth to Armthorpe, 192, 194
M18/A1 Interchange, 192
M180, 189
   Brigg By-pass, 208, 209
   Sandtoft to Trent, 197
   Scunthorpe Southern By-pass, 208
   South Humberside Motorway, 195
   Thorne to Sandtoft, 196, 197
   Trent Approaches Advanced Earthworks, 200
   Trent Bridge, 202
   Trent to Scunthorpe, 207
   Tudworth to Sandtoft, 196
M181, 208
M606, 155
   Bradford South Radial M'way, 155, 187
M62, 157, 227, 228, 240
   Balkholme to Caves, 173, 198
   Construction Contracts, 136
   Contracts, 134
   East Roads Contract, 172
   Ferrybridge to Pollington, 162
   Gildersome to Lofthouse, 157
   Hartshead to Gildersome, 155, 188
   Hopetown to Ferrybridge, 162
   Lancs Boundary to Pole Moor, 138
   Lancashire-Yorkshire Motorway, 99, 126, 127, 128, 185
   Lofthouse to Hopetown, 159
   Outlane to Hartshead, 151
   Pennine Contract, 138
   Pole Moor to Outlane, 150
   Pollington to Rawcliffe, 167, 189
   Prologue, 126
   Rawcliffe to Balkholme, 169
   Trans-Pennine Motorway, 86, 172, 173
   West Roads Contract, 169
M62/M1 Interchange, 157
M621, 155, 184
   Gildersome Street to Leeds Mway, 158, 185
   Leeds SW Urban Motorway, 184, 185
   Stourton Link, 181
magnesian limestone, 15, 23, 29, 39, 54, 57, 136, 163
Malton, Mick, 222, 224
Manzoni, Sir Herbert, 114
Marples, Ernest MP, 18, 53, 109
Marsh, Rt Hon. Richard MP, 62, 116
Marshall, Ivor, 42, 43
Marshall Meadows, 84
Martin Cowley, 27
McKeith, Peter, 76, 81
McKenzie, Jim, 53, 124
McLauchlan (Knottingley) Ltd, 26
McVey, Stewart, 138, 150
Mead, Peter, 62, 124
Meadowhall, 93
   retaining wall, 103
Melling, Brian, 162, 176, 198
Merrison, 104, 110, 112, 113, 147, 156

Committee, 154
Report, 160
Sir Alec, 154
Messer, Gordon, 75, 81
Metcalfe, 'Blind' Jack, 2, 41
Micklefield, 19, 228
By-pass, 32
Millard, Rosie, 126
Miller Construction Northern Ltd, 82
Mills Scaffolding Co. Ltd, 24
mine workings, 88, 118
mining subsidence, 9, 10, 111, 120
Minister-Transport and Civil Aviation, 85
Ministry
Defence, 165
Housing and Local Government, 177
Standards, 15, 38
Transport, 8, 9, 22, 105, 110, 123
Moglia, John, 95, 151, 190
Monk & Co. Ltd, 37, 41, 42, 94, 98, 187, 191, 196
Monk Construction Ltd, 215, 216, 244
Moore, Brian, 78, 79
Moore, Mike, 50
Morley, 97, 129
Mott Hay and Anderson, 74
MVA Consultancy, 226

Nash, Professor, 130, 131, 132
National
Coal Board, 23, 61, 63, 88, 98, 99, 179
Farmers Union, 89
Maritime Institute, 212
Roads Board, 123
Navigation Authority, 29
Naylor, Eddie, 43
Needle Eye, 95
Bridge, 103
Neolithic, 228, 232

Network Management Division, 225
New Civil Engineer, 112, 113, 171
Newcastle, 44, 234, 236
Central Motorway East, 64
City Council, 3
Metro, 68
University, 44
Western By-pass, 64, 71
Newton on the Moor, 79
Norris, Gilbert, 124, 151, 236
North-Eastern Road Construction Unit, 123, 151, 236
Northern (Regional Office), 225
Northumberland, 64, 81, 236
Contracting, 79
Duke of, 79, 80, 81
Nottinghamshire, 12, 17, 86

Observer, 126
Ordnance Survey, 128
origin and destination survey, 128
Ossett, 97
Ouse Bridge, 169, 170
Outlane, 136, 149, 150

parallel widening, 233
patent, 163, 164, 165, 166
peat, 140
Pell Frischmann Consultants, 214, 215, 238
Pennine Way, 127, 138, 146
Petrie, John, 62, 124
piling, 26, 27, 41, 58, 69, 156, 171, 190
pillars, 61, 81, 88, 98
Pole Moor, 129, 132, 138
Policy for Roads, England, 64
Pollington, 162, 167
Pontefract, 162, 189
Porter, John, 134
Post Office Telephone, 193
Powell, John, 42, 93
preferred route, 226, 232

Prescott, Rt Hon. John, MP, 243
Preston By-pass, 7
Private Finance Initiative, 238
PTFE, 101
Public Consultation, 226, 229
Public Inquiry, 105, 185, 203, 237
Public Utilities Street Works Act, 90
Pulverised Fuel Ash (PFA), 33
Purver, Ted, 209, 210

Race, Gordon, 9
Railway
Barnard Castle–Darlington, 53
Bishop Auckland–Darlington, 53
Bradford–Cleckheaton, 156
East Coast Main Line, 12, 58, 192, 193
Ferryhill and Pelaw Branch, 59
Harrogate and York, 40, 41
Harworth Colliery, 18
Horbury–Wakefield, 97
Hull–Barnsley, 21, 173
Hunslet East–Beeston Junction, 181
Leeds–Derby, 183
Leeds–Doncaster, 20
Leeds–London, 185
Merrybent Mineral, 52
Middleton Colliery, 182
Mirfield–Brighouse, 153
Newcastle Metro, 68
Newcastle–Carlisle, 70
Selby to Hull, 173, 175
Wakefield–Ossett, 98
Rainstorth Bridge, 102
Rawcliffe Interchange, 167
Raymond International (UK) Ltd, 171
Redhouse, 19, 227
Redpath Dorman Long (Contracting) Ltd, 170, 171, 212
Regional Development Fund, 66
reinforced earth, 44, 70, 163, 166, 167

Rhodes, Wayne, 66, 70, 83
rhubarb, 85, 98, 186
Richards and Wallington, 62
Ridley, Rt Hon. Nicholas, MP, 77, 83
Ripon, 227, 237
Ripon, Rt Hon. Geoffrey, 184
River
    Aire, 27, 29, 31, 180, 228, 241
    Aln, 80
    Altofts, 160
    Blyth, 73, 75
    Calder, 96, 97, 100, 152, 153, 160
    Coquet, 77
        Bridge, 77
    Don, 12, 15, 17, 107, 167, 196
    Dutch, 167, 168
        Bridge, 201
    Ouse, 169, 170, 171, 172
    Tees, 52, 53, 54
    Trent, 197, 198, 200, 202, 207, 208
    Tweed, 73, 82
        Bridge, 82
    Tyne, 64
    Ure, 1, 41, 48, 232
    Wear, 54, 60, 61
    Wharfe, 37, 38, 218, 229
        Bridge, 38, 219
Rivers Board, 29
Road Research Laboratory, 129, 165, 197, 198, 235
Robert McGregor & Sons Ltd, 62
Roberts, Henry, 9
Robin Hood, 20, 21, 22
Robinson, George, 62, 82
rock
    anchors, 179
    blanket, 97, 192
    bolts, 179
rockfill, 141, 142, 201
Rockingstone, 139
    Moss Interchange, 139, 146

Roebuck, Paul, 66, 70
Rogers, Bill, MP, 124, 208
Roman, 12, 41, 46, 47, 226, 232, 233, 243
Roman Road, 151
Rotherham, 189
    Museum, 21
Royal Fine Arts Commission, 8, 15, 102, 104
Royal Tweed Bridge, 73, 76
RSPB Nature Reserve, 228
Rutter, Ken, 222, 230

Saltmarsh, David, 42, 162, 216, 222
Sandtoft, 197
Sargent, Derek, 90, 124
Sawtell, Ronald, 6, 7, 45, 46, 48, 49, 52
Scammonden, 25, 131, 149
    Bridge, 146, 147, 148, 150
    Dam, 138, 141, 143, 150
Scheduled Ancient Monument (SAM), 228, 233
Scotch Corner, 45, 226, 233
Scotswood, 65, 70
Scott Wilson Kirkpatrick & Partners, 169, 195, 209, 210
Scott, Desmond, 64, 69, 230
Scott, Fred, 9, 37
Scunthorpe, 207
Secretary of State, 153, 215, 230, 237, 239
Selby Fork, 34, 127, 129
sheep, 129, 132, 133, 139, 146
Sheffield County Borough Council, 91
Sheffield Star, 110
Sheffield University, 201
Shelbourn, Jack, 9, 85, 86, 129
Shepherd Hill & Co. Ltd, 201
Shields, Eddie, 41, 192, 197
Side Road Orders, 46, 75
Simpson, Frank, 95, 157, 162
Simpson, Ted, 62, 66

Sims, F.A. ('Joe'), 100, 106, 150, 151, 244, 248
Sir Alfred McAlpine & Son Ltd, 96, 138, 162, 170, 173, 189, 196, 197, 200, 210, 227, 230
Sir Owen Williams and Partners, 116, 119, 226
Sir Robert McAlpine and Sons Ltd, 18
Site of Special Scientific Interest (SSSI), 228, 243
Skellow, 20, 226
Slater, Ken, 82, 230
slip-form paver, 175, 199
soil survey, 109, 201
South Humberside Feasibility Study, 195
South Leeds Interchange, 182
Special Roads Act, 7, 52
Speed, Keith, MP, 157
Sprotborough, 14
Sriskandan, 'Sri', 23, 32, 154
Stannington Bridge, 73, 74
Stantec Zebra computer, 100
Statutory Orders, 89, 226
Statutory Undertakers, 90, 193
steel box girders, 99, 154, 156, 170
Stephens, Howard, 198
Stothard, John, 23, 131
Stourton, 90, 98, 99, 181, 240
    Interchange, 102, 181
subsidence, 61, 96
Surveyor, The, 111
Sutherland, Maurice, 98, 138, 150
Swingler, Stephen, MP, 121

Tankersley, 85, 94
Tarmac Civil Engineering Ltd, 80, 93, 118
Tarmac Construction Ltd, 183
Tayler, 'Palf', 27, 32
Taylor, Denis, 27, 28, 125, 136
Taylor Woodrow Construction Ltd, 23, 24

Teesside, 53
Telford, Len, 73, 80, 84
temporary works, 24, 115, 203
Thirwell, Geoffrey, 6
Thomas Telford, 2, 79
Thurcroft, 86, 93, 101, 117, 118
Tingley
   Common Bridge, 159
   Interchange, 157
Tinsley, 86
   Viaduct, 91, 107
      construction, 111
      strengthening, 112
Towton Field, 32
Transpennine Pressure Group, 126
Transport, Minister of, 14, 127, 165
Treasury Solicitors, 105
trial embankments, 129, 130
Trunk Road A1, 3, 7, 215
Trunk Road Order, 52, 80
Tudworth, 196
   Hall Link, 190, 195
   Hill, 197
Tully, John, 125
tunnel, 179, 182, 185
Tyne
   Bridge, 64, 66
   Tunnel, 62, 74
Tyne and Wear, 236
   Plan (TWP), 177
tyre wall, 157, 167

Universal Beams, 31, 47
Urban Motorway, 64, 177
Urban Traffic Control (UTC), 182
Urn Farm, 99, 102

Varley, Bill, 3, 27, 100, 102, 105, 124
Vidal, Henri, 163

W & C French Ltd, 57, 93, 118, 120, 150, 151, 167, 189
W.S. Atkins, 225, 233
Wadsworth, Trevor, 40
Wadworth, 14, 117, 118, 189
   Interchange Bridges, 121
   Viaduct, 189, 194
Wakefield, 95
Wakefield and District Water Board, 145, 146
Walsh, George, 34, 94
Walshford, 220, 229, 230
Walshford Bridge, 40
Wansbeck Viaduct, 76
War of the Roses, 32, 36
Warenford, 81
Warmsley, Bill, 136
Warmsworth, 15
   Railway Bridge, 17
Washington New Town, 62
Waterside Interchange, 189
Watkinson, Harold, 7, 85
Watts, John, MP, 232
Wear Valley, 57
weather station, 128
Wentbridge, 19, 22, 42
   scaffold, 24
   Viaduct, 22, 227
West Mains, 82
West Moor, 77, 79, 191
   Interchange, 192
   Link, 191
West Riding Sub-Unit, 123, 151, 189

West Riding Special Review Area, 177
West Yorkshire Sub-Unit, 189, 213
West Yorks Trans'n Study (WYTS), 177
wet mix, 47
Wetherby, 37, 215, 228, 229, 237
   By-pass, 9, 19, 36, 40
   Grange Park, 217
   Racecourse, 38, 40, 218, 229
Whitehaughs Arch, 153
Whitley Bridge, 163, 164, 165, 166
Wichert, 95, 102
Wilkinson, Deryk, 46, 50
Williams, Eddie, 9
Williams, Harold, 9, 35, 40, 86, 90, 91
wind tunnel, 129, 212
Windy Hill, 128, 129, 130, 139, 141
Woodall Service Area, 118
Woodhead, Stewart, 201
Wooley, Malcolm, 96, 114
Woolley Edge, 85, 96
   Service Area, 103
WYCET, 166

York Method, 164, 165
York Road, 217, 230
   Bridge, 229
Yorkshire and Humberside, 217, 225, 236
   Regional Strategy Report, 195
Yorkshire coalfields, 12, 88, 155, 159
Yorkshire Link Ltd, 239, 242